Coin Clinic

By Alan Herbert

1,001 FREQUENTLY ASKED QUESTIONS

© 1995 by
Krause Publications, Inc.

krause publications

700 E. State Street • Iola, WI 54990-0001

Please call or write for our free catalog of numismatic publications. Our toll-free number to place an order or obtain a free catalog is 800-258-0929 or please use our regular business telephone 715-445-2214 for editorial comment
and further information.

Library of Congress Catalog Number: 95-77303
ISBN: 0-87341-380-6
Printed in the United States of America

TABLE OF CONTENTS

Table Of Contents (Continued)

FOREWORD

I've always been impressed when I buy something—a new camera or other electronic gizmo—and, upon arriving at home, look at the instructions and find I am greeted with a "congratulations" for purchasing a fine product. Maybe it's just me, but anytime I find that word in conjunction with my introduction to what I've just purchased, I generally end up agreeing with the manufacturer: I did buy the top of the line.

Perhaps it is stretching it a bit to say the same about a book, but having known this book's author for a good many years and having been consistently impressed by the depth of his knowledge of numismatics, I have no hesitation in offering you congratulations if you have just acquired a copy of *Coin Clinic, 1,001 Frequently Asked Questions* for your numismatic library. You have tapped into the numismatic knowledge of one of the hobby's premier writers and beyond a doubt one of its best known and most highly regarded.

Whether you're a neophyte or a seasoned collector you will likely benefit from having Alan Herbert's wealth of knowledge at your fingertips. For example, if you've ever had even a basic question relating to how to buy or sell coins or how to safely store your most valuable items against damage from the environment, you're likely to find the answer inside. Likewise, if your question is of a historical or technical nature, there's a good chance you'll find reference within. You're even likely to come across answers to questions you hadn't thought of but would have liked to have asked.

Based on "Coin Clinic," the ever-popular column Alan has and continues to prepare for *Numismatic News* and *Coins* magazine (and under different titles for *World Coin News* and *Bank Note Reporter*), *Coin Clinic*, the book, is a reflection of Alan's thorough attention to detail and willingness to treat even the most oft-asked question with the same intensity as one that requires considerable research—a trait that has endeared him with collectors throughout the United States and, indeed, throughout the world.

In 1994, this dedication to sharing knowledge with others earned Alan Herbert the American Numismatic Association's prestigious Medal of Merit for his contributions to the hobby and the national association for coin collectors. It is a major award but only slight recognition for a lifetime of selfless devotion to answering the questions of others. From his early days in South Dakota, where he engineered a fight to have the image of Mount Rushmore placed on U.S. currency, to his rise to national recognition as a leading error and variety authority, Alan has displayed an unflappable dedication to teaching the hows and whys of coin collecting that readily shines through in his writings.

They say you should never stop learning, never stop seeking sources for new information, never stop expanding your horizons. Alan's career is proof that this is sage advice—that as long as we, as collectors, keep seeking knowledge we can only enrich our enjoyment of the hobby and thereby enlighten and improve our futures.

In preparing *Coin Clinic, 1,001 Frequently Asked Questions* it was not a question of how to come up with 1,001 questions and answers, it was a matter of how to *limit* the number of questions maintained within his extensive computer files to fit the parameters set forth by the publisher. It was a tough task, but illustrates that this book is the result of years of preparation, study and re-analysis of prior numismatic literature. As such, it's the best one-volume course on numismatics you're likely ever to find—one that will appeal to collectors at all hobby levels.

I am proud to count Alan among my friends and honored to have been asked to write this opening message for what I am certain will be a popular, sought-after book.

Again, congratulations. You hold in your hands the work of a hobby master and an indispensable reference for years to come.

Robert R. Van Ryzin
Editor, *Coins* magazine
April 1995

INTRODUCTION

The Coin Clinic column has been appearing in *Numismatic News* under that title since 1961, although it started two years earlier as "The Question Box." There have been four previous conductors, who guided readers with answers to their questions about virtually every facet of numismatics. I've been on the job since mid-1981 and in that period I've compiled more than 13,000 questions and answers in a data base that is constantly growing. I'm answering questions from readers of three other publications as well: *World Coin News*, *Coins Magazine*, and *Bank Note Reporter*.

Recently I've added a vast new group of inquisitive collectors on CompuServe, Prodigy, America Online, and the Internet. Many of these people have never seen a hobby publication, so a lot of the questions are repeats of questions that our readers are familiar with, or are based on misinformation that has long since been refuted by researchers in the hobby. It has been a challenge working with this wide audience, but one that I welcome, and enjoy.

The idea of putting a group of the common questions into a book is one that has been under discussion for more than a decade. Many *News* readers have either suggested such a book, or have inquired about the prospects of one, so now that it has become a reality this book should reach a large audience.

Readers often marvel about my "vast knowledge" of the hobby when they meet me or write to me. The secret is not my memory, but the very excellent research library maintained at Krause Publications. With this resource to draw on, it has been a real pleasure to answer the hundreds of letters that pour into the mailroom for me every month. However, it has reached the point where there simply is more mail than I can handle, so I have to try to pick questions of general interest to answer, either in the columns, in this book, or by mail.

As you can imagine, sorting 13,000 questions is not quickly accomplished. This has been the first major update of my data base, combining and cross-checking duplicate questions, and in many cases combining facts from several answers into a single comprehensive discussion. Even with this sorting, you will find some comments repeated in different forms in several answers. In the main, these are points that bear repeating.

My style is informal, hopefully informative. You may find the categories confusing, but I didn't feel that the system should be rigid, rather that you could browse through, picking and choosing information as you go. If you are unfamiliar with Coin Clinic— the column, it has always been a source for unusual, interesting sidelights on the roots of the hobby, as well as a source for vital information, such as how to safely store your coins and why cleaning coins is not in your best interest.

If you are not a reader of one of the Krause publications in which my columns appear, when you reach the end of the book you will find a chapter with information about them. I will be pleased to have a sample copy sent to you with my compliments.

No doubt, after reading through this book you will have questions of your own that I haven't answered. You are welcome to write to me, but please include a first class stamp for return postage. I can authenticate and photograph your minting varieties, but only by prior arrangement. Do not send any coins until you have received mailing instructions from me.

The address is:

Alan Herbert
Krause Publications—Dept. CCB
700 E. State St.
Iola, WI 54990-0001

Chapter 1

ABBREVIATIONS

Listed here are some common abbreviations you may run into while reading about your hobby. It's by no means all of them, but it's a start.

Q: An abbreviation that somehow got mixed up is A.A. Right?

A.A. stands for after date, or ante diem. However, ante diem is Latin and translates as "before the day." Seems to be a slight conflict there. Spell it "anti," which appears to have been the intent, and it then picks up the Greek meaning of "after."

Q: What do ASW or AGW stand for?

Actual silver weight or actual gold weight.

Q: How did we get AR and AU as abbreviations for silver and gold?

They trace to the Latin, Argentum for silver and Aurum for gold. They are still used in Europe, but in the U.S. we use Ag and Au.

Q: What are the symbols for brass and bronze?

Br is sometimes used for Brass, while AE is used for bronze, or any copper alloy.

Q: What is meant by a "DMPL" coin?

DMPL is the abbreviation for Deep Mirror Proof-Like, or a coin with a mirror-like field surface which exhibits some, but not all of the characteristics of a true proof coin.

Q: Some write it EF, some XF, meaning extra fine grade. Which is correct?

Either or both. This is just more confusion for the hobby to clear up.

Q: What is the abbreviation for grams? I never know whether someone is talking about grams, grammes, or grains, and there's a big difference!

Either spelling of grams is correct, although common usage in the United States is the shorter, gram. A scientific minded reader furnished us with the internationally approved symbol (not abbreviation) used for gram. It is the small letter "g" used without a period, and without an s, as the symbol is either singular or plural. For grains, use "gr" also without a period or s. However not all writers or editors are aware of these symbols and you may find "variations."

To point up the problem, the accepted abbreviations for grain are: gr., G., and g. for either the singular or the plural.

Q: What do IA and IB stand for ?

They mean included above and included below. They are used in coin charts to show where mintage figures are included together for the same mint. The early mint records frequently mixed dates.

Q: What does NM mean?

It has two meanings, either none minted, or no motto.

Q: What do the initials P.N.C. stand for?

PNC is a Philatelic Numismatic Combination. One of the first was by Lyle Roe of Wisconsin with a Kennedy half dollar postmarked on the first day of issue, March 24, 1964. The term includes coins on stamps, stamps on coins, stock certificates with a revenue stamp, encased stamps as currency, etc.

Q: What is a P D S Set?

It's a set of coins from the three principal mints: Philadelphia, Denver, and San Francisco.

Q: Does RPM have a different meaning to coin collectors?

It is the abbreviation for repunched mint mark.

Q: What do 7T or 7 TF mean in a coin listing?

Either one refers to the 7 tailfeathers design, the first eagle design on the Morgan dollars. There are also the 8T or 8TF, and 7/8T or 7/8TF (7 over 8 tailfeathers).

Q: What are VAM numbers?

These are Van Allen and Mallis catalog numbers for die varieties in the Morgan and Peace dollars.

Chapter 2

ADVERTISING

The hobby regrettably has a secret language of its own. Coin dealers frequently use terms in their ads that are unfamiliar to the novice. I've assembled some typical examples in this chapter to help you unlock the secrets.

Q: What is meant by a dealer's ad offering "Unsearched coins?"

Unsearched coins supposedly have not been checked by anyone for the rare dates and mints. Since there is no way of proving this the claim has to be taken on faith. The odds against a 1916-D dime turning up in "unsearched" coins are just as great as they are in any given quantity of coins, so the dealers aren't taking much of a chance. They usually don't have the time to go through very many coins themselves, but it's a good idea to discuss the dealer's definition of unsearched before buying.

Q: What does an ad mean when it says "A mixed roll of Lincoln cents?"

The usually accepted meaning is that it will be a roll with a number of different dates and mints, in various grades. Left unsaid is whether there are or aren't a number of duplicates. Again, it's best to query before buying.

Q: Don't they "make" any coins in grades below MS-65 anymore? That's all I see advertised.

For an apt comparison, check the display ads from your local car dealers. In most cases all they will list are the models from the last couple of years on the lot, even though they have hundreds of older cars. It's much the same for coin dealers, who spend their ad dollars on coins which have a larger profit potential because of their higher value. The lower grade coins are out there, so with a little looking you can find one to fit your pocketbook or your checkbook.

Q: How can one date be better than another?

In ads, a "better" date means one of the lower mintage dates, in contrast to common dates.

Q: What does it mean when a dealer says in his ads that he guarantees the grade of the coins being sold?

Usually it means that if the ad says that the coin is (for example) an MS-63 grade, the coin you receive will be that grade, or he will refund your money. You do need to read the fine print in the ad to pick up any special provisions in connection with that guarantee, which in effect is a limited warranty. I say usually, because there may be the occasional bad apple who offers a meaningless guarantee, pays off the one collector in a thousand smart enough to complain that his coin was overgraded, and goes right on making regular trips to the bank. The solution, at the risk of repeating good advice, is to learn to grade your coins yourself, so you can see at a glance if they are the correct grade. Grading is the first thing to learn before you buy a single coin.

Q: Are there any U.S. coins with ads on them?

The Ft. Vancouver commemorative half, has the words "Founded by Hudsons Bay Company." Also, there's the Pass & Stowe firm name on the Liberty Bell. Canada has "H.B. Co." on the furs on the Canadian dollar for the Hudsons Bay Co.

Q: An old-timer told me that it was once possible to get a coin series with "Green" stamps. Any truth to it?

Not as tall a tale as it might sound. While I'm relatively sure that the S&H Green Stamp company didn't offer coins as a premium for their stamps, at least one coin dealer back in the early 1960's was offering in his ads to trade a complete set of 1941-1962 cents for one book of the S&H stamps. The ad, which appeared in *Numismatic News*, didn't state the grade of the coins, so it's hard to tell exactly how good a bargain the trade might have been.

Q: An ad offers, "Lincoln Cent Set, no Small Dates." What does it mean?

It refers to the small date 1960 and 1960-D cents, the so called "small" date 1970-S cent, and small 1982 and 1982-D cent dates.

Q: I've noted a number of ads for coins, offering "Dates of our choice." Is this some sort of scam? I want to pick my own dates, not have someone do it for me, and charge me for the privilege.

The offer of "dates of our choice" is a perfectly legitimate offer that is frequently made, directed toward the individual who is interested in a type coin, as opposed to a coin of a specific date and mint. Since many collectors collect by type, especially in the more expensive (gold) series, these ads offer a convenient way of getting a common date coin without the hassle of asking for several dates until you find one a dealer has. It allows the dealer to fill orders without having to spend a lot of time jockeying for a particular date.

Q: Could you give me the address of (A specific firm)?

To the best of my knowledge the firm you inquired about has never advertised with our publications. I always urge readers to be extremely wary of doing business with any firm which does not run ads in the hobby publications as this is a possible indication that they are not meeting hobby standards. While it is not actual proof, it is grounds to be suspicious, especially if the company uses a name which suggests or implies that it is a "Federal," "National" or some other term that makes it sound like the official U.S. Mint.

Q: What dates do these ads refer to which offer to pay huge amounts for "certain dates before.....?" I saw the ad in (a non-numismatic publication.)

Reading the fine print won't help either. Most of these ads are designed to lure non-collectors into buying the firm's "price guides" with the end result that the company gets a chance to purchase coins for a fraction of their real worth. Frequently the "come-on" prices are based very loosely on minting varieties that require a trained expert to identify. The aim is to sell coin books rather than to buy coins, and it apparently has been a highly profitable scam over the years. One of the first mentions I found of this deceptive advertising was in an article in a 1935 *Numismatist* magazine, and from the tone of the article it had been going on for some time even then. Before you answer one of those ads, check the Coin Market prices in *Numismatic News* and save yourself a lot of fruitless searching.

Q: Is there anything that can be done about misleading ads in the lay press or the computer online services?

Complain to the publisher. If it is an organizational publication, complain through your local chapter or unit if you are a member. Cite the correct figures or other facts as to why the ads should be refused.

Chapter 3

ALLOY, BULLION, BULLION COINS, COIN METALS

The makeup of the metal used for a coin has a major bearing on the collectibility of the piece. Questions about bullion, alloys, and coin metals are frequent, the answers important.

Q: Wasn't there a proposal back in the Depression years to issue a "Lindberg" bullion coin?

Perhaps anticipating the art bars of the 1970s and the current "hockey puck" rounds of various sizes, Senator Borah introduced a bill in 1932 to authorize a one-ounce silver coin and a similar note to be backed by silver, with Lindberg on one side and the Spirit of St. Louis on the other.

Q: Is there a legal definition of the fineness of bullion?

While not strictly a matter of law, the general world standard is .995 fine to be classed as bullion, but this does not directly apply to coins. Usually coins must contain at least 50 percent of a precious metal to be considered bullion coins, but in practice most coins classed as bullion coins sold today are .995 or higher fineness.

Q: Please send me information on how to buy the gold and silver coins.

I assume you mean the gold and silver American Eagles. The regular issues are available from local coin dealers in your area, while the proof versions may be purchased directly from the Mint, or from a dealer. To get on the Mint mailing list to receive order blanks and notification of when the sale periods are open, write to: U.S. Mint, Account Maintenance, 10001 Aerospace Drive, Lanham, MD 20706, Tel. (202) 283-2646.

Q: I have a Babe Ruth "art bar" which has the wrong date for his death. Is this a rarity?

It depends on whether the manufacturer corrected it or not. The bar "boom" in the 1970s saw thousands of silver bar designs, and an unusually large number turned out to be "errors" with the wrong number of wheels on the locomotive, the wrong dates, or other mistakes, some of which seemed to occur more to promote sales than from other causes. The principal problem was the total lack of official control over mintages, announced mintage figures, and other factors affecting value.

Q: I have a ten-ounce silver bar that was issued by the U.S. Assay Office in 1981. Do you have any idea what it is worth?

First of all, the bar you have was not an issue of the U.S. Assay Office. The legend on the bar says, "Minted From U.S. Strategic Stockpile Silver, Formerly Stored at the U.S. Assay Office San Francisco." The minting was done after the silver was sold by the government to a private firm. These bars were struck by the Continental Coin Corporation in one-ounce rounds and bars and five- and ten-ounce bars. The Indexed Guide Book of Silver Art Bars lists two varieties for the one ounce-bars, both fairly common. As a guess, your ten-ounce bar might bring $1 to $2 an ounce over the spot price of silver.

Q: Supposedly there are eight "noble" metals, but my buddies are arguing about some of the less well known. Could you please list them?

Besides gold, platinum, and silver, the other five are members of the platinum group: palladium, rhodium, ruthenium, iridium, and osmium.

The noble metals are another way of designating those metals that are considered to be bullion, such as gold, silver, and more recently platinum. The noble metals are contrasted with the base metals, such as lead, copper, tin, zinc, or iron.

Q: Is 100 percent pure silver possible?

Only in a lab. Usually the best you can get is .999 fine, which means it has a trace of impurities.

Q: With gold close to $400 isn't it about time we mined all the gold that is contained in the ocean water?

According to some sources there is one gram of gold in solution in each ton of sea water. Back when gold was $20 an ounce this figured out to about 4.2 cents per ton of water. At $380, we're up to 79.2 cents per ton which is still a long way from an economical and profitable recovery effort. When someone does figure out a cheap way to do it they'll be rich, as there are quite a few tons of water out there to work on.

Q: What's the difference between gold leaf and gold foil?

Gold leaf is thinner, only 1/200,000th of an inch thick, and nearly transparent.

Q: Where is gold found in the U.S.?

21 states have commercial deposits; every state has at least traces.

Q: Since the start of the "modern era" of gold mining (1850) how much of the gold that was mined was struck into coins?

I don't have the exact figures, but up to 1933 almost all of the gold mined between 1850-1933 was minted into coins, or about 900 million ounces. Roughly 1.5 billion ounces of gold has been mined or recovered from placers since humans first began to use gold as a medium of value or exchange. Approximately 80 to 85 percent of that figure has been produced since 1900.

Q: If gold is so "common" why don't they make coins or bars for collectors out of some of the more exotic metals that are truly rare, such as osmium?

Current quotes on osmium are something less than three times the current gold prices ($950) , even though available stocks are substantially lower. Gold has a built in "prestige," which is lacking for the exotics. If you have a couple of million with nothing to do, you could probably corner the osmium market, but profiting from it would be another matter.

Q: What causes the difference in color in gold coins and gold jewelry?

This is a fairly regular question, with an answer based on the metal with which the gold is alloyed. Of the two combinations frequently used for coins, copper tends to turn gold reddish, while silver will produce a green gold alloy.

Q: On the topic of early American history, I'm told that the miners were reluctant to use gold from the Black Hills of South Dakota for fillings for their teeth. Can you track down the story?

Over the years a lot of gold coins and nuggets were transformed into tooth fillings, or even bridgework. California gold was preferred, according to one source, because it retained its color in the wearer's mouth. In contrast, the gold from the Black Hills always showed the copper content, and stained badly if the teeth were used to chew tobacco. I'm a little dubious of the possible bias here, as I lived in the Black Hills for 30 years and never once heard this tale.

Q: Did the Mint do anything special to make the 1983-84 Olympic gold coins look better?

Dr. George Hunter, the Mint's Assistant Director for Technology, is quoted as saying that the Mint "blanched" the planchets, to give them a more golden color rather than the reddish or brassy look associated with a copper-gold alloy.

Q: Silver solder I know, but is there a gold solder?

There is, and the formula is 12 parts of gold, two of silver, and two of copper.

Q: I'm confused by a reference to "electron" in an article about ancient Greece, which did not seem to refer to the silver-gold alloy. Can you clear this up?

Electron was an alloy of three parts gold to one part silver, and it also was the name for amber, which was highly prized both then and now.

Q: Is there such a thing as a "base bullion" alloy?

This sounds like a confusion of two differing terms but there actually is a mixture of metals called base bullion. It is an alloy of lead and silver, which may or may not contain gold. The alloy is such that the silver or gold can be recovered from the mixture.

Q: By base silver does one mean a low grade silver alloy?

That's the generally accepted numismatic meaning, the same thing as billon, an alloy containing less than 50% silver.

The Ikes are often called "silver" dollars, but only the S-mint coins contain silver.

Q: Would the Ike dollars have circulated as 90% silver?

By 1971, silver was already too expensive, worth more than the face value of a 90 percent silver coin. However, it probably would not have helped even if silver was cheap. The general public simply doesn't like the big dollars, and has little use even for the down-sized Anthony dollar.

Q: Is it true that two war nickels contain more silver than a 90% silver dime?

This fact is usually overlooked. A 90% silver dime contains .0724 ounce of silver, while a single wartime nickel contained .0563 ounce. Thus two nickels contain .1126 ounce of silver. For that matter, three nickels contain .1689 ounce and a silver quarter contains just .1809 ounce.

Q: Why did they use silver in the wartime nickels during World War II?

The principal reason was an effort to save both copper and nickel that were in short supply and urgently needed for a variety of wartime needs. A major factor in selecting silver was that—for the government at least—it was both plentiful and cheap. We are so used to seeing silver worth at least several dollars an ounce in recent years that it is hard to realize that during the 1940s, the government stockpile of silver included metal that had been purchased for much less, some of it probably during the 1930s when silver prices had dropped to less than 30 cents an ounce. The relatively crude vending machine coin rejecters would accept the silver nickels as identical to the copper-nickel alloy, which was another factor in its favor. The Mint came close to settling on an alloy of 50 percent silver, but dropped the percentage at the last minute because, at 50 percent, the silver value would have exceeded the face value of the coins.

Q: Did the early silver proof sets contain only silver coins?

They also contained the "minor" coins, first the cent, later the two cent, then the copper-nickel three cent and nickel.

Q: Wasn't there some controversy over the silver Ike dollars and the Canadian dollars?

Critics called both pseudo coins, since the proofs were not in circulation metals.

Q: Isn't the government now selling us back the silver they took away in 1965 when they grabbed all the silver coins and issued copper-nickel ones?

If you read the record book, you will find that just about every country in the world switched away from silver as a coin metal in the 1960s, so the U.S. was protecting its coins in the same fashion as everyone else. With the price of silver rising, and beyond the control of the government, there was really no choice.

Q: When were our silver coins demonetized?

They haven't been. All our silver coins are still legal tender, but all are worth more for their numismatic or bullion value, so they don't circulate.

Q: I'm told that the Chinese laborers in the California gold fields were more interested in silver than in gold. Is this correct?

Silver was much more popular as a matter of tradition and availability, and accounts of the gold rush indicate that laborers who were paid in gold dust would quickly trade it for silver coins.

Q: How much silver is estimated to exist above ground worldwide?

A rather staggering amount: the estimates center on a figure of 9.5 million tons.

Q: Are there any estimates available as to the amount of silver in storage in the U.S.?

One source puts the estimate at 3.9 billion ounces, indicating that there are tremendous quantities of unreported holdings, which amount to over 1.6 billion of that figure.

Q: Were the aluminum proof sets sold directly to collectors by the U.S. Mint, as they did with other collector coins struck in the last half of the 1800s?

From what I can determine they seem to have had a special status, and very few went to collectors until after 1900, when many of them passed through the hands of William H. Woodin. There are several theories but little factual information beyond this.

Q: Why didn't the U.S. Mint go to a better alloy than copper plated zinc for its coins, such as aluminum, bronze clad steel, or stainless steel, such as other countries use?

Back in 1973-74, the Mint commissioned a study of various alloys, and at that time found that each of the suggested metals had its problems. Aluminum would cause vending machine problems, bronze clad steel is hard to strike and three times as expensive as brass, and stainless steel is also hard to strike and more expensive. Other materials considered included plastics, chromized steel, zinc alloys, and clad (Cu-Ni) zinc.

Q: Is there some kind of a process that will turn a bronze or brass medal or coin a dark red?

There is a method of treating a bronze piece with potassium nitrate which will produce a dark red finish, not to be confused with the fairly bright red resulting from a coin or other piece being in a fire.

Q: What is silver powder?

One thing it is not, is silver. It is a powdered alloy of tin, bismuth, and mercury used in applying a varnish coating known as japanning.

Q: If an object, such as a pattern coin, is "gilded" does that mean it is gold plated?

Gilding may mean either plated with gold or with some material (such as bronze powder) which simulates or resembles the appearance of gold. In most cases gilding on pattern coins is something other than gold, as gold plated pieces usually are described as plated.

Q: What is the composition of "nickel-bronze?"

To answer the question we need to be specific about the time period involved. From the 1940s to about the 1950s in the United States, the regular copper-nickel coin alloy was referred to as nickel bronze, apparently an outgrowth of some wartime change in specifications. Before and since, a nickel bronze would require at least some tin in the alloy to meet the standards.

Q: Did the U.S. Mint consider a different alloy for the Anthony dollar?

An SBA trial piece exists which is 82 percent copper and 18 percent nickel.

Q: Why are the 1946 and later nickels cataloged as "Prewar alloy?"

This is a simple way of indicating that they reverted to the copper-nickel alloy which was used until 1942.

Q: Nickel coins are supposed to be magnetic. Doesn't mixing nickel with other metals in an alloy destroy this magnetic property?

Pure nickel is slightly magnetic, but as little as 20 percent of some other metal added to it will destroy this magnetic property. This is important to the coin maker, as slug rejection devices can be readily made to detect the magnetic properties of the metal that are missing from a counterfeit.

Q: What alloy is my light colored 1861 cent?

From 1859 to 1864 the coins were minted with a copper-nickel alloy, which contained 12 percent nickel. For obvious reasons they were called "white cents."

Q: Was there any effort or support by the United States Mint for the idea of going back to nickel as a metal for the cent?

The Bureau of the Mint more than once complained about the "gilding metal" alloy used for the cent. Typically, in 1911 the Mint Director, George E. Roberts, stated, "The Mint officials have always regarded the change (from an alloy of 88 percent copper and 12 percent nickel) as a backward step, and in the opinion of the Bureau, the percentage of nickel should have been increased instead of being reduced." He complained of the then current cents as "Unsatisfactory, as the coins soon become dull and dirty in appearance and when exposed to the salt air of the seacoast are rendered unfit for circulation."

Q: Is it possible to have an allergy to coins?

An allergy to nickel is well known. The effect is cumulative, and can cause dermatitis within one hour of handling nickel-alloy coins.

Q: When did they make the switch from calling the alloy "German silver" to "nickel silver?

The switch came during World War I when anything German was unpopular. However, even with the common usage changed, the old term never was completely eradicated, and still is used today. The term "German silver" was introduced in 1830 when a German brought the first sample of the alloy to Sheffield, England. The alloy invention is laid at the door of the Chinese at a much earlier date. German silver and nickel silver are the common names of an alloy of 65% copper, 23% zinc, and 12% nickel.

Q: Is copper considered to be bullion?

Normally no, but even mint people refer to copper as bullion. Mint records show that both Troy and avoirdupois pounds and ounces were used in the internal and public reports, making for some monumental problems in checking through the records.

Q: What is meant when a coin is described as having a porous surface?

Porosity is a problem with many of the early coins, especially the large cents. I think the generally accepted cause is a problem in getting the coin metal alloy fully mixed while in a molten state, compounded by problems in rolling it out. Typically porosity will give the piece a surface broken by a multitude of tiny irregular holes. Another possible cause is the use of an acid base cleaner, which dissolves one of the base metals out of the alloy, leaving a sponge-like remainder.

Q: What is a copper bronzed medal?

It's a medal struck in copper, then put through a bronzing process. Most early U.S. Mint medals are copper bronzed, but are listed as bronze.

Q: Please give me the alloy figures for the two 1982 cents.

The brass cents of 1962-1982 are 95% copper and 5% zinc, weighing 48.0 grains. The copper plated zinc cents substituted in 1982, and struck since, have a core of 99.2% zinc and 0.8% copper, plated with pure copper, making them 97.6% zinc and 2.4% copper, weighing 38.58 grains. Since the zinc cents are about 20% lighter, they can readily be detected by using a simple balance scale, made with a ruler and a known (pre1982) brass cent.

Q: Some old books say that the 1944-1946 cents were "shell casing brass," made from salvaged shell casings, with a composition of 70 percent copper and 30 percent zinc. Modern catalogs call them "shell casing brass," but give the composition as 95 percent copper and 5 percent zinc. Which is correct?

According to Ed Rochette, the original plan was to use the 70-30 alloy of the shell casings, but at the last moment enough copper became available to avoid the need for a third change in the composition in three years. To keep the patriotic flavor, a few shell casings were actually melted down, but the alloy remained the same 95 percent copper and 5 percent zinc. Some of the old books and catalogs missed the last-minute change, but did mention the "shell-casing brass." If the 70-30 alloy had been used, the cents would have been a bright golden color.

Q: I've been told that our cents, prior to the switch to copper plated zinc in 1982 were made out of "Dutch metal." Am I having my leg pulled?

Almost. The last brass cents were 95 percent copper and five percent zinc. The formula for Dutch metal is 11 parts copper to two parts zinc, which figures out to 84.6 percent copper.

Q: Did the United States Mint stick closely to the alloy specifications for the cent or were there variations?

There were many times when the specs got "bent" for one reason or another. The Mint reports usually ignored them, although they were cited in isolated reports, as for example, in 1902, where they were given as 95 percent copper and 2.5 percent each of tin and zinc. Figures given in the 1910 report imply that at Denver the actual alloy had even then turned to brass, since only 1.93 percent tin and 3.07 percent zinc were being used. From a variety of other evidence I would strongly suspect that anyone who cared to spend the time and money to check samples would find that a lot more brass cents have been struck since 1864 than those that are true bronze—with a majority of tin in the alloy.

Q: What is really meant by a "copper" coin?

It's one that is more than 95% copper. Anything less is a copper alloy.

Q: What's the life span of a brass or bronze cent?

The Mint figure is 25 years. No figure is available for the copper plated zinc.

Q: Is there a precedent for clad coinage?

The Greeks instituted a silver-clad copper coinage after C.E. 700.

Q: How are the clad layers bonded to the copper core for our clad coinage?

Originally they used an explosion bonding process, later a pressure method. A top Mint official told me explosive bonding was discarded in 1967 as too expensive, so the pressure bonding method was developed and used.

Q: I'm involved in an argument about clad coins. Doesn't a clad coin have layers of nickel, or are they silver, or what?

There are copper-nickel clad coins, with layers of 75% copper and 25% nickel bonded to a copper core, which contain no silver. There are silver clad coins with layers of silver and copper alloy bonded to copper cores, and there are silver clad coins with layers of silver-copper bonded to silver-copper cores. A "clad" coin can contain any alloy in the clad layers or the core, not limited to any specific metal.

Q: Are the 1982 zinc cents the same as the 1943 "lead" cents?

The 1943 cents were zinc-plated steel. The 1982 (and later) cents are copper plated zinc. The 1943 cents are magnetic, the 1982 cents are not. The latter is about 20 percent lighter than brass.

Q: I have a 1983 cent which seems to have been struck in some strange metal. It is a shiny grey color.

Somewhat puzzling is a recent rash of questions which very obviously come from people who assume that all our cents are still "copper." For those readers still living in the brass age, beginning in mid-1982 all U.S. cents have been struck on copper plated zinc planchets, which weigh about 20 percent less than the pre-1982 brass cents. Your coin is either on a planchet that missed the plating process, or has been altered by removing the copper plating.

Q: What was the medical objection that was raised when Congress was debating making aluminum cents?

The principal medical objection to the aluminum cents was that if they are accidentally swallowed they are difficult to pick up with an X-ray machine. At the 1974 hearings on an aluminum cent before the House Banking Committee, Dr. Richard E. Reichelderfer of Johns Hopkins University testified that aluminum coins are more difficult to detect with X-rays, and thus could cause medical problems if swallowed.

Q: A couple of times I've been told that the copper-plated zinc cents can be dangerous if swallowed. Is this true, or just a myth?

The zinc core does pose a potential medical problem, but I have yet to hear of a serious illness from ingesting a zinc coin—at least as far as humans are concerned. There have been a number of reports of dogs becoming sick from swallowing a zinc coin. These reports indicate that the stomach acids would cause problems if a human were to swallow a zinc cent. A random check of several poison centers showed that for the most part they were unaware of the hazard, although this situation may have been corrected by now.

Q: Coins have a long life expectancy, but wasn't there an unusual period estimated for the steel cents?

When the 1943 zinc plated steel cents went into circulation, Moses E. Smith, Superintendent of the Denver Mint is quoted as stating, "Steel pennies (sic) will probably be in circulation for the next 100 years." This ranks with President Johnson's statement that silver coins would remain in circulation alongside the clad coins in 1965.

Q: Why wasn't the goloid alloy accepted for our coinage?

Goloid is an alloy of gold, silver and copper, patented in 1877 by Wheeler H. Hubbell. It was used for several 1880 patterns for metric dollars. The untreated coins failed to show any special identification features and were easily counterfeited, and it was impossible to control the value of the silver and gold, requiring a constantly changing ratio.

An 1878 goloid metric dollar.

Chapter 4

ALTERATIONS

Alterations, or changes in the original or intended design for a coin, token or medal, are the bane of the collector. Knowing what to look for, or expect, from an alteration is half the battle.

Q: Why do dealer ads refer to "full date" Buffalo nickels? Is there something here that I'm missing in the description?

The Buffalo nickel design is such that the date wears off first, long before the rest of the design is seriously affected. Coins with partial dates have only slight value, if any, and those with the date completely gone are worth only a couple of cents over face value. The dealer is telling you his coins are in good enough shape so that you can distinguish all four digits in the date.

Q: A coin I sent to a grading service was returned with the notation that it had been "whizzed." What does this mean?

It means that your coin has been altered by some method (buffing, polishing, etc.) which moved the surface metal of the coin around. This is often done to simulate a higher grade coin, a practice frowned on by ANA, PNG, and reputable coin dealers. The ANA definition is: "The artificial treatment of a coin by wire brushing, acid dipping, or otherwise removing metal from the coin's surface to give it the artificial appearance of being in a higher grade." If this is the case it will reduce the value sharply, as responsible coin dealers will not handle whizzed coins. Although I am unaware of anyone ever being prosecuted for whizzing a coin, federal law states that "fraudulent....diminishing of a coin" is illegal. Whizzing a coin will remove some of the metal, decreasing the weight. Since this "diminishes" the coin, it could be grounds for a criminal action, especially if the coin happened to be gold or silver, although the law (Title 18—Sect. 331) specifically says "...any of the coins coined at the mints of the United States, or any foreign coins."

Q: I was recently offered several semi-key and key date Buffalo nickels that had the dates restored with some sort of acid. Isn't that illegal?

Restored date Buffalo nickels have been around for a long time. The method used is the same as that used to bring up serial numbers on a gun, that have been filed off. The use of an acid to show the date on a worn coin is not illegal, but it does place the coin in the altered class. Altered coins are not considered collectible, so they have no collector value. If you want to collect them, that's your business, but don't do it with the supposition that "someday" they might have some value. You can go down to the beach and collect a bucket of sand with as much prospect of future profit.

Q: Enameled coins have been a popular collectible in other countries. How about U.S. coins?

The topic came up during the Columbian Exposition in Chicago in 1893. An enterprising American jeweler on a trip abroad spotted the enameled coins, and took a quantity of the Columbian commemorative halves with him to London and had them reworked. When he brought them back to the states they readily sold for $5 to $10. However, when an attempt was made to get 100,000 of the surplus halves from the Treasury, the Secret Service stepped in and announced that any enameled coins would be seized. While there was no law preventing the mutilation of the coins, the Secret Service argued that if the enamel was scraped off, the innocent possessor of the coin would only be able to get bullion value (then about 25 cents) for it. The scheme collapsed under the Government pressure, so no doubt the original samples would be pretty rare items.

Q: A friend of mine has an early Washington quarter with a crude swastika punched into it. Any idea as to the source?

American sympathizers for the Nazi cause took a lesson from the Austrian Nazi party and started altering coins with the swastika shortly after the German invasion of Poland in 1939. Enough of them were altered to bring them to the attention of Treasury officials, but other than passing notice in the press, the coins attracted little attention. Once the U.S. entered the war the practice pretty well stopped as anyone attempting to pass such an altered coin was exposed to the patriotic wrath of the public. Many of the alterations were crude, often done with a screwdriver as a punch.

Q: I have a clad coin with a recessed core. The clad layers hang over the edges, but you can see the reeding on the smaller diameter core. What caused this?

I'm sorry, but from your description you have an altered coin. The quarter has been dipped in acid, which cut down the core more rapidly than the rest of the coin, leaving a "slot" between the clad layers, but still showing the reeding on the edge of the copper core. As an altered coin it has no value. Acid can do strange things to a coin. I recently authenticated a large cent which to the unaided eye appeared normal and was believed to have been struck on a half cent planchet. However, under close examination it turned out to have been reduced with acid, the weight significantly below normal, but still above that of a half cent. The design will remain legible on an acid treated coin even when it has been reduced to paper thinness.

Q: I have a thin coin that is smaller than normal. The diameter is less, and the design seems to be reduced to match. What's wrong?

 Smaller and thinner usually means the coin has been reduced with acid. There are hundreds of cents of all dates which have been altered with acid, but these pieces usually are thinner than a normal cent and have a generally "fuzzy" surface appearance. The key point in identification is that the design is essentially complete even on a paper thin coin. This would not happen with a genuine thin planchet strike, which would show missing or weak detail because of a lack of metal to fill the dies.

Q: I have a quarter which has no reeding. What caused this?

This is a popular question with several answers. If the coin has a larger than normal diameter with "stretched" letters around the rim it is probably a broadstrike, struck without the collar, and worth a premium. If it is normal size or slightly smaller, it probably has been altered by hammering or grinding the reeding off the coin. If it has been altered by hammering the rim you can usually find traces of the reeding using a magnifier.

Q: I have a coin which has a date one or more years from now, or several years before or after a series began or ended. How valuable is this?

Very likely it has no value. There is no way that a coin could be struck, even accidentally, with a 1998 date in 1994, so it is undoubtedly an alteration or a fake. To produce a coin with such a date at the mint it would be necessary to make a hub with the date, make a die and then strike the coin, actions involving several dozen people. Obviously a conspiracy of that magnitude just to produce a single coin that you found in circulation is completely unbelievable. Thus, your coin is worthless, and technically illegal to own since the date has been altered. It should be turned in to a local bank for transmittal to the Secret Service as it is also illegal to sell, trade, or even give the coin to someone else.

Q: Wasn't there a flurry of altered Buffalo nickels back in the early 1980s that had a mint mark embossed on them?

A quantity of Buffalo nickels, most dated between 1913 and 1926 were altered in this fashion. The work was done by drilling a small hole in the edge of the coin. An embossing tool was then inserted in the hole which was used to force the surface metal up to form either a D or an S. Once the fakes were publicized, the source dried up, but not before at least one 1909-S VDB cent was similarly faked. Some of the coins may have gone into collections, so the coin edge should always be closely checked for signs of tampering.

Q: There are still stories circulating about the reeded 1937 U.S. cents and nickels. What's the true story?

300 sets of the coins were reeded, apparently by a mint employee, but it is unclear whether in the mint or someone's garage workshop. Whichever, the reeding was done after the coins were struck, was not authorized by the Mint, and constitutes an alteration of the coins. Ira Reed had the coins reeded and brought them to the 1941 ANA convention where they were sold. In 1960, a pair of the coins sold at auction for $87.50, but they have since been discredited as mint products. They were altered after being struck, using at least three different knurling tools, making them virtually impossible to authenticate as "original" pieces. The statement stands: there are no genuine mint product, modern reeded cents or nickels of any date.

Q: I have a coin which is larger than normal in diameter, slightly thinner than normal, but the weight is normal. Any idea what happened to it?

You have a so-called "Texas" coin, an alteration produced by placing the coin between two pieces of heavy leather, and hand hammering it until it expands. When expertly done there will be little if any distortion of the design. As an altered coin it has no value. This isn't just done to nickels either, as other letters reported a similar quarter and a dime.

Q: In previous columns you have mentioned the "Texas" nickels and other coins pounded to a larger diameter. Isn't that illegal?

Right you are! President Harry Truman signed a law in July 1951 which made the practice illegal, and tacked on a $2,000 fine and five years in prison to make it smart. This law appears as Sect. 331, Title 18, U.S. Code, which prohibits "fraudulent alteration and muti-lation of a coin." The fraud involved is implicit in changing the diameter of a coin to that of a larger denomination, so that it could be used in a vending machine, telephone, etc.

Q: I have a coin with incuse, reversed designs on both sides. How could that happen?

You have a "sandwich" alteration. It was produced by sandwiching a coin between two others, then hammering the pile, producing a coin which has incused, reversed images of the two outside coins in the pile. These are often mistaken for a double strike. There are at least two numismatic meanings for the term "sandwich coin." The second meaning is attached to the clad coin, which has a solid core surrounded by clad layers.

Q: I've been offered a gold-plated "Racketeer" 1883 nickel. Can I get it authenticated?

Since the gold plating was applied after the coin was minted, there is no way to prove when, or where the coin received the plating. As a result, nobody is going to be able to authenticate the coin. There have been numerous modern copies of the "originals," some even plated with brass, so this is not something you would want to pay good money to buy. It is a hard and fast rule governing the minting process, that anything that occurs after the final impact of the die pair is not part of the minting process and cannot be accurately traced or fixed as to when or where it occurred. This applies even to recognized countermarks and counterstamps, which are much easier to fake than the actual struck coin. They however can usually be authenticated by a qualified expert. The Racketeer nickels should exhibit no wear under the gold plating.

Q: I have a coin with an impression of another coin on top of it, that is raised, rather than being into the metal. How could this occur?

Clear glue on a coin is one of the most common accidents that is mistaken for a minting variety, especially when another coin has been pressed into the surface of the glue. Always be suspicious of anything raised above the normal surface of the coin, especially

1883 Racketeer nickel.

if it doesn't look like coin metal. In many cases you can use your fingernail to separate the glue, but don't use anything harder than the nail or you will damage the coin. If left on the coin, this glue will protect the original surface, while where there is no glue, the coin will "age" normally, and turn dark. Clear glue will often fool people when it has been impressed with the design from another coin, so always check a strange looking coin for glue as one of the first tests you make on it.

Q: I have a coin which has a very thick edge, but no reeding. Was this done at the Mint?

From your description your coin has had the edge hammered. This will thicken it and eliminate the reeding. On larger coins this was frequently done as the first steps in making a silver coin into a ring. Many GIs used a mess-kit spoon to repeatedly hammer the edge until it was quite thick. A genuine reedless coin would show a rough, broken edge surface but there would be no thickening.

Q: I have a cent struck in what appears to be wrong metal. Can this be?

The usual answer is that it has been plated. Check the weight, or if it is out of round, thin, etc. Resist the temptation to perform a destructive test such as scratching, cutting, cleaning or filing the piece. A plated cent will weigh very close to the normal 48.0 grains for the pre-1982 brass, or 38.6 grains for the post-1982 copper plated zinc. A cent on a wrong planchet will usually be out of round, with weak or missing design areas, and the weight will match that of the intended coin, such as 35.0 grains for a cent on a silver dime planchet. Many of these plated pieces have been produced to take advantage of the tale of the 1974 dated aluminum cents which disappeared into the possession of a number of members of Congress and were never returned. The Mint passed out samples to support a change in alloy for the cent. None of those genuine aluminum cents have ever turned up in the hobby.

Q: I have inherited a collection which includes a 1943 cent struck on a brass or bronze planchet. I have examined it closely and there is no evidence of tampering and the 3 is the same as on the regular steel cents. How can I get it authenticated?

The quickest check is to use a magnet. If your coin is attracted, then it is a steel cent which has been plated, with no collector value. Even if this is not the case, the chances are very slim that your coin is genuine. The next step is weight. A steel cent weighs about 41-42 grains, while a brass or bronze planchet weighs 48 grains. If the weight is correct then the piece would have to be authenticated. There are several possible ways of faking these cents, including some that were made with counterfeit dies. Others were made by altering 1933 or 1953 cents, but these will have a different shaped 3. On the genuine 1943 cents, the elongated tail extends down to the left, rather than being sharply curved. Thousands of steel cents were commercially copper plated. A genuine coin must be a sharp, clear strike, undamaged, and very high grade. Don't cut, file, scratch, or polish to "test" the metal. Instead, use a non destructive test: weigh the piece.

Q: I have a 1943 lead cent which shows some copper on it. Was this one of the first 1943 cents struck?

First of all, your 1943 cent is not lead, but zinc plated steel, which will be attracted by a magnet. The copper on your coin undoubtedly is a plating applied after the piece left the mint, as thousands were plated and sold as "novelty" coins, so it has no extra value.

Q: I was offered a gold plated coin recently. Isn't this illegal?

Immoral, but not illegal. Under the provisions of Section 331, Title 18, U.S. Code, you can do almost anything to a coin, except alter the date or value. (The prohibitions on gold plating were rescinded in 1969.) For those of you beginning your collections, a word of caution: "All that glitters is not gold," and a gold plated coin in your collection is a dead item. It has been altered, so it will never appreciate in value. The gold plating involves only a few cents worth of gold, so even if the price of gold doubled or tripled, you would not get your money back from a plated coin.

Q: I have a coin with a bubble under one of the clad layers. Is this a minting variety, and if so, what is it worth?

This seems to be one of our more popular questions recently. You can create bubbles in most any clad coin by the sudden application of heat, as with a welding torch. Telltale signs are black soot in among the letters and discolored metal, but even if genuine these are so easy to fake that none—good or bad—have any value.

Q: I have a cent which appears to be normal, except that the reverse is smooth. Is this a known variety?

Sorry, but your cent has been altered by grinding off the reverse. It's impossible to strike only one side of a coin, so this is definitely not a minting variety and has no collector value. The reverse design is in such low relief that removing it lowers the coin weight by only 3 grains, out of the 48.0 grain total weight. Unless you weigh the coin this weight loss is so small that you might not notice it.

Q: What is a tooled coin?

It's a coin which has been worked over with engraving tools, an alteration. It's a coin you want to stay away from. In the late 1800s and even as recently as the 1920s, it was an accepted practice among collectors to "enhance" the appearance of a worn or poorly struck coin by using engraving tools to cut into the coin metal to restore parts of the design, such as locks of hair or a weak date digit. Today such coins are not acceptable to collectors, any more than are coins that have been whizzed or otherwise damaged. A coin struck from a reworked die is perfectly acceptable, but nothing done to the coin after it leaves the mint is going to improve its value.

Q: A long time collector once told me that a chop marked trade dollar is scarcer, and thus worth more than one without the chop marks. Is this still true?

As late as the 1940s collectors would pay a slight premium for chop marked coins, on the theory that this proved they had actually circulated in the Orient. Chop marks are alterations or mutilations of the coin, and when the trade dollars were called in and redeemed, those with chop marks were rejected. The story that those with chops were worth more traces back to a coin dealer who was attempting to unload an accumulation of chop marked coins several decades ago.

Q: What is meant by a "reprocessed" steel cent?

The 1943 zinc plated steel cents were reprocessed by stripping the zinc plating and replating the coins. Reprocessed steel cents have a totally different surface than the original coins. This plating has a completely different appearance because it has not been struck by the die. The reprocessed coins have a different, brighter appearance than the normal coins, and examination under magnification will usually show wear and damage covered by the replating. Since this is an alteration of the coin, it reduces the collector value, usually to face value. Reprocessed coins are altered coins and cannot be sold as "genuine." They have been tolerated by the hobby for many years, but only if clearly labeled as reprocessed when sold.

Q: I have found a wheat cent which has steps in the rims on both sides. The coin appears slightly undersize and somewhat bent, and the edge is concave. Did this happen at the mint?

This is an altered coin, one that was squeezed into a lucky token. The cent is placed in the (full size) center hole of the token, and then struck by the token dies. This squeezes the token metal against the edge of the coin, which reduces the diameter of the cent, buckles the field, and causes the concave edge. It would be impossible for a coin to be struck in this fashion at the mint.

Q: I have a large cent which has a misspelling of "CENT." I've never seen anything in any of the catalogs about it, so am I right in assuming it is rare and valuable?

You will progress a lot farther as a variety collector if you assume exactly the opposite about any coin variety that you find, as the principal reason for NOT finding a listing is that it either is so common that it isn't worth wasting paper on, or that it is—as in this case—an alteration. This particular case is a very popular alteration of the large cent, as examples are known for just about every date that they were struck. Since it is an alteration, it is worthless to a collector. Rule two of variety collecting is to always assume that a new find is common and of little or no value until you can prove otherwise.

Q: What is a soft die?

A soft die is an aluminum or hard plastic tool used to alter a coin. It's squeezed or hammered onto the face of one coin, and the resulting incuse image is used to alter another coin. One example was a 1977/6 overdate cent, reported from Florida. The piece was a hoax which was featured by a hobby publication after the Mint declared it genuine. When it was too late to retract the story, the Mint did some further checking and found that the coin had been faked with a so called "soft" die. Two Floridians were arrested for making the altered coin and other similar pieces. The method used was similar to that used to fake the multi-strike 1964 cents, many of which are still around. There is an aluminum alloy often used which becomes almost as soft as butter when heat treated and then hardens overnight to equal soft steel. I have no idea how long they have been doing this, but I would suspect back at least to World War I. Coins struck with soft dies can usually be detected by the spreading out of the design, because both the die and the coin expand as the die is being made.

Q: What would cause my cent to be smaller than normal?

Correct diameter should be .750 (3/4 inch), so the immediate suspicion is that the coin has been altered, as there is no normal way of striking an undersized coin. It would require the special manufacture of a pair of dies and a matching collar. One possibility is that the coin has been "swedged," or forced through a tapered tube, which will reduce the diameter, or it may have been struck into a lucky token. Smaller, thinner coins have been reduced with acid. The collars used by the mint to surround the planchet as it is struck by the dies can vary only a couple of thousandths of an inch before they are discarded. Thus we have to look in another direction for a cause for your small cent.

Q: My silver dollar has a clearly defined, and relief (raised) "X" in the field in front of Liberty's face. There seems to be a lot of controversy, as I can't get the same answer from anyone that I show it to. Is it a minting variety, or not?

If you put your coin under a microscope, you will undoubtedly find that someone has cut the "X" in the field with a sharp instrument, such as a knife blade. This shoves the metal up and out of the cut, and when this metal is pressed or hammered down, it will spread out and hide the cut, and unless carefully examined under magnification will be quite deceptive. This is the most popular grafitti found on such altered coins. Dies are sometimes cancelled by cutting deep lines across them, resulting in raised ridges on a coin struck with a cancelled die, but the appearance is quite different.

Q: I have a cent which has the design strangely flattened on both sides, with the metal looking like it squeezed out between the die and the coin around the letters. What caused it?

I haven't seen one of these in some time, but the coin has been altered by placing it between two blocks of wood and hammering it. Two virtually identical coins came in the same mail, the first I've seen in several years. Both of the coins were altered by hammering them between two blocks of wood. The metal driven into the field from the rims is a key clue here. This was a very popular alteration back in the 1960s, when you were likely to run across one or two a month.

Chapter 5

ASSAY, U.S. ASSAY COMMISSION

One government control over the quality of our coins is the assay. While politics may get involved too, the intent is to ensure that our coins are up to standard.

Q: When did the U.S. Mint institute the practice of having its coins checked annually by an outside group?

The first commission to examine and weigh the currency was established in 1823. This would ultimately become the Assay Commission, which was a group of private citizens appointed each year to conduct tests and review the coin production records of the Mint. One of the principal duties over the years was to compare the weight of the standard pound, made and used by the Mint, with the original standard pound sent over from England in 1827.

Q: Have coin collectors ever gone on "strike" against the Mint?

Collectors picketed the Philadelphia Mint on Feb. 9, 1977 because of President Carter's order eliminating the civilian membership in the annual Assay Commission. Billed as an "economy" move, the protests were ignored and the Assay Commission became a part of history.

Q: What was the Trial of the Pyx?

It was the traditional check of weight, bullion content, and fineness of English coins. It was initiated during the reign of Edward III in England, 1327-1376. It's still conducted by the Company of Goldsmiths. The pyx is the box into which the Mint Master placed the coins to be tested. Boxes of coins were called pyxides, and the shortened form came down to us as a standard for coin tests. Assays of a similar nature were made in 1208 during the reign of King John, and in 1248, by King Henry III and the Lord Mayor of London.

Chapter 6

AUCTIONS

Auctions are a key method of obtaining the best possible price for a coin. Not for everyone, but for the collector who has a valuable coin, or a significant collection, the auction is a mecca.

Q: What's the point of a collector attending an auction? Seems to me the dealers get all the good coins.

This is a popular fallacy. Any knowledgeable collector can outbid most dealers who have to keep their profit margin in mind. A collector who has a specific coin in mind for his collection usually can get it because of the leeway the dealer must have to come out ahead on the deal. There are exceptions of course, such as when a dealer is representing a client who also wants a specific coin and has instructed the dealer to bid whatever it takes to get the coin. However, that comes down to a head-to-head competition between two collectors for the same coin. As a typical example, a collector trying to buy a $100 coin can afford to bid $100 for it, while a dealer buying it for his stock can only afford to bid from $50 to $80. Also, the collector usually is interested in a relatively small number of coins while the dealer has to spread his available cash over as many coins as he needs.

Q: Old-timers frequently refer to "buy" bids. Please explain.

"Buy" bids were the bane of any auctioneer, and coin auctions were no exception. A bidder (usually by mail or telephone) would tell the auctioneer to bid on his behalf for whatever amount was necessary to win a particular lot. In theory this worked, but when more than one "buy" bid was entered for a given lot, the situation became impossible, because there could be only one sale. Such bids are no longer accepted, except in rare instances.

Q: When was the first million dollar sale of a single private coin collection?

The Stack's auction of the George F. Scanlon collection, October 24-27, 1973 realized $1,093,890. Scanlon began collecting at the age of 65 and the collection sold was less than ten years old.

Q: I have a quantity of old auction catalogs that I would like to dispose of. Is there any market for them?

You may not get rich out of the deal, but most such catalogs are in demand and if you happen to have a really rare or hard to find item, you may be pleasantly surprised by what it will bring. Reading old catalogs is one way of learning a lot about your hobby.

Q: Weren't most old-time coin auctions by the piece rather than by lots?

This was the common and traditional practice in the coin business in the U.S. up until about the 1950s, even though stamp auctions were run so as to include both individual stamps and lots containing numbers of stamps. The coin dealers and collectors wanted each coin sold separately to avoid problems such as acquiring unwanted duplicates, or having to buy several low grade coins to get one valuable piece. European coin dealers usually sold coins at auction in lots, along with individual coins.

Q: What is a "private treaty" sale?

The term is used for any private sale where a buyer and a seller agree on a price for some item and complete the transaction. Technically, almost any purchase you make is a private treaty sale, although the term usually is reserved for a sale where there is at least some bargaining back and forth between buyer and seller.

Chapter 7

AUTHENTICATION

Is it genuine? Has it been faked in some way? The authenticator is the one with the answer. The collector should recognize the need for, and the importance of getting qualified advice.

Q: I have an unstruck planchet that I can't identify. Can you help?

Unless the planchet is for a regular U.S. coin it may be difficult, especially if the edge is not upset, to produce a raised area where the rim of the coin will be. The problem is that anyone who has access to a punch press can produce a simulated Type I blank. Producing a Type II planchet with the raised rim is more difficult, but even that can be faked. Type I blanks for the recent copper-plated zinc cents are virtually impossible to authenticate.

Q: My friend showed me a half dollar which he believes to be 90 percent silver, even though it weighs the same as a normal clad half. How can I convince him?

If showing him the answer in print will help, here goes. A 90 percent silver half weighs 192.9 grains. A 40 percent silver half weighs 177.5 grains, and a copper-nickel clad half weighs 175 grains. If the coin matches the clad weight, it would be impossible for it to be silver. You are likely to run into halves which show little sign of the copper core, and even some which have been silver plated.

Q: I have a Kennedy half dollar (1968) which doesn't "ring" right. When dropped on a table it makes a dull thud. Is it a counterfeit?

The usual reason for a coin not "ringing" when dropped is that it has some sort of internal flaw, a split or void, which may not reach the surface. This is one reason why ringing a coin is at best only a negative test, besides being potentially damaging to the coin. The key rule here is that you should never, ever perform a destructive, or potentially destructive test on any coin which might have some collector value. The best non-destructive test in this case would be to weigh the coin to see if it is normal weight. That would help to confirm that this is probably an internal flaw, without taking the chance of denting or scratching the piece.

Q: I have a half dollar which appears to be solid copper. It has a nick in it where someone cut into the metal, but it shows solid copper. Can you tell me anything about it?

I wish I had a dollar for every coin that has been ruined by the stupidity of using a destructive test for being on a wrong metal planchet. It is doubly unfortunate that the person that would cut into a coin lacked the knowledge that it is virtually impossible to cut through plating with any sharp instrument. The act of cutting drags the plating down the sides of the cut, making the piece look like solid metal. Although there is a possibility that your half dollar might have been struck on a planchet that was from the end of a piece of strip which had been rolled out without the cladding, I'm more inclined to think that it probably has been plated. There is a very simple, non-destructive test that everyone in the hobby should know about, and that is to WEIGH the coin. If the coin is normal weight—175 grains—then it has been plated. If it is significantly over or under that figure—at least 5 grains—then there is a possibility that it might be a wrong metal strike, and would be worth having authenticated.

Q: What is a "dumb" coin?

Its an old term applied to a coin or planchet which, although genuine, lacked the "ring" of a normal piece. The most usual cause was an internal crack. These pieces are ample reason for classing the "ringing" of a coin as only a negative test, as well as being dangerous to the condition of a high grade coin.

Q: What was the purpose of the marble shelf on the old-time cash registers?

While I doubt that many people have ever stopped to consider that there might have been some specific purpose other than decoration for this particular part of the ornate brass and bronze machines, it did have a purpose. The marble was used as a test for counterfeit silver coins.Genuine pieces would "ring" on the stone while a fake would sound differently. Join in a collective shudder as we consider how many collectible coins were permanently damaged by this destructive testing.

Q: What is the so called "pencil point" test for proof coins?

This is a method for testing the reflectivity of a proof coin, as opposed to a coin which is a first strike from new dies. A proof struck twice or more on a polished planchet by polished dies will accurately reflect the point of a pencil or a finger held above the coin, while "usually" a first strike will not show this reflection. The test is not infallible, so it is not a positive guarantee that a coin is, or isn't a proof, but it is one way of running a preliminary check on a suspect coin before more detailed analysis is undertaken. The test fails if the coin has been cleaned.

Q: I found a coin in circulation that is quite rare and quite valuable. Since it was circulating I intend to sell it without getting it authenticated. Any problems with that?

There's a basic premise here that needs to be discussed very frankly. Many collectors make the grave mistake of presuming that anything found in circulation "has" to be genuine, merely because it was in fact circulating. This is a potentially serious miscalculation, frequently made for both regular coins and for minting varieties. While it's true that the grossest fakes and alterations are going to be quickly spotted, many coins that have been altered or damaged, whether accidentally or deliberately, get into circulation. As collectors, we usually look closely at our coins. The vast majority of the public look only to confirm the denomination, often only by outline or "feel," so all sorts of fakes and alterations can get by. A coin found in circulation has to be judged just as carefully as any other coin from any source.

Q: Why won't a magnet attract one of the new copper plated zinc cents?

This is a throwback to the 1943 zinc plated steel cents, which were magnetic. Zinc is not magnetic, so a magnet has no effect on it.

Chapter 8

BAGS OF COINS

Coin bags are a popular and easily recognized method of handling bulk coins. Obtaining a fresh, sealed bag of coins is one possible source of a new minting variety, such as the recent 1955 doubled-die cents. But, bags have their problems too.

Q: Where can I get a mint sealed bag of coins?

Try a local bank, an armored car service, or a coin dealer. A bank that is a member of the Federal Reserve Bank can order coins, but you may have to pay transportation charges. There is no guarantee that ordered bags will be new coins. The U.S. Mint deals only with Federal Reserve Banks, and they deal only with local member banks.

Q: I searched a mint-sealed bag and found one example of a die variety. Shouldn't my coin be quite valuable?

It's not at all unusual to find a single coin in a bag like that. If you spend the time you probably will be able to identify from four or five to as many as twenty other dies in that bag, each with a differing number of examples. Bags are not filled at the coin press. The coins go to a bin into which the production from a number of coin presses has been dumped, either directly or by a conveyor system. The coins are further mixed when the bin is dumped into the counting machines, which is where the bags are filled. Finding one coin in a bag of 5,000 cents means that you have examined less than five minutes of production from 10 to 20 coin presses or die pairs, out of the hundreds that are running. To examine every coin from one die alone you'd have to go through up to 200 bags, assuming that all of the coins from that one die were put into the same bag. After going through the 200 bags and still finding only one coin, then you could say that it may be rare.

Q: What can you tell me about the miniature bags the Mint sold?

Miniature bags were sold through 1973, but sale was discontinued in 1974 because of the speculation in 1974-S cents. The 1973 and 1972 bags of 15 coins (5 each from the three mints) sold over the counter for 25 cents and by mail for 40 cents. The 1971 bags each had 20 coins of one mint, and also sold for 25 cents. In 1970 bags of 25 cents were made up for each of the three mints (Philadelphia, Denver, and San Francisco) and sold at a slight premium. They were dated, and were quite popular with collectors, even though bags are a poor way of storing coins.

Multiples of five bags up to 25 were sold. Costs including insured mail were $2 for 5 bags, $3.75 for 10, $5 for 15, $6.50 for 20, and $8 for 25 bags.

Q: What is meant by a "bag" of coins?

Coins are bagged at the mint in cloth bags, or at the Federal Reserve Banks. Bag sizes are standardized with 1,000 dollars; 1,000 halves; 2,000 quarters; 10,000 dimes; 4,000 nickels; or 5,000 cents.

Chapter 9

BICENTENNIAL COINS

The bicentennial coins and medals make up an integral part of U.S. coinage history. While the billions of coins minted make them pointless from an investment standpoint, they are a commemorative piece of memorabilia.

Q: For a number of years after 1976, the Mint reports included listings of the Bicentennial coin sets. I thought they halted production in 1976?

They did. The figures, which were sometimes labeled, and sometimes not, covered the number of sets sold from the surplus that the Mint had on hand, and did not indicate any new production. None of the Bicentennial coins were struck after 1976. The last coin was struck by the Mint Director, Mary Brooks, at San Francisco on June 22, 1976. It isn't just the collector who has problems, as I know of an official of a foreign mint who had made the same mistake in assuming that production had gone on. The Mint has officially stated that no silver coins were struck between 1976 and 1982, when the Washington halves were struck, but there were a few accidental strikes on silver planchets.

Q: How were the bicentennial designs able to be used without an eagle?

The enabling act authorizing the designs omitted the exemption, but the designs were accepted as the "intent" of Congress, even if not actually authorized. The eagle was not specifically exempted from the law, but the House report on the bill indicated the Congressional intent to leave the eagle off the bicentennial coins.

Q: Was the Statue of Liberty in the finals for the bicentennial coin designs?

The statue got to the semi-finals, but was knocked out because it was not a direct part of revolutionary history. Despite this, it was the central design of more than 800 entries.

Q: Did soldiers from Haiti fight in the American Revolution?

The bicentennial 1000 gourdes of 1974 depicts the Battle of Savannah in which Haitian troops under French command fought against the British.

Q: What was the Troy weight of the ARBA gold and silver medals? The selling prices?

The American Revolution Bicentennial Administration issued several medals between 1972 and 1976. The 9/10-inch gold contained .370 ounce. The 3-inch sterling silver contained 7.822 ounces, the 1-1/2-inch sterling .925 ounce. There also were gold plated bronze medals, with a negligible amount of gold. The gold 3-inch sold for $4000, the 1-5/16-inch for $400, the .906-inch for $100. The 1-1/2-inch gold plated bronze was $15, the silver 3-inch $150, the 1-1/2-inch $25, the Bronze 1-1/2-inch $5. All of the pieces had the Statue of Liberty design.

Q: I know there are two varieties of the bicentennial Ike dollar, but did they ever determine a way of identifying the 1975 from the 1976 strikes for the Bicentennial quarters and halves?

Outside of a few individual dies with defects there was no discernable difference between the coins struck in the two years with the 1976 date.

A sampling of various bicentennial coins.

Chapter 10

BLAKE $20 COPIES

One of the most common and recurring questions that I answer concerns the myriad of copies of the Blake & Co. gold piece. Virtually every other early colonial and major territorial coins have been copied, but none have caused as much consternation and disappointment as the Blake copies.

Q: I have a Blake & Co. coin which appears to be gold, pictures a coin press, and has an incuse 20 on it. What is it worth?

I'm sorry to disappoint you, but you have a very common copy of an early California piece. The original was gold, but your piece is probably brass. The Chrysler Corporation had scores of thousands of the copies (brass) of the $20 gold coin made in 1969 to promote the introduction of the 1970 Gold Duster Valiant. They are a perennial problem for collectors. There is one original in the Lily collection in the Smithsonian, and a second in the John J. Ford collection and that is all. The rest are just worthless copies. If you are clinging to one of the copies of the 20, thinking it may be genuine, weigh the piece. The genuine Blake $20 gold piece weighs 507.7 grains or 32.9 grams. The $50 piece weighs 1284.6 grains or 83.241 grams. By contrast the 1915-S Pan Pacific $50 gold pieces officially weighed 1,290 grains or 83.592 grams.

A fake $20 gold piece dated 1855.

Q: Was one of the $20 Blake & Co. gold coins the subject of a lawsuit?

In the Aug. 7, 1976 issue of *Numismatic News* we reported a lawsuit in Michigan between members of a family who were fighting over one that was found in an estate. A jeweler finally weighed the piece that was in contention and found it to be one of the worthless copies.

Q: You've mentioned the Blake and Co. $20 gold pieces numerous times, but wasn't there a matching $50 piece?

Because of the hundreds of thousands of brass copies of the $20 gold piece with the coin press on the obverse, the $20 is much more well known. The coin you inquired about is from the same obverse die, but with 50 punched into the center of the reverse. Only one specimen is reported, in the John J. Ford collection.

Chapter 11

BUYING AND SELLING

Buying and selling coins concerns the lifeblood of the hobby. Without the constant interchange over the bourse table, across the coin shop counter, or by mail, there could be no collecting as we know it.

Q: I bought a coin and took it out of the holder to have it authenticated. Now the dealer I bought it from says I broke an implied contract with him by doing this. Is this correct?

Most coin dealers, for their own protection, stipulate that once a coin is removed from their holder, then any guarantee is void. The recommended way to avoid such problems is to have the dealer get the coin authenticated before you take possession of it. You may have to pay the authentication fee, but it's a small price to pay for peace of mind. Otherwise, work out some sort of agreement with the dealer before you open the holder.

Q: How can dealers offer proof and mint sets for less than the original issue price? Did they get a rakeoff from the Mint, or aren't these Mint packaged sets?

There is no law requiring coin dealers, or any other merchant, to charge more than he pays for an item, which is why you see "loss leader" ads in the papers every day. Dealers usually pay the same prices for Mint-issued coins as anyone else. When they are over-stocked the only way to liquidate is to sell below cost. This is a periodic complaint from readers who were brought up to believe that coins were government property that have a fixed value. This view causes a lot of confusion for the novice collector since it is not based on fact. Coins, once issued, are a commodity, like cars or nuts or screws. A car dealer faced with today's market offers "cash back." The coin dealer offers the coin at less than he paid for it, even less than face value if he is willing to take a loss to clear out his stock and get his hands on some cash.

Q: Where do the dealers get their huge stocks of upper grade proof coins?

Many dealers break up sets by the thousands and hand pick the best struck coins. A lot of collectors are doing the same thing, and assembling their own high grade proof sets. There is no rule that says you have to leave the coins in their original packaging. Dealers plan ahead and buy surplus sets from local collectors.

Q: I have a number of coins that I bought, which have two and three letter combinations printed on the holders in ink, but I can't make any sense out of them. Are they grade abbreviations or what?

The symbols you describe are a dealer price code, and have nothing to do with grading. The usual procedure is to take a 10 letter word and assign each letter to one of the 10 digits, so that the price paid for a piece can be coded. If you have enough of them you can undoubtedly break the code.

Q: How do I go about becoming a coin dealer? Do I have to have a license to become a coin dealer, and where would I get schooling for the job?

This question comes across my desk with great regularity, and it is a frustrating experience each time it occurs. This is a situation very similar to the old saw about "If you need to ask the price you can't afford it." In most cases, if you write to me to ask the question, you are probably lacking one or more of the basic qualities needed to become a successful coin dealer. One possible place to start is with your local coin dealer, who can tell you more about what you need to know in five minutes than I could if I used this entire book. If you don't know more than the average collector about coins, don't have a head for figures, don't know grading backward and forward, don't know how to run a business of any kind, and aren't an aggressive or successful salesman, then you probably should consider another line of work and leave coin dealing to those who do have the right qualifications.

There are no licensing requirements—at least in this country—and there are no schools that you could attend. The only tax and other licenses required are the same for any business, although some states may impose licensing requirements on some aspects, such as handling bullion sales. The best suggestion I can offer is to find a job with a local coin dealer and learn the trade.

Q: How do I buy coins at wholesale?

Another frequent question that comes in, and one that is extremely difficult for me to answer, because of our firm's policy of not recommending any specific dealer or service. I hesitate to point a finger, but the question itself is evidence that the writer needs to learn a lot more about the coin business before getting involved. Coin dealers give established dealers wholesale discounts. Until, and unless, you become a recognized dealer, you will not get a wholesale discount.

Q: As a coin dealer, I have a serious problem. When I ask for an SASE in my ads, your readers don't know what that means. Is there any way of getting the message across?

I wish I knew of a way! I have fought this problem for 27 years because most people who write for information either don't include postage or enclose an undersize or odd shaped envelope. As a result, I've made a practice of asking readers to enclose an unused, unlicked first class stamp instead. It is a matter of common courtesy to include postage when asking for information, but it is pure folly to affix it to an undersize envelope which is too small to hold brochures, copies, or other materials. The point is that you are imposing a limitation on what can be sent to you and that you are subjecting your source to the possibility of having to pay extra postage, as there is a surcharge for undersize envelopes that are too thick. SASE means "Self Addressed Stamped Envelope," but make sure it is a legal size, long envelope, for your own benefit. When ordering coins by mail, read the instructions closely, and if they ask for an SASE, be sure to include it.

Q: What sort of return privileges may I expect from a coin dealer?

Return privileges are usually stated in the dealer ad and may vary from dealer to dealer. In general, most offer a seven day period, but the return must be for a legitimate reason such as overgrading, wrong coin sent, etc. Individual dealers may accept returns for other reasons, but that is something that you and the dealer have to work out between you, as there is no provision for third party intervention. The usual outcome is that the dealer will refund your original payment, but not your postage to return the coins to him.

Q: I'm disappointed with coin collecting. Nobody wants to buy the coins that I've collected (mostly from circulation).

Most common, or low value coins are not wanted by dealers, just as with any other collectible, whether antiques or rocks. There is simply too large a supply and too small a profit margin for them to afford to buy them. While you may have spent some time searching for them, this time does not automatically increase the value of the pieces. At the same time, the prices you see quoted for coins are retail figures. That means that in order to stay in business the dealer has to buy at wholesale in order to sell at retail. This is no different than any other business. Prices quoted for many low value coins are figured to include the dealer's time and material to sort and grade them and put them in holders.

Q: I see lots of ads in your publications offering coins for sale, but who buys coins?

This question comes in with surprising frequency, indicating a communication problem with many dealers' ads. Almost all dealers who sell coins also buy them, as they have to keep their stock up, so in most cases any "sell" ad you see is also a "buy" ad. However, unless the ad specifically states that the dealer is buying, and specifies coins that can be shipped without confirmation, it is an absolute must that you contact the dealer first and make an agreement about shipping any coins that you want to sell. Unsolicited items sent through the mail don't have to be returned. While they usually are, it is pointless to go through the time, hazard, and expense of shipping coins only to have them returned unwanted. The one thing to watch for here is specialization. If a particular dealer offers only Colonial coins, or only gold, then he or she is not likely to be interested in current copper coinage, minting varieties, or Roman coins. A letter or a phone call to the dealer will quickly confirm the dealer's interest, and as a matter of courtesy include return postage.

Q: I noticed when I got my bill from my credit card company that the U.S. Mint had billed me for coins I didn't order. Can you help?

Unfortunately, by the time this reader wrote to me it was too late. Instead of notifying his credit card company he first wrote to the Mint. When the Mint didn't respond he wrote to me. Upon reading his letter I called his credit card company and found that like all of them, this firm has a 120 day period after you receive your bill during which you can notify them of any discrepancies. In this case the deadline expired 12 days before I received his letter. However, my call to the Mint did start some action at that end, and I was notified by letter that they are requesting the customer's billing receipt so that they can investigate the extra charge. The customer had ordered one set of coins and received it, but was billed a similar amount by the credit card company for coins he neither ordered nor received.

Best advice, read your credit card bill when it comes in. If there is any problem, call them at once. By not doing this, the customer probably has lost the more than $100 that he was billed. Your credit card company may have a different reporting period, so do it immediately to avoid problems like this.

Q: Recently I've had several phone calls from people offering coins for sale. How can I determine whether their offers are worthwhile?

There are three general rules that apply here. First, learn as much as you can, especially about grading, before you buy any coins. Second, never buy coins, or anything else of value, over the phone. Third, never buy coins from dealers who don't advertise in the specialized hobby publications. While there are exceptions, following these three suggestions will help you avoid many of the problems. I'm an expert and I can't even tell you what a coin is worth without seeing it, so how can you tell what you are getting over the phone?

Chapter 12

CANADIAN COINS

Because of the proximity, a lot of U.S. collectors go for Canadian coins. Certainly the Royal Canadian Mint has done far more for collectors with their circulating commemoratives than has the U.S. Mint, so the interest is increasing.

Q: Do Canadians call their coins pennies, nickels, dimes, and quarters?

These are all U.S. names, so they are incorrect. A lawsuit over parking meters which used this "American" language resulted in an ordinance at Halifax, Nova Scotia which says: "penny shall mean cent, nickel five cents, etc." It was my experience that they did not use the terms, and even got a bit hostile if you referred to them that way. However, in the last decade this has changed, and they are now generally accepted. I did field one comment from a Canadian who blames the Americans for intruding the terms into the Canadian "language."

Q: What's the difference in the 1968 Canada dimes? Did Canada have a coin shortage in the mid-1960s?

In 1968 the Royal Mint at Ottawa struck 70,460,000 .500 fine silver dimes. It also struck 87,412,930 pure nickel dimes, with V-shaped reeding. The U.S. Mint struck 85,170,000 nickel dimes with U-shaped reeding. It takes a magnet to detect the nickel version. The Philadelphia strikes were technically illegal under Canadian law, which requires that anything imported has to show the country of origin. The Royal Mint later admitted bending the rule. The Canadians suffered a coin shortage three years later than the U.S., resulting in the need for the coins struck at Philadelphia.

Q: What is a "blackout" nickel?

This question drew a lot of blank stares from the experts until it was finally traced to our northern neighbors, where it was one of the less objectionable nicknames for the despised tombac nickels of World War II fame, struck by the Canadian government in 1942 and 1943. The 88 percent copper and 12 percent zinc (brass) alloy quickly turned the color of a cent, and in dim light could easily be confused with it; much the same problem as with the 1943 U.S. cent which more than once was mistaken for a dime. The Royal Mint, like the U.S. Mint, had a penchant for calling copper-zinc alloy coins bronze, but since this alloy was too obviously a brass, it was fixed up with a fancy name to keep the public from realizing its true nature.

Q: What's the difference between Canadian coins with the shoulder strap or the shoulder fold?

The 1953 design had detail missing, which was modified in midyear to add a fold to the Queen's gown. It resembles a strap, so it got the nickname. The name and nickname apply to the same design. Much rarer are 1954 and 1955 dated coins without the fold, which was also used in the 1954 prooflike sets and a few 1955 circulation strikes.

Q: What's the "diving goose" Canada dollar? Is it possible to fake the "diving goose" variety?

These are 1967 dollars with a rotated reverse—not the double strikes of the same coin. The rotated reverse put the goose into a power dive when the coin was turned over. Both varieties were apparently "helped," and then smuggled out of the mint. They can be faked by cutting down one coin and hollowing out a second, then joining the two together. The joint would be along the inside edge of the rim on either side, so this would be the first place to check. Look for signs that the metal has been burnished in this area, as it is fairly easy to "work" the metal with engraving tools to hide most of the evidence. On a prooflike coin the job would be harder than on one of the regular "two headed" or "two tailed" alterations, but not impossible. The result would be a headache for the lawyers, as it would be a fantasy (copy) of a fake minting variety.

Q: When did Canada begin striking its own coins?

The date was January 2, 1908, at Ottawa. The Ottawa Mint opened in 1908 as a branch of the Royal Mint of England. Prior Canadian coins were struck at London.

Q: I have a 1962 Canadian cent (nickel) with a "double struck" or "recut" date. What's it worth?

It's impossible to have part of the design on one side of a coin "double struck." In this case, it's abrasion doubling, which is worthless. The 1962 Canadian cents, nickels of the same year, and a number of other Canadian coins exhibit abrasion doubling, which is a repeating, very high mintage die variety with little or no value, on a par with the abraded doubled dates on the 1935-1958 U.S. wheat cents. A recut die involves the use of an engraving tool to remove die metal, which leaves its own distinctive markings, totally different from the effects of die abrasion.

Q: In examining my Canadian Olympic coins, I noticed that there is a mistake in the design, as the Olympic rings don't overlap properly. Has this been reported?

It made headlines in the numismatic press, along with at least two other mistakes in the Olympic issues. At the time it was discovered, the Canadian Postmaster General discounted it as a "stylized representation,...(not) meant to be a replica of the original." The official design has five rings alternating over and under. The Canada version (1976 Y-76 $5 for the XXI Olympiad) has the rings over and over. All were struck that way.

Q: How long has the term "prooflike" been around?

It's a relatively recent arrival in the numismatic language, with general use dating back to the early 1950s when the Canadian Mint began calling some of their collector coins "prooflike." Just like the parent word, the term is often misused as a grade, rather than a condition. However, author J. E. Charlton claims credit for it, saying he used it beginning in 1953 for coins better than circulation strikes, but not to proof standards.

Q: Why will a magnet attract a Canadian but not a U.S. nickel?

Canadian nickels are pure nickel up to 1982, while the U.S. coins are only 25% nickel. Anything less than 80% nickel in an alloy is nonmagnetic. Nickel is the only other metal besides iron that you are likely to find in a coin that is at least weakly magnetic. The pure nickel Canadian coins will stick to a strong magnet.

Q: What's the story of the disappearing island on the Canadian dollars?

This is just one of a series of abrasion varieties found on Canadian coins which, lacking very heavy dealer promotion, would have been ignored. Most collectors of Canadian coins apparently are unaware that die abrasion can remove detail or add it in the form of doubling of design elements. This is another example of a very high mintage abrasion variety which has been oversold because of ignorance of the actual cause or relative scarcity.

Q: Is there any truth to the story that the 1902 Canadian five cent pieces were struck with the "wrong" crown?

The tale took on credence because it was quoted in several old numismatic reference works, but the facts are at odds with the myth. The crown used was the same one used on English coins from George III onward, so the assumption by the uninformed that it was an accidental use of the Victoria crown caused the rumors. The decision to change to the heraldic crown was made with the advent of coins of Edward VII, but there wasn't time to complete the five cent dies for Canada before the 1902 coins were struck. The switch was made on the five cent dies for the 1903 coinage.

Q: How long has the beaver been used as a symbol for Canada?

The beaver has a long and close relationship with Canada, beginning with the Indian use of the beaver as a totem symbol long before the first Europeans arrived. The beaver was part of the arms granted by Charles I of France to Sir William Alexander in 1633. The arms of the city of Quebec included a black beaver on a gold background. The first Canadian postage stamps issued in 1851 included a beaver design, and the animal was included in the arms of Montreal in 1833. The beaver, after all that, was adopted as the official Canadian symbol on March 23, 1975. It appeared on the Canadian 5 cent coin beginning with the 1937 issue.

Q: What is the significance of the dots and dashes around the edge of the Canadian 1943-45 five cent reverse?

It's International Morse Code, which differs on several letters from standard code. The dots and dashes translate as "We Win When We Work Willingly."

Q: How do I tell the small and large bead varieties of the 1965 Canadian dollars?

Actually, there are three size rim beads for that year, the small, medium, and large, as well as combinations with the pointed 5 in the date or the blunt 5. One of several markers is the I in REGINA. On the dollars with small beads, the I points directly at a bead. On the medium bead variety it points left of the bead, and on the large bead variety the I points to the right of the bead. This is the easiest way to tell them apart. The pointed 5 has a sharp lower tip, while the blunt 5 in the date has the tip squared off. The "point" referred to is the lower tip of the 5. On some coins the tip is pointed, and on others it is rounded or blunt, giving rise to the names for the varieties.

Q: Why do some Canadian coins of the 1942-45 period have a bright finish on one side and a duller finish on the other?

The Canadian Mint was in the process of expanding the use of chrome plated dies, which struck a glossy finish on the coin, but because of the problems of wartime production it was often necessary to match a plated and an unplated die pair, resulting in coins with two different finishes.

Q: Canadian Maple Leaf bullion coins I'm familiar with, but Canadian "Beavers?"

You won't find the beaver in the official record books, as it was a privately issued bullion "round" from some years back. It "looks" official, carries the word "CANADA" and the 1977 date, but the reverse bears the name of the manufacturer. It is not a coin.

Q: Isn't there a museum or something in Canada which has very large replicas of coins on display?

You're probably thinking of the Canadian Centennial Numismatic Park at Sudbury, Ontario, built in the 1960s. They had a 30-foot replica of the 1951 Canadian nickel, a 10-foot replica of a 1965 Canadian cent, and plans were made for a 20-foot copy of the 1964 U.S. half dollar and a 12-foot British Churchill crown. The most recent word that I have is that the displays at Sudbury have been dismantled, except for the 1951 nickel.

Q: Has there been more than one official name for the Canadian Mint?

It began January 2, 1908 as The Royal Mint, Ottawa Branch. On Dec. 1, 1931 the name was changed to The Royal Canadian Mint.

Q: Is there any record of the dates on the Canadian silver dollars that have been found with the "J.O.P." initials as a countermark?

Supposedly there are four known complete sets of the coins which were purchased and stamped by Joseph O. Patenaude, a jeweler in Nelson, British Columbia. The full set includes the 1935, 1936, 1939, 1947, 1948, 1949, and 1953 dates. At one time the individual coins were being quoted at up to $100, and the asking price for a complete set was $2,000.

Q: Weren't the New Brunswick half cents of 1861 minted by accident?

They were accidentally struck by The British Royal Mint, and were nearly identical to the 1861 Nova Scotia half cents. More than 222,800 were melted down. The survivors were mixed with Nova Scotia half cents and shipped to Halifax. Technically, they were not a legal coin. They were sent to New Brunswick, but they were unwanted and were returned to London. Later they were shipped to Newfoundland and circulated there.

Chapter 13

BOOKS, CATALOGS, PRICE GUIDES, LISTINGS

Books, reference catalogs and price guides are vital to a thriving hobby. Without books, there is no way to know the history or background of the coins you collect. A ready price reference helps the collector who has no idea of rarity, value, or any other real facts about a coin. They are a major resource, which should not be neglected.

Q: Who originated the slogan "Buy the book before you buy the coin?"

The late Aaron Feldman. Among other noted parts of his career was the operation of what was billed as the "smallest coin shop in the world," a booth in a jewelry exchange. His purpose was to get collectors to educate themselves as they progressed in the hobby. I have modified the slogan to read: "Buy the book before you buy—or sell—the coin." You can lose just as much selling a coin for less than it's worth as you can buying one for more than it's worth.

Q: What books would you recommend that I read? I'm just getting started in coin collecting.

It's extremely difficult to suggest books since numismatics covers such a wide area, with many specialty books to match. Since you didn't indicate your specific interests, the one universal suggestion that I can make is to get yourself a copy of the *ANA Grading Guide, 4th Edition*, as learning how to grade your coins is vital to success in every area of the hobby. Beyond that, visit your local coin dealers' shops to see what is available, as most carry books and supplies.

Q: I've found a coin that I can't find listed in any catalog or guide book. A friend has advised me that if a coin isn't cataloged it is because it is very rare and very valuable. What should I do?

I'm tempted to tell you to get a new friend, because this one is giving you some potentially very bad advice. For example, one of the primary reasons for some coins not being listed is that they are fakes or fantasies. Often, die varieties or other minting varieties are listed only in specialty catalogs which may have a very limited circulation. Even in those catalogs many varieties which are very common (and valueless) are not listed. Other pieces which are assumed to be coins turn out to be tokens or even medals, which of course are not listed in any coin catalog, but again only in specialized listings. The solution is to make a foil rubbing and a drawing of the piece, spelling out all the letters and numbers on both sides and the edge, and indicate the exact diameter, apparent metal, and if possible, the approximate grade. Send the information to me with a loose first class stamp. Be sure to protect the foil in a reversed 2 x 2 or small box.

Q: Why can't I get the prices that are quoted in your catalog for my coins?

The prices quoted are retail, while dealers pay wholesale. Price listings in any publication other than a dealer sale catalog are not meant to be "fixed," and this is usually clearly stated, if not always understood. They are intended to show an approximate value, based on what the current market is doing, with changes reflecting the frequency with which the charts are published. Nobody is required to exactly match the quoted prices, as they are intended merely as a guide to values. These questions invariably turn up whenever coin pricing is discussed, especially by new collectors. Most coin charts reflect retail values—the approximate amount what you would expect to pay if you purchased a coin from a coin dealer. A dealer must buy at wholesale, like any merchant, if he expects to make a profit. If you sell a coin to a fellow collector (thereby becoming a dealer) then the retail value figure is likely to be the one you would use as a basis for your offer to sell.

Q: Why do some catalogs—especially older ones—list the mints in P S D order, rather than the normal P D S order (alphabetical order)?

Part of the answer is tradition, and the rest is the sequence in which the mints began operating. Denver was the last of the mints to begin operating, hence was listed last. Most old collectors and dealers also attached more importance to the San Francisco mintages because of the several rarities produced at that mint. Today, most authors and writers use the alphabetical system of listing the Mints. The Mint appears currently to list the mints in alphabetical order, but earlier used a different approach, listing the currently operating mints in ABC order, but the inactive mints in random order.

Q: Why are mintage figures incomplete or missing, especially when two different series were struck in the same year?

Chalk this up to government style bookkeeping, which centered strictly on numbers, not designs. The same problem occurs with dates on coins struck in more than one calendar of fiscal year.

Chapter 14

CLUBS, COLLECTORS, COLLECTING

Strength in numbers means a lot to the collector, so the clubs, societies,and associations are vital. Without collectors, where would we be? Without experience, who would be able to collect anything with certainty? Going up the scale from novice to expert, collectors make up the majority of the hobby.

Q: Can you give me the address of a local coin club in my area?

You probably have an active state organization that would be glad to steer you to a local member club. If you'll send me a letter, with a loose first class stamp, we have an annual listing of all the numismatic clubs in the U.S. that I'll be glad to send you.

Q: Which is older, the American Numismatic Society, or the American Numismatic Association?

The American Numismatic Society is the older of the two major coin collector groups by a wide margin. The ANS was established in 1858, as was the Numismatic and Antiquarian Society of Philadelphia. It would be another 33 years before the ANA was founded in 1891. The ANS is headquartered in New York City, while ANA has its headquarters in Colorado Springs, Colorado. The French Numismatic Society began in 1865. The Canadian Numismatic Association was founded in 1950.

Q: When did the Boy Scouts of America add a merit badge for coin collecting?

The first record of a coin collecting merit badge that I can find is in 1937. When Clem Bailey was conducting this column back in the 1970s, I recall he was involved in updating the requirements for the badge. The new badge was added to the list in 1937, according to Harry X Boosel. Requirements included collecting at least 100 types of coins, with specimens from at least 15 countries, which had to be identified.

Q: I have a piece of glassware which depicts 1892 dated coins, but they are not the Barber designs of that year. Was this done to circumvent the law?

The pieces were made in 1891 for the 1892 Columbian Exposition, on the assumption that the Seated Liberty designs would continue. Later this coin glass, as it is called, did run afoul of the law. It is now legal to own.

Q: What are the most popular coins to collect?

Although in commerce the quarter is the most popular and most used coin, when it comes to collecting, the big ones are the cent, nickel, and silver dollar. Probably 95 percent of all U.S. collectors either collect, or have collected cents. The Jefferson nickel is sometimes listed second, or third, after silver dollars.

Q: It seems to me that numismatics is just becoming a case of one fad after another, with a mad rush to anything new. Care to comment?

Fads have been with us since the first coin was put away and saved. Walter Breen cited such fads as the popularity of Washingtonian items during the era of 1859-67, and the collecting of store cards and political items during the Civil War era. During World War I it was patterns and pioneer gold. There were large cents in several periods, medals up to the mid-1950s, and foreign series and silver bars in the 1970s. A good case could be made for "follow the leader" collecting. One of the earliest in U.S. coin collecting was the search for half penny varieties in the last decade of the 1700s, when quite a number of mules and other oddities were struck specifically for collectors.

Q: What's the difference between type collecting and series collecting?

Series collecting means to assemble a collection that includes every date and mint for a particular series, such as the Lincoln cent. A type collection requires just one example of each series, so they are relatively easy to put together.

Q: How do I get started in coin collecting? Please give me some advice.

It's very difficult to suggest anything without sitting down with you and discussing your interests, finances, and other factors affecting what you collect. The best initial advice I can offer is to buy the book before you buy—or sell—a coin. Do your homework first, then reach (slowly) for your checkbook. Your local coin dealers, or those who offer books in our publications, can help recommend some good books. "How to" manuals with lots of general interest information are a good place to start.

What you collect should depend on what you like, what you want, and what you can afford. That last point is the underlying reason why so many new collectors start with cents, then work up to more valuable and expensive coins. A hobby is to enjoy, so go at it with that in mind. If you work hard enough at learning all you can about your hobby, eventually you will reach the point where it will become profitable for you as well, and nothing is more fun than having fun and making money at the same time. Collecting is basically a hobby, intended to be enjoyed, so don't let someone else regiment you or tell you what you "must" collect. There are literally thousands of possible ways of collecting coins so keep trying until you find what you like.

Q: What is the earliest date for a coin collection in the U.S.?

The earliest date I can find for the beginning of a coin collection is 1817. This date is mentioned in several references, but all trace to a single early source—presumed to be correct. Both Matthew Adams Stickney and Joseph J. Mickley got their start in that year, Mickley looking for the rare 1799 cent from the year of his birth.

Chapter 15

COLONIAL, STATE ISSUES

The richest part of our numismatic history surrounds the coins which were struck during the colonial period, through the formative years of our country. As a group they encompass many singular rarities, marked by "unique," or numbers less than a handful. They also have the greatest number of copies, making knowledge a key weapon.

Q: How many of the original colonies minted coins?

Prior to the Revolutionary War, Massachusetts was the only one. John Hull was awarded a monopoly to coin money and a mint was erected in 1652, first producing the coins with NE on one side and the denomination on the other, later striking the famed pine tree shilling. Hull became rich, collecting 15 pence out of every 20 shillings he minted.

Q: Before the Federal Mint was established at Philadelphia, did any of the states strike a half cent coin?

The State of Massachusetts was the only state to strike half cents, issuing several varieties, dated 1787 and 1788. The coins bore the denomination on the eagle's breast in incuse letters because the relief letters on the cents wore away rapidly. Along with the cents of the same dates they were the only state coinage to conform to the 1786 Acts of Congress which proposed standards for a federal coinage.

Q: Are there any proofs of our early colonial coins?

One list I have says that there are proofs known for several of the American colonials, especially the Lord Baltimore shilling, the Rosa Americana twopence, the Hibernia coinage of William Wood, the Newby halfpence, and the George III Virginia "penny" and "shilling." The proofs are expectedly rare.

Q: Isn't there some historical fact surrounding the elimination of wampum from colonial trade because of widespread counterfeiting?

I've run across references to the practice both in Massachusetts, where the General Court investigated, but never charged a Bill Pynchon with running a wampum factory (using Indian labor) and in New York, where similar "mass production" drove the value of the genuine wampum down. New Amsterdam passed a law in 1650 banning the makers of porcelain and bone beads for the fakes.

Q: Didn't the different colored beads (wampum) have different values?

They had different values for colors, depending upon where the trading occured. The white beads were the cheapest, going at a rate of 6 to a penny, (Massachusetts law of 1627) while the black beads were fixed at 3 to a penny. Technically, the term wampum can be applied only to the white beads, as the name for the black (sometimes purple or blue) was suckauhock. It wasn't until after the arrival of the Europeans in America that the Indians changed their currency to accommodate different colors and different values.

Q: Were all of the Rosa Americana coins struck in Bath metal?

All of the coins were in that metal alloy, but there are trial strikes of the obverse of the 1733 pattern in steel, a distinction which has escaped most catalogs. William Wood, who held the King's patent to strike the coins, was the first to use coal, rather than charcoal, in the manufacture of iron. According to Sylvester Crosby, a steel strike of the obverse is in the British Museum, and Crosby lists "two others known." He suggests that the steel trial strikes were made to display the malleability of the steel produced by his new method of processing the iron ore.

1723 Rosa Americana Halfpenny.

A Rosa Americana Twopence. No date.

1733 Rosa Americana Twopence.

Q: What is the weight of the Brasher doubloon?

The weights vary from 409 to 412 grains, matching that of the Spanish doubloon, hence the name. This is a good way to check your coin to see if you have a copy, as most are significantly underweight. The Spanish coin had a weight of 408 grains or 26.4 grams.

1787 Brasher doubloon.

Q: Didn't Ephraim Brasher have a direct connection with George Washington and our first coinage?

A receipt exists showing that Brasher sold "sundry articles of plate" valued at 283 pounds, 3 shillings, and 7 pence to the Washington household, which at the time was located at 3 Cherry Street, next door to where Brasher lived in New York. The plate was never found among Washington's effects, and the possibility exists that this was the silver furnished to strike the first half dismes and dismes in 1792.

Q: Are there any instances of brides being purchased in the American colonies?

In the Colony of Virginia in the 1620s, arrangements were made to bring brides over from England in exchange for 100 pounds of tobacco. Later, inflation set in and the bride price was raised to 150 pounds.

Q: What are the "Bar" cents?

The coin, which has 13 raised bars on one side and the letters "USA" on the other, is of uncertain origin, although some sources credit it to Thomas Wyon of Birmingham, England. It appeared first in New York in 1785. The originals have the letter "U" under the "S," with the "A" over it. The Bolen copies, made in 1862 have the "A" under the "S."

Q: What is the most commonly faked early American token or coin?

Although there seems to be a number of candidates for this dubious "honor," Walter Breen stated that the so called "bar cent," or bar copper, was the one forged the most often. The originals, made by the Wyon Mint in Birmingham, England have a small spur pointing downward from the left end of the second bar and a small die crack from the sixth to seventh bar near the middle of the coin. Die struck forgeries do not have these markings, but some cast or electrotype copies may show them. This and just about every other early American rarity have been copied profusely right through the mid-1960s.

The "Bar" cents appeared first in New York in 1785.

Q: Is there a coin which has its varieties explained as "long" or "short" worms?
Something of a surprise is this listing for the John Chalmers silver shilling of 1783 from Maryland. There are three varieties, the two most common have a reverse with two seagulls having a tug-of-war with a worm. One variety has a short worm and the slightly more common piece has a long worm. Auction prices for the coin in 1988 ranged from $1,100 in VF for the short worm to $2,090 for the long worm in the same grade.

The John Chalmers silver shilling of 1783 from Maryland.

Chapter 16

COMMEMORATIVE COINS

Commemorative coins hold a special place in the hearts of collectors. With a history that is so tarnished that they were literally banned from production between 1954 and 1982, they attract far more attention than their numbers would seem to warrant.

Q: Which was the first commemorative coin to bear the "IN GOD WE TRUST motto?"

It was the Pan-Pacific half dollar of 1915. The commemorative coins were struck under the provisions of special acts of Congress, and thus did not have to abide by the specific regulations which prescribed the mottos and designs of our circulating coins.

1900 Lafayette dollar.

Q: I'm told the 1900 Lafayette dollars were issued in 1899, rather than 1900. How did they get away with predating the coins?

On a technicality. The coins were struck to raise money for a statue honoring Lafayette, which was installed in 1900, so it was claimed that the 1900 date is intended to show the installation date, rather than the issue date of the coin.

1926 Sesquicentennial commemorative half dollar.

1984 Olympic gold $10 commemorative coin.

1983 Olympic silver dollar.

Q: The U.S. celebrated the Bicentennial with three special coins. How about the 100th birthday?

That event was marked with medals rather than special coins. However, by the 150th anniversary (1926) the idea of a coin had caught hold, and there were two commemoratives: the Sesquicentennial half dollar and the $2.50 gold Sesquicentennial, which is usually listed as a Philadelphia Sesquicentennial.

Q: What was the last U.S. gold commemorative before the 1984 Olympic eagles?

Before the 1984 Olympic eagles, the 1926 Sesquicentennial gold quarter eagle was the last gold commemorative coin to be produced, marking the 150th anniversary of the founding of the United States. Like most of the commemoratives, some 200,000 were struck, but all but about 40,000 were melted because the promoters overestimated the market.

Q: Are there any specific distinguishing marks which can be used to detect the genuine Grant Commemorative with star?

The genuine pieces with star have a die clash of the space between the leaves extending from Grant's chin to the G in GRANT and another of the tops of the trees above the letters F DO. Some early reference works describe these marks as "die lines," die cracks, or die breaks, all of which are incorrect.

Grant commemorative half dollar.

Q: Which was the first U.S. commemorative coin?

Most sources list the Columbian half dollar of 1892-93, but technically the first were the 1848 quarter eagles which were countermarked with "CAL" to recognize the discovery of gold in California.

The first U.S. commemorative coin was the 1848 "CAL" $2.50.

Q: One writer made the point that the Lincoln cent was a commemorative, when first issued. Comment?

The Lincoln cent was struck in 1909 to mark the 100th anniversary of Lincoln's birth, just as the later Washington quarter. Since they are circulating coins struck in succeeding years they are not considered to be true commemoratives, although one might form a new class of "circulating commemoratives" for them.

Q: Were the first Washington quarters hoarded when they were issued in 1932?

Contemporary accounts indicate that few showed up in circulation because, like the Kennedy half dollars of 1964, the public wanted them as souvenirs. It must be remembered that when they originally were issued they were billed as a one year commemorative, and it wasn't until later that the decision to continue them was made.

Q: Would you describe the Peace dollars as a circulating commemorative?

Certainly. The purpose of the coin was to celebrate peace, and it was therefore issued as a commemorative. Since it was intended to circulate, even if it did not fully meet the criteria, it would be classed as a circulating commemorative. The statement has been made that it was the only such commemorative issued between 1922 and 1935, but several of the commemorative half dollars actually circulated, and the Washington quarter, issued originally as a circulating commemorative in 1932, continued as a regular circulating coin by popular demand.

Q: Did the U.S. Mint issue any two-obverse coins?

The 1904 and 1905 Lewis and Clark gold commemorative dollar, has the head of Lewis on one side and Clark's head on the other. Otherwise, there is no circulation strike with two obverses. The side with the date is considered the obverse, with the bust of Lewis, while Clark is on the reverse with the denomination.

1905 Lewis and Clark gold commemorative dollar.

Q: Supposedly there are three U.S. commemorative coins which depict a foreign ruler. Which ones are they?

Queen Isabella of Spain is on the 1893 Columbian Expo quarter. A native chief is depicted on the Hawaiian Sesquicentennial half of 1928 and the Texas Centennial 1934-38 shows General Sam Houston, first president of the Republic of Texas.

Q: The "D" mint mark on my 1921-D Pilgrim Tercentenary commemorative half dollar is incuse. Is this a mistake?

Sorry, but the D is the designer's initial, for Cyrus E. Dallin, and is intended to be incuse as is the F on the Buffalo nickel. All of the 1920 and 1921 issues of this design were struck at Philadelphia, without a mint mark. There is no known U.S. incuse mint mark.

Chapter 17

COPIES, FANTASIES, REPRODUCTIONS, RESTRIKES

This category overlaps into several others, because copies are so pervasive in the hobby. If a collector wished to collect just these copies he or she would have a never-ending supply of new items to add to the mix.

Q: What can you tell me about J. A. Bolen?

If the gentlemen had been alive today he would either have spent time behind bars or changed his occupation. He was a well-known 19th century medalist of Springfield, Massachusetts who gained a wide reputation by making copies of rare colonial coins. They were struck in limited numbers, and are as avidly collected as the originals. Among his copies are examples of the Confederato cent, the Higley cent, and the New York cent.

Q: I have been given a set of five Confederate coins: a half dollar, a quarter, a dime, a half dime, and a cent. What can you tell me about it?

The pieces are fantasy coins, produced in the early 1960s. The set sold at the time for $3.95 plus 25 cents postage. Incidentally, the half dollar in this set is not the one that is listed in our "Unusual World Coins" catalog which is a copy of the Confederate half which was actually produced. These pieces have a different design.

1776 Continental dollar.

Q: Are there Continental dollar restrikes?

Dr. M.W. Dickeson made dies and struck copies for the Philadelphia U.S. Exposition in 1876. Since then, more copies have been made from the same dies, incorrectly identified as "restrikes," which applies only to official dies. There are some "genuine" copies of the Continental dollar and of course there are hundreds of thousands of worthless cast copies. The early copies, such as those produced by Dickeson, are recognized and have some value.

Q: I have a Mercury dime which is considerably smaller than normal, about 3/8 of an inch in diameter. Was this some special issue?

This question came from a reader in Canada, who perhaps is not as familiar with the U.S. coinage. From the description, you apparently have a copy of the U.S. Mercury dime. None of the real coins were minted in a smaller size such as you describe. As a medal, the piece would have no more than a few cents value. These small size copies are frequently found offered for sale at dealers' tables at coin shows. There have been several companies over the years who have put out miniature copies like this. They are collectible as a "novelty" piece, with very minor value, but that is all, as they are not genuine coins and are technically illegal to own, as coin reproductions must be larger than three inches in diameter.

Q: I have a coin which is listed in the catalogs as "unique." I'm not sure just how many are in existence, so what can you tell me about it?

This is a composite of frequent questions from readers who have found a specimen of an apparently rare American Colonial coin. Unique in numismatics means there is only one specimen known. Whenever you see a coin listed as unique or extremely rare, it is a tipoff that the piece you have is probably a replica or copy. There are thousands upon thousands of copies of these and other rare Colonial era coins in the hands of the public. The chances of your coins being genuine are extremely slim. The first check is the edge of the piece. If it shows a flange or thin raised edge of metal sticking out from the middle of the edge, then the piece is a cast copy. These are usually some other metal than the genuine alloy.

Q: How is an electrotype made?

A graphite-coated mold of a coin is plated, then this thin shell is filled with base metal, and joined to the shell for the other side. If expertly done it's difficult to detect. Lots were made after the Civil War for educational purposes. When two electrotypes of the obverse and reverse of a coin are skillfully soldered together and then plated to hide the joint, they can be very deceptive. More than one has been accepted as genuine by gullible collectors. A solid electrotype is one in which the plating process was continued until the inside of the mold was completely filled with the plating.

Q: I have a copper uniface piece with the "Washington Born Virginia" design. Is this an original strike?

It probably is one of the restrikes, made in the early 1960s by Albert Collis, a coin dealer in Massachusetts, who obtained the original obverse die and reportedly struck some 2,000 uniface pieces.

Q: I purchased a California gold coin at a private auction, and I need to know what it is worth. It has a bear, 1852 date, and 1/2 on it.

If the auctioneer described it as a gold coin he was mistaken, and you have purchased a nearly worthless souvenir. Unless the piece has "DOLLAR," "CENTS," or an abbreviation of either word, it is probably just a copy. It may or may not be gold, and if it is, it's very probably low grade.

Q: I have a U.S. coin dated 1851. It is a silver dollar and it has an Indian head design. I can't find it in any of my catalogs. Can you help me please?

This question came to me from the Czech republic, but the same pieces are showing up here in the U.S. It appears to combine the obverse of an Indian Head cent with the gold dollar reverse. I'm sorry to disappoint this reader, but these are fantasy coins that are being made in Italy for sale to the tourists. A reader in Italy recently sent us copies of this piece and several other imitations and fantasy pieces.

Q: Somewhere I read something about an 1818 quarter which had a large cent reverse. Was this a mule?

This one is a bit difficult to label. Judd lists it (J-45) as a cent mule, with an 1818 quarter dollar obverse die and a large cent reverse, and says it is "struck over a quarter dollar." The unique coin was offered by Bowers and Ruddy in a 1976 fixed price list as a pattern cent (or quarter) with the additional information that it was struck over a Seated Liberty quarter (1838-1891) sometime in the 1858-1862 period. The obvious conclusion is that the piece is a fantasy, produced during the period when the Mint would make anything for anybody.

Chapter 18

GAME COUNTERS, JETONS, TOKENS, MEDALS

Q: What are Kettle "coins?"

These are gaming counters from Kettle & Sons of Birmingham, England. In the early 1800s the firm produced a quantity of gaming counters which were close reproductions of a number of earlier coins. Among them were copies of 1803-dated U.S. quarter eagles, which are often mistaken for pattern coins. The Kettle game counters carried the word "KETTLE" to the right of the date, but it was not unusual for the letters to be scraped off and the counter sold as a coin. Other designs matched the U.S. gold $1, $2.50, $5, and $20 coins, and the pieces were often gold plated. The Secret Service at one time was confiscating the counters because one dealer was selling large quantities of the altered pieces. There are no genuine 1803 quarter eagles.

Q: I have a piece which looks a lot like a U.S. $20 gold piece but it has the word "Spiele-munze" on it. What is it?

You will find variations, such as "Composition Spielmarke" or abbreviations, many of them with designs copied from various world coins, including several U.S. gold coin designs. The pieces are collected, so they provide another specialty area for you to enjoy. The word "Spielemunze" is the clue to identifying your piece. It is a game token, similar to a poker chip, the word being German for playing money, or game counter. These were struck in large quantities in Germany and usually are worth at best a couple of dollars.

Q: Where can I get some information on my coin? It is an undated mule of an Argentine 5 pesos and a U.S. $5 gold half eagle.

Without knowing where to look for this one, you undoubtedly could spend a lot of time searching coin catalogs. The piece is not a coin. It's a fantasy design, struck as a game counter in the mid-1800s in large quantities. Examples of the piece don't turn up as often now as they did a few years ago, but they are still around and still puzzling the uninitiated.

Q: I have a "California Model Dollar," dated 1849, that I am unable to find listed in any catalog. Can you tell me anything about it?

This is an exception to the rule that applies to most California gold coins, as the word "Dollar" does not indicate that the piece is a genuine coin. Instead, it is a poker chip, or game counter, and incidentally one of a series of "models" which ran from the half dollar up to the half eagle. All of them had an eagle and 13 stars on the reverse. These pieces were brass and not gold, and originally came in a brass box that housed the full set. They are not a pattern.

Q: Is there a coin known as the Jefferson Davis dime?

The piece is a Confederate Civil War silver token or medalet, with the bust of Davis, and the wording "CSA FIRST PRESIDENT." The nickname arose from the size and metal, and the piece is fairly rare.

Chapter 19

COIN VALUES

The most common question by far—and the one that I can't answer—is: "What is my coin worth?" The coin itself has to be examined to determine the grade, or amount of wear. With that established, then the eyes swing to the price charts to find that grade and the value attached to it.

Q: I see in your price charts where a Mercury dime is worth over $2000. I have one which has a 1941 or a 1943 date that I'd like to sell, if you can help.

I've had a surprising rash of questions similar to this, indicating a fresh supply of collectors entering the hobby. The three and four figure prices quoted are for coins that have never been in circulation, and are just about perfectly struck. To the novice any coin may appear to match these specifications, but if the coin shows the slightest wear it is worth far less. Best advice is to first buy a magnifier and second learn how to grade your coins.

Q: What are the factors that affect the value of a coin? In what order should one consider the following: the number of a given coin minted, the grade, the mint where they were struck, and the age of the coin?

It's virtually impossible to "rank" the criteria. The mint is actually unimportant, except as a means of identifying a low mintage coin, but another factor that is important is the survival rate, as some low mintage issues are common because they were hoarded, while some high mintage pieces were heavily melted, shipped out of the country, etc. For the same reason, age is often unimportant. For example, look how many 16th and 17th century British coins can be had for a few dollars. Collector popularity and the amount of promotion a given coin has received also affect value. Date, mintage, design, amount of wear, collector demand, preservation—all have varying amounts of influence on the value of a given coin.

Q: Why do rare coins have more value than other rare numismatic items?

Coins are struck under much stricter controls. The mint is a branch of government, and as such is responsible to authority. Most private minters of medals and tokens are under no restraint. They can easily falsify mintage records, dilute bullion, or engage in other shady practices. This does not mean that they do, just that the opportunity exists. Also there are far more collectors interested in coins, so there is more demand and competition for rare pieces.

Q: Aren't older coins more valuable?

Most non-collectors equate coins with antiques. It's an assumption that is frequently applied to coins, but it's a false assumption. For a coin to be valuable, the number minted and the grade are much more important. That's why collectors and dealers pay so much attention to mintages and the exact grade of any coin. There are other factors as well, so age is of relatively minor importance.

Q: Why do silver coins carry a premium over silver bars which have a higher silver content?

Since most U.S. silver coins are only 90% or 40% silver, this is a good question. The principal reason is that the coins are of recognized value, while the bars must be assayed or subjected to other tests which add to the expense of handling.

Q: Didn't Abe Kosoff once predict silver coins would be worth 30 times face value?

In 1970 Kosoff made the statement: "20 years from now silver coins probably will be up to 10, 20, or even 30 times face value." As it turned out, he was off by a decade, but sooner rather than later, as silver jumped in 1980 to double digit multiples of face value (as high as $52 an ounce) before crashing.

Q: What happened to all of the experts who predicted gold would go to $2000 and silver to $100 an ounce in "less than five years?"

Most are still working on revised estimates.

Q: Was the silver in a silver dollar always worth face value or more?

That phase is a fairly recent development. In 1873 the dollar contained $1.004 worth of silver, but by 1878 it dropped to 89.1 cents, in 1885 to 82.3 cents, dropping below 80 cents in 1886. In 1893 it fell to an average of 60.3 cents, and in December of that year to only 54.3 cents. The value dropped to as low as 47 cents in 1900, even lower by 1910, and by the 1930s contained less than 30 cents worth, actually dropping in 1932 to 20 cents.

Q: What's the earliest auction record of a U.S. cent being sold?

The Dr. Lewis Roper collection was sold at auction in 1851. An uncirculated Chain cent of 1793 sold for 10 cents.

1792 cent pattern with silver center plug.

Q: What was the first U.S. cent to exceed the $100,000 mark in collector value?

The 1792 cent pattern with silver center plug sold at auction at the Great Eastern Numismatic Association convention Sept. 20, 1974 for $105,000, setting a new record for the lowly cent. For the regular issue cents, the 1793 Chain cent brought $120,000 in Auction '80.

Q: Shouldn't the 1835 cent be worth more than other dates because so many of them were shipped to Venezuela?

Venezuela purchased a total of 1,100,000 cents in 1835. Mintage for the year was 3,878,400, so with almost a third shipped out of the country they should be in shorter supply, and consequently worth more. However, as you will note from reading the price charts, catalog prices for the cents of that era are almost identical for years with less than two million and more than six million minted.

Q: For the Lincoln cents there are four dates which have a mintage of about 75 million, but which are worth widely varying prices in MS-60 grade. The four are the 1909, 1913, 1914, and 1924. Why the difference?

Mintage figures often are only part of the story. For instance, because it was the first year of issue, many more of the 1909 cents were saved, so there are more available (in all, but especially the higher grades) now. For the 1913 and 1914 coins, note that there are plenty of low grades available, so they are much lower in value. This is also true of the 1924, which jumps sharply in value in the higher grades.

1909-S VDB cent.

Q: A fellow collector and I are having a discussion about the rarity of the 1909-S VDB cent. Isn't it the key coin of the Lincoln cent series?

At the risk of getting into a discussion of the relative values of apples and oranges, I might note that as but one example, the 1909 VDB proofs are a much rarer, and more valuable coin. Only 420 of the proofs were struck, compared to the 484,000 circulation strikes of the 1909-S VDB cent. Current values give the very low mintage proof a price tag that's nearly twice the value of the S mint coin in MS-65. Even in the circulating coins, the 1914-D and 1914-S cents outrank the '09-S VDB in the same MS-65 grade, but all of them are pikers compared to the 1969-S doubled die at $8,000 or the 1922 cent without mint mark which currently lists at $23,500.

Q: Why does the low mintage 1931-S cent have such a narrow spread in circulated prices?

Everybody knew the '31-S was a low mintage coin (866,000). It was offered by the Treasury at face value for two years, so an unusually large number were saved in the higher grades. Collectors jumped on the coin as soon as it was released and large quantities were saved in original rolls. Even after it was determined to be a low mintage coin, they could still be purchased over the counter from the Mint. As a result, few of the coins circulated, hence the flat price curve for the circulated grades.

Q: Why are prices for uncirculated rolls of 1968 through 1971 cents so high?

It's difficult to find clean, spot free examples. Billions were minted, but in each case, the Philadelphia mintage was lower than that at Denver. Even so, few bags or rolls of Philadelphia cents for those years were saved.

Q: I read that there are several die varieties of the 1988-D cent. How do I identify them, and will they be as valuable some day as the varieties of the 1982 P and D cents?

You didn't indicate the source of the comment on the 1988-D cents, but I should point out that there are hundreds, even thousands of minor die varieties which occur every year, at every mint, so saving any but the most important - such as the large and small date, and the brass or zinc varieties of 1982 - becomes a matter of both space and a lack of potential market. The majority of such minor varieties probably never will be in demand as there is only a very limited single piece - rather than roll - market for the vast majority of such die varieties.

Q: Why is it that the "No Cents" variety of the 1883 Liberty nickels rates a lower price than the much higher mintage "With Cents" variety?

The reason for the difference in current prices is that many more of the "No Cents" variety were saved, so today the "With Cents" are much harder to find. Mintage doesn't always tell the whole story. This is by no means the only instance where a low mintage coin is now more common than some of the higher mintage dates. Because of the publicity surrounding the racketeer nickels and the change in the design, everyone at the time thought that the "No Cents" variety would be the rarity and hoarded them, so that today there are many more available than the "common" with cents variety. The other factor involved is the almost automatic saving of any first issue of a new series, which has the same effect on the number available to collectors, almost regardless of the mintage. It still rates a key coin status, but there is very little spread between the uncirculated and lower grades.

Q: I have several rolls of worn Buffalo nickels, most of which have no dates or just partial dates. I've been told they are not worth saving. True?

You've got your money tied up in a dead end. Dateless coins have no prospects of ever increasing significantly in value, so you would be much better off to sell them for whatever slight premium you might get, or face value, and invest the money in coins with a potential of increasing in value.

Q: Why isn't the 1926-S Buffalo nickel recognized as a key coin? It is the lowest mintage of the series.

The coin is recognized as such, but mintage is not the only factor. As shown by the prices, some of the nickels are more scarce in the lower grades, and some of the higher mintage coins have fewer surviving high grade coins. The '26-S ties for 7th place in G-4 grade, and ties with two others for 1st in MS-65. This helps make the point that it isn't just low mintage that makes a coin a key coin.

1926-S Buffalo nickel.

Q: Why the low price of the 1946-S nickel in MS-65?

This is a "rumor" coin. It was the subject of a number of widely published stories as to scarcity, including that "most" if not "all" were shipped to military bases in the Pacific after World War II. As a result, everybody hoarded the coin and lots are still available. West Coast collectors complained that the few put in circulation were in bad shape.

Q: Several years ago a 1961-D nickel worth $2,500 was mentioned in Numismatic News. What made it so valuable?

Sounds almost like one of the "come on" ads in the mass media, but the $2,500 price tag was for a full strike 1961-D nickel with six full steps, a very rare piece because the majority of the 1961-D (and several other date) nickels are poor strikes.

Q: Why is there such a low premium on 1955 and 1955-D dimes?

The reason for the low premium on the 1955 and 1955-D dimes is that everyone knew that San Francisco was closing, so they saved every "last year" coin they could, meaning that now there are plenty of high grade examples available.

Q: What 20th century U.S. coin has increased the most in value over the years?

Ignoring gold, it's the 1918/1917-S quarter, which has been as high as $78,000. Coming in second is the 1901-S Barber quarter at $38,500.

Q: Wasn't there a 1964 Kennedy half dollar which sold for $18,000?

All in all a remarkable sum for a coin which was (at the time) only five years old. The Kennedy half dollar was glued to the outside of an envelope which was postmarked on March 24, 1964, the first day of issue of the new Kennedy half dollars. The coin was purchased and affixed to the envelope by John M. Baker. It was sold for $2,000 in 1967 and then sold for $18,000 at an auction held by the Collectors of Certified Coins on September 27, 1969. The piece sold to John Marquardt, who indicated after the sale that he had been prepared to go as high as $30,000 to buy the piece, which was one of two that Baker had cancelled on the first day of issue.

Q: Was the 1903-O dollar the only rare New Orleans dollar which suffered a price drop from the process of cleaning out the Treasury vaults back in the 1960s?

The 1903-O got most of the publicity because up until they began finding bags of the coins among the millions in storage, the coin was selling for $500 or more. The reports of bag quantities reaching the market quickly dropped the piece below the $100 mark, and at the same time at least two other high priced New Orleans dollars, the 1898-O (cataloging for $300) and the 1904-O, which had been selling for $150, showed up in quantity, sharply dropping the market price.

1903-O dollar.

Q: Why don't you quote values on circulated Ike dollars, or on most recent coins?

Principally because most recent circulated coins, Ikes included, aren't worth more than face value to collectors. As they get older, and scarcer, you will find the values being added to the price charts as the values increase to the point where lists are warranted.

Q: Was there ever a time when it was possible to convert a silver dollar into more money by turning it in to the government?

If you think the idea of something for nothing is a pipe dream, consider this: In 1863 it was possible to walk into the Mint with 100 silver dollars, and walk out the door with $104 in small change, legally. The point was that the standard silver dollar contained .7736 of an ounce of silver. Two half dollars, four quarters, or ten dimes contained .7200 of an ounce of bullion, so more were required to match the silver in a dollar. The money making method was written up in a rare numismatic publication of that era, and referred to transactions at the San Francisco Mint.

Q: I have one of the three coin sets of SBA dollars sold at the 1980 ANA Convention. Do you remember what the issue price was?

The sets were sold by the Mint for $4. They contained examples with the P, D and S mint marks.

Q: One often sees figures giving the dollar value of gold as far back as the 13th century. Since the dollar didn't exist back then, just how did they go about figuring the dollar value?

The answer lies in another currency which existed and was relatively stable for the 500 year period ending when the United States came into being in 1776. The British pound varied only slightly in value between 1250 C.E. and 1776, so the value of the pound in 1776 dollars was used as the established base, or a figure of approximately $21.50 an ounce. Ignoring inflation, this pegged the price of gold in dollars at about $4.50 in 1250 C.E. It would also put the value of an ounce of gold at $10 in 1492 when Columbus discovered America. 1792 to 1834—$19.39; 1834/1837 to May 12, 1933—$20.67; 1933-March 31, 1972—$35; 1972-Oct. 18, 1973—$38. On that date it was raised to $42.22.

Q: Why was California gold worth only $16 an ounce, when gold was priced at $20.67?

You missed a key word in making the comparison. Pure gold was worth $20.67 an ounce, (troy ounce) but gold dust or nuggets from California contained silver and other metals which reduced the actual gold content. After considerable discussion, the "average" value of gold dust from California was established at $16.

Q: Did the U.S. $5 gold half eagle match any foreign coins in value during the early 1800s?

Probably one reason why it was struck during that period was that it matched closely with several world coins, among them the Portuguese 4000 reis and 2 escudo, the French Louis d'or and 24 livres, and the British guinea and sovereign. The eagle by contrast matched only a couple of low mintage coins.

Q: I found a reference to the offer of the single specimen of the 1849 $20 gold piece for $100,000 many years ago. Can you help track it down?

The coin is a star member of the Mint Cabinet, and thus not for sale. The $100,000 figure you refer to probably came from a published comment from Faran Zerbe in 1899 that "if" the coin were offered for sale that "the rivalry among the wealthy collectors of the world would make that coin worth $100,000." Speculation, but a remarkable figure for that era.

1849 $20 Gold Liberty. This is the only one in existence and is kept in the vaults of The Numismatic Museum of the Smithsonian Institution in Washington, DC.

Q: Will proof coins always retain their value?

There is no guarantee that any coin will maintain its value, but as a practical matter most coins do become more valuable over the long term. Although many collectors treat proof coins as if they were completely different from circulating coins, the fact is that their value is dependent on the same factors, the ultimate key being the numbers minted. For some years the U.S. Mint has oversold proof coins, and as a result, you may have noted that some of the proof sets from a few years ago are selling for less than the issue price because the mintages were so high.

Q: What was the original issue price for a Seated Liberty proof dollar prior to the Civil War?

The Mint priced such pieces at $1.08. Today the cheapest demands a catalog price of $13,500. Actually, beginning in 1853 the Mint charged collectors the same price for both circulation and proof dollars.

Q: Would it be worthwhile to try to assemble a complete date set of U.S. proof sets since 1936?

Certainly an expensive idea, but it's doubtful that there would be any particular benefit (profit) to having a complete group of sets. More important would be the quality of any of the individual proof coins prior to 1950, as the ultimate value of the early proofs is determined on a coin by coin, rather than set, price.

Q: Why are the prices you quote higher for the proof cent than most of the other denominations?

The proof cents cost more because there are many more collectors of cents than the other denominations, the greater demand boosting the price. This may come as a surprise, but the answer shows the power of the collector who is interested in filling a coin board or album.

These have a hole for each date and mint, and the only way to fill the S mint holes after 1974, when they stopped striking S mint cents for circulation, is with proof cents with an S mint mark. Many of these sets have been broken up for the half dollars, so there are lots of loose proof coins around, but the demand remains strong for the proof cents.

Q: What was so unusual about the 1982 proof sets that they were worth double face value right after they were issued?

For a time it was thought there would be no regular 1982 dated half dollars so the proof sets were in demand to fill that gap. When halves were struck for circulation the price dropped for the proofs.

Q: How did the surcharge work on the U.S. Olympic commemorative coins sold in 1983 and 1984?

The surcharge applied to the 1983 and 1984 Olympic coins amounted to $50 on each gold coin and $10 for each silver coin, which was included in the purchase price. As orders were received, 50 percent of the surcharge was turned over to the United States Olympic Committee. As a result, when the program was over the committee had received a total of $73.4 million for the athletes who competed under the American banner.

Q: What were the issue prices for the Pan-Pacific commemorative coins?

The Columbia half dollar sold for $1, the gold dollar for $2.25, the gold $2.50 for $4, and the round or octagonal $50 gold for $100 each. A complete set with choice of round or octagonal was also $100, a set with both was $200, or a double set mounted to show the obverses and reverses was $400. Also offered was a "small" set of the three small denomination coins for $7.50.

Q: How high will the price of gold have to go before the face value of a gold coin will be an exact multiple of the gold value?

Let's back up and start over. I think you are mixing some facts and some fantasy here. No U.S. gold coin contains, or ever contained, the exact value in gold to match the face value, always slightly less. No matter what the price of gold does, it isn't going to change that ratio a bit. Even if gold went to a million dollars an ounce, it won't alter the fact that a $20 gold coin contains less than an ounce of gold. Actually to answer the question, gold would have to drop below $11 for the face value to be twice the gold value.

Q: What were the Spanish gold escudos worth in terms of the dollar when they were still legal tender in the U.S.?

Probably not nearly as well known as the Spanish dollar, the escudo turns out to be a very simple denomination to figure. The smallest gold coin, the half escudo, equalled the value of the Spanish (and U.S.) dollar, so the escudo was worth $2, and the multiples were worth 4, 8, and 16 dollars.

Chapter 20

COUNTERFEITS

From copies to counterfeits is just a short hop. Although counterfeit bank notes get much of the publicity, fake coins have been bothersome to our country since its founding. Today, most counterfeits are aimed straight at collectors, but the odd bum dime or quarter still turns up in the casino slot machines.

Q: Is there a quick check for an 1856 Flying Eagle cent to see if it's counterfeit?

Check the back of the 5. The genuine has a round serif on the lower tip which will project beyond a line down the back. The 1858 counterfeits will show the ball to the right of the line.

1856 Flying Eagle cent.

Q: Are there any counterfeit Lincoln cents?

Lots of the key coins have been counterfeited. The 1943 cents are said to be the most commonly counterfeited Lincoln cent. There are 1941 brass cents which weigh 32.95 grains, and there's a counterfeit 1942 "trial strike" for the 1943 cents. The 1955 and 1972 doubled-die cents have also been counterfeited.

Q: A 1959 cent with wheat reverse was authenticated by the old ANACS. Isn't there more to that story?

There is, as reported in "Insight on Coinage," published by the Institute for Applied Numismatics and Research in Washington, D.C. F.M. Fazzari, who in the 1970s was one of the authenticators who looked at this particular coin, writing in the June 1991 issue, related the story of this particular coin. He admits that it got by them simply because they considered it a common date possibly submitted as a joke by a dealer and failed to connect the date with the incorrect wheat reverse. When the coin was brought to their attention by a reporter, it was re-examined and determined to be a very high quality counterfeit. Fazzari wrote, "At the time, this was the finest counterfeit cent we had seen." The coin and a Photo-Certificate attesting that it is genuine are still out there, because the coin's owner refused to return the certificate.

Q: In past references to the rare 1969-S doubled die cent, I've seen statistics indicating the Secret Service confiscated several thousand of the coins, and in other places only a small number. Which is correct?

The lower figure is correct, and I am at least partially at fault for the "2000-3000" figure getting into print. In discussing the piece with Mint officials, those figures were quoted to me, but actually applied to counterfeit 1969 doubled die cents without a mint mark.

Q: Are any of the 1944 nickels without mint marks genuine?

It's possible to have one that was struck with a filled die, but almost all are copper-nickel counterfeits, made by Francis L. Henning. These counterfeit nickels are still turning up, and are still illegal to own, as is any counterfeit coin. You can dispose of them by sending them to: U.S. Secret Service, Counterfeit Division, 1800 G St., Washington, DC 20223.

Almost all of the 1944 Jefferson nickels without mint marks are copper-nickel counterfeits made by Francis L. Henning.

Q: I found what appears to be a Standing Liberty quarter with my metal detector, but it's lead and the weight isn't right. Can you identify it from my photo?

From your description and the photos, this appears to be one of the many crude lead counterfeits produced during the Great Depression. If so, it is illegal to own, sell, trade, or otherwise dispose of, and should be turned in to your local bank for transmittal to the Secret Service.

Q: Is it true that the design change on the 1917 quarters resulted in the new issue being considered counterfeits?

Secret Service records show that there were numerous complaints in Denver about the new design, with much of the public convinced they were fakes. The Mint didn't bother to advise the public of the new designs. It took several public pronouncements by the then Superintendent of the Denver Mint, Thomas Annear, before the public settled down and accepted Liberty with more of a dress, and the eagle flying above three stars on the reverse.

Q: What can you tell me about several copper pieces I have? They are the size of quarters, and some have reeded edges.

From your description, if you have unstruck, reeded copper pieces the size of quarters, then they are slugs, or fake coins, and not unstruck planchets. The reeding can only be applied by the striking of the coin, so it is impossible to have a reeded planchet. The unreeded pieces, if approximately 95-105 grains, are made to use in slot machines and telephones. They are illegal to own, sell, trade, or otherwise dispose of, and should be turned over to the Secret Service. These pieces have a varied history, turning up in the 1970s in large quantities, some with a 6 or 8 sided depression on both sides. A normal clad quarter weighs 87.5 grains; minus the clad layers it weighs about 65 grains. These slugs are the same diameter as a struck quarter, so they are too large to be a two cent planchet.

Q: What's the story on my 1838 half dollar, with lettered edge and 50 C.?

They are Mexican counterfeits, in a non-silver alloy. The dates faked ranged from 1837 up to 1842, six years after the lettered edge was dropped. An article in a 1943 *Numismatist* is cited as proof they are genuine, based on an examination by a Mint official, but this was later refuted.

The U.S. Mint switched to a reeded edge in 1836, and all 1837 and later halves have reeded edges. Lots of the counterfeits were made and circulated at the time the coins were current and examples keep turning up in the hands of unsuspecting collectors, and in several cases have been declared a new and unlisted variety. It's interesting to note that Mexican counterfeits of the silver dollar were a follow-up export during the 1930s.

A quote from the New York Evening News of July 13, 1846 says: "Counterfeit half dollars, dated 1838, are very common. They are made of German silver, and ring well, but the die is imperfect, and by comparing them with a genuine coin they can be very easily detected." There is at least one book which (mistakenly) lists the German silver half dollars with dates in the 1830s as patterns. The problem points up the need to cross check and double check any reference work, as I can speak from experience that mistakes do creep in.

Q: I've been told to be suspicious of 1899 and 1912 Barber halves as there are many counterfeits of them. Is this true?

Whether still true is questionable, but back in the 1930s there were perhaps as many cottage shop counterfeiters as there were moonshiners. One man was arrested in Iowa for faking the two dates you mention and apparently had been pretty busy, as the Feds confiscated a bushel basket of worn out dies from his private mint. The pieces he made reportedly had the right amount of silver in them but the planchets were cast and tended to flake and pit, giving them away. No doubt a few of these made their way into collections and may still turn up. Quarters and halves were faked literally by the ton during the Depression as one way to solve financial woes, so there are still plenty of the old fakes around. Remember they are illegal to own, in case you have thoughts of acquiring one.

Q: I have a 1922 Peace dollar which has a countermark—"ALP"—on the reverse, just above the eagle's tail. Can you tell me the source of the countermark?

I hate to be the bearer of bad news but you have a counterfeit coin. A large scale operation in Málaga, on the southern coast of Spain, was making them. Large quantities of these coins turned up in the early 1980s as well as copies of German five mark pieces, Straits Settlements coins, and a number of different Spanish and Portuguese coins. The pieces were sold through flea markets and antique shops and many of them were undoubtedly brought into the U.S. by tourists. The ALP stands for alpaca, which is the name of the nickel-zinc alloy used to strike the pieces.

Q: Are there any counterfeits of the clad coins?

You bet. Large quantities of them appeared two decades ago in Nevada where the slugs were used to operate slot machines which had unsophisticated slug rejecters. Both dimes and quarters were faked. Curiously, some of the earliest English counterfeits were clad pieces, consisting of thin silver layers attached to a pewter core.

Q: What's the most counterfeited U.S. coin?

This question gets several answers as there doesn't seem to be general agreement. The old ANACS says the 1882 $3 gold is the winner, with the 1916-D dime in second place. Hancock and Spanbauer said that the 1950-D is the most counterfeited nickel. The British Royal Mint, which authenticates coins, lists the 1853 $1 gold. Undoubtedly there are other contenders, such as the 1943 steel cent on brass, etc.

Q: What was the so called "Platinum Menace" during the early 1860s?

Counterfeiters had discovered a method of sawing gold coins in two, hollowing them out and filling the cavity with platinum, which matched the weight and ring of a normal gold coin. These very deceptive counterfeits were a problem even for the Mint as far as identification was concerned. By 1878 the price of platinum had risen enough to make this kind of fake unprofitable.

Q: What is a "collar" or "ring" counterfeit?

Back in the mid-1800s some smart counterfeiters discovered that it was possible to take the $20 gold pieces and saw them in two, scoop out the gold and replace it with a platinum disc, then solder the halves together and hide the joint with a reeded ring which was placed around the coin. The scheme worked until the price of platinum rose above the price of gold. These pieces still turn up in old collections.

Q: I've seen the statement several times that a die break or die crack cannot be duplicated on a fake coin. Is this statement correct?

This is a canard with a 20 foot long beard, dating back to the era when little was known about the minting process. I have seen lengthy arguments supporting this claim, but the fact of the matter is that a die break or die crack is a form of relief design, in that it raises above the normal surface of the coin, and like any of the rest of the design, it can be readily duplicated by anyone intent on copying the coin. Restating this in another way, a die break or die crack appearing on a coin is not an indication that the piece is genuine. Counterfeit dies are frequently made by copying a struck coin. In the process, the die cracks and die breaks that occurred on the example coin are copied right along with the rest of the relief design. In addition, the counterfeit dies themselves are subject to the same stresses and strains that genuine dies experience during the striking of coins, so they can crack and break at least as easily. A good copy will also duplicate minting varieties such as hub doubling as well.

Q: Please tell me how many different copies, reproductions, restrikes or counterfeits of (a specific rare coin) have been produced?

Unfortunately counterfeiters have a habit of not broadcasting their production figures, so quantities, types of metals used, and when they were made are statistics that are rarely available, or accurate. You'll have to be satisfied with general statements that the rarer the coin the more likely it is to be copied in quantity, with a correspondingly minute chance of your example being genuine.

Q: Can frosting on a coin be faked?

You bet! Some quite dangerous fakes turned up in the 1970s with homemade "frosting" that was added after the coin left the mint. At least two forms are known, one of which disappears in commercial dipping solutions, the other vanishing when treated with acetone or alcohol. Real frosting occurs from the irregularities in the surface of a new proof die, and can be enhanced or "extended" to additional coins—but by treating the die itself—not the coin.

Q: I know it's not legal to counterfeit U.S. coins, but is there any prohibition against making counterfeits of coins of other countries in the U.S.?

The same laws which prohibit counterfeiting U.S. coins also cover foreign coins.

Q: Did any of the people who counterfeited coins in the American colonial period get put to death, or was that a European custom?

According to the records, several counterfeiters were put to death in the early days of our country. Somewhat surprisingly, one of the first two was a woman. In 1720, Martha Hunt and her husband, whose first name is lost to us, were hanged in Philadelphia on being found guilty of a charge of making and issuing counterfeit coins. When the United States Mint was established in 1792, one of the first laws governing it provided for the death penalty for an official who tampered with the coinage.

Q: Some time ago I read something about the English having counterfeited a quantity of Spanish dollars for trade. Can you find it for me?

The reference is in a letter in the National Archives, written in 1793 to Thomas Jefferson, describing the making of fake Spanish 8 reales with dates between 1772 and 1788. The fineness was reduced by "a value of nine pence to the coin." Some six tons of the fakes were made in an eight month period, apparently for the East India Co, which also had fakes made in China.

Q: What can you tell me about "Becker Reproductions?"

The original Becker was a notorious German counterfeiter, who made museum quality reproductions of ancient Greek and Roman coins and more modern issues. Becker Reproductions was a company doing business in New York City in the 1960s which, besides copying the Becker forgeries, also made copies of early American coins by the hundreds of thousands. The coins are made of an alloy of 80 percent lead, 12 percent tin and 6 percent antimony, or just about the same as the old linotype type alloy. A substantial percentage of the questions that come in to me are based on possession of one of these reproductions that a novice has assumed to be a genuine rare coin.

Q: What can you tell me about the Wyatt counterfeit Colonial coins?

Thomas Wyatt of New York could be considered one of the more clumsy fakers of history. He hired diecutters and had them make copies from illustrations which had in turn been copied from a previous book, including mistakes. His dies fell into the hands of Edwin Bishop of New York, who proceeded to strike what Eric Newman described as one of "the phoniest coins in the history of numismatics." It was an overstrike on an English guinea using Wyatt's obverse for the Good Samaritan shilling and the obverse of the Oak Tree shilling, making it "a muled restrike of Wyatt's reproduction of an incorrect drawing of a fantasized illustration of a fake coin."

Chapter 21

CUSTOMS AND PRACTICES, SUPERSTITIONS

There are numerous customs and superstitions connected to coins. I have room for just a few, to tantalize your interest.

Q: Was President Woodrow Wilson superstitious about the number of letters in his name?

Wilson was what you might call "counter" superstitious about the number 13, considering it his lucky number, and he delighted in inviting 13 guests to a dinner or party. Which reminds me, there are 13 letters in the motto appearing on our coins—E Pluribus Unum.

Q: Is there a difference between a bent love token and a bent witches coin?

The old custom was that a coin was bent once or broken in two as a love token, with half to each lover. A coin was bent twice to ward off witches. This eventually grew into the lucky coin. Back in those days coins usually were much thinner that today's, and easily bent.

Q: My bride to be and I are both collectors. Are there any bridal customs involving coins that we can incorporate in our wedding plans?

There are literally dozens of such customs, so pick and choose. The bride may put a coin in her shoe or her right stocking. The bride's shoes will bring luck if they are purchased entirely with pfennigs, pennies or cents—although that one went out of fashion when shoe prices went over $2. The bride should hide some coins just before the wedding to ensure she isn't marrying the wrong man. Save some coins, because it is also a custom to throw coins from the vehicle on the way to the church. In some places the way will be blocked, and the bride must pay a toll to pass through.

Q: What's the old story about the dime and churning butter?

This is a bit of folklore, which alleged that if milk was "witched" so it wouldn't churn, all one had to do was drop in a (silver) dime to remove the spell. Silver holds a prominent place in literature concerning protection from witchcraft.

Q: Why is the 1928 silver dollar sometimes called the "cornerstone" dollar?

The 1928 had a mintage of 360,649, which one source indicated "were mostly struck to be put in cornerstones." That story got started because the Treasury for a time refused to release the coins except for that specific purpose. However, since there weren't that many new buildings built that year, they ultimately were released to join the other dates in circulation. The low mintages of that year were the result of the fulfillment of the requirements of the Pittman Act of 1918.

Q: What is the reason behind putting coins in the cornerstone of a building that is being built?

The custom traces back to several ancient religions where it was customary to place coins in the foundation to buy the good will of the gods and demons or evil spirits.

Chapter 22

DAMAGE - ACCIDENTAL, DELIBERATE

Minting varieties have a lure for many collectors, but the downfall of a substantial number is trying to figure which is a mint product and which is damage. A key problem is that a lot of accidental damage can occur in the mint after the coin is struck, so it's not part of the minting process, and has no collector value.

Q: I've seen ads asking several hundred dollars for a 1969-S cent with machine doubling. Is this a legitimate price?

Machine doubling damage is not a minting variety, so it has no collector value. It is damage to the coin after the strike and I don't know of any form of damage after the striking process ends which has any value. It is the most frequent form of doubling found on all coins, so frequent that bags of San Francisco cents often contained up to 60 percent of the coins with such damage. My advice is to never pay a cent more than face value for any coin that has been damaged after striking, whether it's called machine doubling, strike doubling, shelf doubling, ejection doubling, shift doubling, micro doubling, or any of the numerous obsolete names for die bounce doubling. Another good rule, if you don't recognize the "language," often "slanguage," then don't buy the coin. Chances are the dealer is either ignorant of what he's selling or is being less than honest in describing it.

Q: You've mentioned machine doubling damage quite often, but something about it still puzzles me. If as you say it is, it is caused by the die bouncing on the struck coin, why does it only affect the date and letters and not the main design?

Machine doubling damage, or MDD usually affects the date and letters and not the design because the edges of the design usually have a gentle slope to the field, while the letters and digits stick up sharply, with much steeper sides. Compare the date for example with the nearby front of the bust on the Lincoln cent, and you will see that the bust comes up from the field at a very low angle, so that the die has nothing to hit there. The chin, nose and forelock of Lincoln's hair rise more sharply from the field, and can and do get damaged by the bouncing die, as do the letters on both sides of the coin.

Q: I have a coin which has some of the rim metal covering the parts of the letters that appear next to the rim. How does this happen?

If this is a thin layer, with a distinct separation from the metal in the letters or field, then it is probable that the coin has been squeezed into a bezel or ring, used to attach the coin to a piece of jewelry. When the band is crimped around the rims of the coin, it sometimes squeezes the metal out in a thin layer over the lettering or design next to the rim. In some cases you may even find the ring still on the coin, where it is often mistaken for a striking problem of some kind. If the ring is still in place, check the inside edge and you will probably find where the attachment tab broke off.

Q: I was referred to you by a coin dealer for information on a 1925 cent which I have, which has a 1 struck over the 9. Is it an overdate?

Highly unlikely. If you examine the coin with a lens you will probably find that the 9 has been damaged by some sharp object which sheared the soft metal and piled it up in a mound which resembles a 1. With modern die manufacturing methods it is almost impossible to make a die with that kind of a mistake, especially on just a single coin.

**A Mercury dime with the
1942/41 overdates.**

Q: Which of the doubled date Mercury dimes are valuable?

A general answer is that almost none of them have any special value. The two major exceptions in the date file are of course the 1942/1941 overdates from both the Philadelphia and Denver Mints, but they are in a class by themselves. Doubling on the Mercury dates is frequent and found for most dates and mints. The reason is that it is machine doubling damage, caused by the die bouncing on the already struck coin. There are a couple of dates that are legitimate doubled dies, but you're much more likely to run into the coins damaged by the die bounce, where the doubling shows as a flat shelf.

Q: I have a 1984-P and a 1984-D Olympic commemorative dollar with what looks like a doubled die. Is this a known variety?

Veteran readers of *Numismatic News* may remember that I got my foot in my mouth on this one a few years back, first identifying it as a doubled die, then having to retract it because the doubling is plain old die bounce, or machine doubling damage. The problem is that when a die bounces on the incuse design it acts as a punch, so the doubling on the incuse dates on the Olympic coins much more closely resembles hub doubling than does die bounce on a relief design. A special rule to help spot this as die bounce is that the doubling on the incuse design will be on the opposite side from where it is on the relief design. In other words, if the doubling on the mint mark is on the left, while it is on the right side of the date, then it is die bounce.

Q: I have a 1941 (1951, 1911, etc.) cent. The last 1 in the date is slanted to the right. How much can I expect to get for this coin if I sell it?

It is worth just face value. The slant 1 on the 1941 and some other date cents is damage. This is frequently blamed on the Federal Reserve Bank rolling machines, which have a crimping finger to make the "shotgun" rolls. The finger catches and damages the 1 in the process. Lots of these have been sold as "genuine" "errors" over the years, but they are worthless. Check the base (or top) of the 1 with a lens, and you will see where the metal has been sheared and shoved to one side. The alloy used for the cent is relatively soft, and it doesn't take much pressure behind a sharp, or even blunt instrument to shear part of a digit or letter and shove it to one side, which is what has happened to your coin. Collectors and dealers could solve a lot of such problems if they would just look at the piece with a magnifying lens. You can clearly see the contact mark where the metal was shoved to one side, and the sheared area where the metal was moved.

Q: I found several coins with circular scratches, with a distinctive purplish color. What happened to them?

Your coins were caught under the fence in a coin counter. This is damage after the strike so it is not a minting variety, and has no collector value. The purple color comes from the coin metal being heated by the friction. The mints have been changing to new machines, which have eliminated much of this sort of damage.

Q: I have a 1963 proof set (or a later date mint set) with a coin which has parallel grooves in the rims. Was this done in the minting process?

This is damage from the jaws of the sealing machine which sealed the coins into the individual compartments in the plastic envelope. You can find this damage on proof sets dated 1955 to 1964, and all of the mint sets dated from 1968 on. It is damage and not a minting variety, so it has no value. The Mint is still using the same method of sealing the sets, so these coins turn up every year, one more reason why you should check your coins carefully when you receive them, and not just toss the unopened box into your safe or bank box. If you catch something like this while it is still current, you can get a replacement. To get the set replaced, write to: U.S. Mint, Account Maintenance, 10001 Aerospace Drive, Lanham, MD 20706, Tel. (202) 283-2646. Ask for instructions on how to return the set and get a replacement, but do not mail the set until you have written first.

Q: Is a fingerprint on a coin considered to be damage, and should it be listed in the description of the coin?

A fingerprint is actually etched into the surface of the coin by the natural acids in the skin, so it is damage to the coin and it should be listed in a description. I believe that the grading services will drop a point or two for such a marking on the coin, so it should be stated. The warning is valid—always hold a coin by the edge. A "fresh" fingerprint on a coin can be removed by dipping the coin, a job best left to an expert, but if the coin has already been dipped one or more times, the cumulative effect is going to reduce the value of the piece. This question came from a reader who purchased several coins through the mail from a dealer who has been denied advertising privileges in any of our numismatic publications because of recurring grading problems.

Example of a fingerprinted damaged coin.

Q: What would cause some of my copper alloy coins to have a mottled, unnatural reddish color?

The most likely cause is that they have been in a fire. Intense heat will cause oxidation and the distinctive reddish appearance, and unfortunately the effects are deep seated and permanent, sharply reducing or eliminating any collector value.

Q: I have a zinc cent which has a number of craters in the copper plating, with a whitish material breaking through the plating. What causes this?

The eruptions you describe are fairly common on the zinc cents, and appear to be a form of corrosion caused by contamination on the zinc core. The whitish excrescence is a zinc oxide. One more reason why perfect examples of the zinc cents are going to be scarce in a decade or two.

Q: What is "PVC" and how do you identify it?

 PVC is short for polyvinyl-chloride, which is a common plastic, containing various amounts of plasticizers, or softeners. It is these softeners which do the damage to coins or paper money, leaving a green slime on them, which corrodes the coin surface, doing permanent damage. There is no easy way to identify or distinguish the amount of dangerous softeners, leaving us at the mercy of the manufacturer. There are other plastics on the market which do not contain plasticizers and are safe for coins, such as Mylar or polystyrene. There are a couple of special products specifically for removing PVC contamination (not regular coin cleaners or dips) which should not harm your coins. However, the green is attacking the surface of the coin, so there will be some permanent damage, which cannot be reversed.

Q: One of the grading services refused to grade my coin because it has PVC contamination on it. How do I remove it?

There are several non-acid products on the market which will remove PVC contamination. Company policy prohibits recommending any specific product, so check the ads. Note that these products will not repair the damage already done by the PVC slime. In advanced stages it will reduce the grade of the coin. All it will do is remove the PVC slime to stop it from doing further damage. Read the directions for use, and follow them EXACTLY!

Q: What happens to damaged or mutilated coins?

The Treasury has long had a salvage policy which recovers the metals contained in coins that are accidentally or intentionally damaged. The usual procedure is for local banks to accept the coins—usually for face value, although some banks may discount them—and they are shipped to the Federal Reserve, which in turn returns them in bulk to the Mint. There they are sorted into the different metals and melted right along with fresh stocks of metals to make new coins. The clad coins get the same treatment, since the alloy was intentionally picked so that it can be mixed directly into the alloy used to make nickels. The Denver Mint has a small melting furnace where damaged coins are dumped in with misstruck coins and melted down to return to the supplier, since they no longer produce their own coin metal strip.

Q: Why are there more bag marks on big coins than on the small ones?

Sheer mass is the answer. The bigger the coin, the more damage it will cause when it scrapes, rubs, or bounces against another coin.

Q: If checks are cancelled and paper money is punched or cut to cancel the value, what is done with our coins?

Some countries use a stamping press which deforms or mutilates the pieces to make sure they don't get back into circulation. The U.S. Mint sends obsolete, mutilated, worn, or damaged coins direct to the melting furnace.

Chapter 23

DENOMINATIONS

Statistics about the different denominations that the U.S. Mint has struck always seem to be fascinating to the reader. There have been a goodly number of questions over the years on this topic, so perhaps it's one of your interests too.

Q: Is the trime and the thrip the same coin by different names?

Technically no, as trime was applied to the U.S. three cent piece to fit with dime. Thrip was another candidate for the coin, but it was originally applied to the English three-pence. Official efforts to use either or both for the U.S. coin failed to catch the public fancy.

Q: Has the U.S. Mint ever issued any pennies?

Although the Mint has struck pennies for other countries, it has never struck one for U.S. issue. Our coins are cents, but even the Mint calls them "pennies" in some of their literature. Internally the official word is cents. However, since 1985 in its news releases and sales literature the Mint has conceded defeat and has gone along with American slang, calling them pennies. Unless Congress were to rebuke the Treasury Department, this two level policy is likely to continue. Pennies have been struck for other countries, including Fiji in 1942 and 1943. Pennies were also struck for Australia during World War II.

Q: Did the public use the names of the official denominations of the gold coins?

Even though Congress used "eagle" as the official denomination, the general public, from what evidence is available, ignored the official name and called the coins by their numerical denomination—$10 gold, $5 gold, $2-1/2 gold, etc. With the modern versions the trend is running the other way, with the pieces being called (silver) Eagles rather than dollars.

Q: What is the source for the discontinued "disme" denomination?

The term traces to the French "Dixieme" which also was the root source for Dixie as the moniker for the Southern states. Dixieme means "one tenth." The "s" was dropped to Americanize the dime. Walter Breen traced it as a French term back to 1585 when Simon Stevin created the term to use in decimal reckoning. He refers to it as a "neologism," which means a new word or a new meaning for an established word.

Q: What is the correct pronunciation of "disme?"

The answer to your question may be a bit surprising—and no doubt controversial when I use them here—but there are two accepted pronunciations: "dime" and "deem." I had to go back to a 1938 Funk & Wagnells dictionary, one of the last to list the term with a pronunciation. There were also a number of slang terms attached to the coin which obviously had their roots in disme, such as: deece, deemer, deemier, dimer, dimmer, dimmo, or dimo. The term I'd pick as the most unusual for a dime though was "hog."

Q: Why were there no denominations on our early silver coins?

It was a matter of ego. The British coins didn't show a value, so ours didn't either. The Act establishing the U.S. coinage did not require denominations on the silver and gold coins, so they followed the British tradition of value denoted by size.

Q: The 1883 nickel got lots of publicity. Was it the only coin without a spelled-out denomination?

Don't forget the three-cent silver, three-cent nickel, the half dime (1794-1805), dimes (1796-1807), the 1796 quarter, the half dollars (1794-1807) which had it on the edge. It was the same for the dollars from 1794 to 1804.

Q: How many different denominations have we had for U.S. coins?

There was the mill, the 1/2, 1, 2, 3, 5, 10, 20, 25, and 50 cents; $1, $2.50, $3, $4, $5, $10, $20,and $50; a total of 18. We're currently down to six, two of which either fail to circulate or pile up unwanted. Included are the nickel and silver 3-cent and 5-cent, and the silver and gold $1. The mill is an official denomination, still on the books, but it never was actually struck as a coin. The 1792 Coinage act called for a mill. This was discarded immediately, but was revived during the Great Depression for tax tokens. It was left on the federal books as part of Title 31, U.S. Code. The dime gets official mention too, although the nickel, quarter, and half dollar are ignored. Here is the full text: "United States money is expressed in dollars, dimes or tenths, cents or hundredths, and mills or thousandths. A dime is a tenth of a dollar, a cent is a hundredth of a dollar and a mill is a thousandth of a dollar."

Q: Has the United States ever struck a U.S. coin denominated in pesos?

Careful before you jump on this one! All of the peso denominated coins used in the Philippines between 1903 and 1947 are U.S. coins, struck at either the mainland U.S. Mints or the U.S. Branch Mint in Manila.

Q: There was a drive at one time to obtain a 7-1/2 cent denomination to cover the increase in the cost of the nickel candy bar. Are there other instances of such odd denominations?

During World War I the price of newspapers doubled from one cent to two, and the American Newspaper Publisher's Association urged Congress to adopt a new 2-cent coin. One contemporary editor, tongue-in-cheek suggested a 3-cent coin to buy a stamp, a 7-cent to buy a pint of milk, a 9-cent for a pound of sugar, and a 23-cent to buy a gallon of gasoline. A bill actually was introduced for a 15-cent coin to "pay movie admissions," although it was noted that such admissions varied widely. The 7-1/2 cent coin was a 1965 candy manufacturer's suggestion for raising the price of a candy bar. The Association of Candy Brokers asked for the coin for vending machines to avoid changing the size of nickel candy bars. The American Institute for Intermediate Coinage, a lobbying group, was founded in 1949 by California soft drink magnate, Edward W. Mehren. It's purpose was to promote the introduction of fractional coins, such as the 2-1/2 and 7-1/2 cent pieces, and it had the membership and support of a number of major business firms and even the American Federation of Labor union.

Q: Several of us got into a discussion recently about the first use of dollar as a denomination. Wasn't the U.S. the first to use it?

The United States was more than a century late in using the term which originated long before the U.S. became a nation. Charles II of Scotland struck the first dollar coins in 1676. Smaller pieces down to the denomination of 1/16 dollar were also issued. The U.S. first authorized the dollar coin by an Act of Congress dated April 2, 1792, but the first dollars weren't struck and issued until 1794. The Scotch dollar incidentally was about the heaviest of the breed, weighing 429 grains.

Q: Several 1815 quarters are known with an E stamped into them. Was this done at the U.S. Mint?

So far as is known it was, but researchers have searched in vain for a reason for the act. The letters "R," "E" and "L" are found countermarked on quarters of that date, supposedly by the Mint. One theory is that the letters stand for "Regular," Excess," and "Light," although this theory has not been fully confirmed. If they are a mint product, they join a very limited number of U.S. coins which had countermarks officially added by the Mint. We use the Standard Catalog of World Coins system, which calls an added mark on one side of a coin a countermark, while marks on both sides, applied at the same time are a counterstamp.

Q: Can you tell me anything about my coin, which has a name, letters, or numbers punched into it?

With limited exceptions, most are worthless, as there is no way to trace anything done after a coin is minted. The punches could have been done by anyone, but some of the early, more important ones have been cataloged. Otherwise your coin has lost, rather than gained value.

Chapter 24

DESIGNS

The designs that appear on our coins have always been the topic of controversy, from the earliest colonial coins right up to the present day. Whether damned as too crude, not artistic, or whatever epithet, the design that pleased a majority seems in the minority.

Q: Which of our coins was ugly enough to be described as the "blowsy barmaid?"

Early collectors were prone to nicknames, a habit which seems to have become a tradition among more modern collectors. There was the "silly" head, the "booby" head, and many more. The man on the street was critical enough of the design used for the 1808-14 Classic Head type to describe it as a "sleepy looking Liberty turbaned with a diaphanous nightcloth," and someone settled on the title of "blowsy barmaid" for the series.

1810 Classic Head cent.

Q: There's a 1794 cent which has what is called "The Drunken Diecutter's Obverse." What can you tell me about it?

They had colorful names for die varieties—and still do! In this case, the die cutter started out on the date, got the first two digits cut, then apparently had a three martini lunch and cut the 9 very high, close to the base of the bust, and then dropped the 4 sharply down to make it fit.

Q: There's a 1794 large cent that has what is nicknamed the "office boy" reverse. Why the title?

Because the die looks like the office boy cut it while the engraver was out to lunch. The wreath is not symmetrical, with variations in the depth of the leaves, and the N in ONE was cut upside down and then corrected.

Q: Has the word "PEACE" appeared on any world coin prior to the 1921 United States Peace dollar?

The proposal originated with the American Numismatic Association, and while it was supported by a Congressional Resolution, the enabling resolution failed to make it out of the hands of Congress, so it was necessary to fall back on the law which allowed design changes for coins that had been struck for 25 years. This is apparently the first usage in the English language on a coin. There are quite a number of Roman and Greek coins with "Peace" on them.

Q: How do you tell which is the obverse and which is the reverse of a foreign coin?

This is a perennial problem, which not too surprisingly has been a bone of contention among coin experts for many years. Traditionally, many countries have their own customs as to which side of a coin is considered the obverse, frequently based on some national symbol, such as the eagle. To settle some of the confusion, our catalog department has evolved a couple of rules which are used for listings in *The Standard Catalog of World Coins* which we publish annually. For countries which have royalty as the head of government, the bust of the ruler is considered to be on the obverse. For those countries with a republican form of government or something similar, the side upon which the name of the country appears is the obverse. This solves the problem for all but the U.S. coins, which continue to be listed in the traditional manner.

Q: I saw a reference to the "naked" bust of Washington on the quarter. What's that supposed to mean?

In artistic terms a bust which is unclothed, even if it only shows the head and neck is "naked." Not to worry, George wasn't being immodest. It's just a technical description.

Q: Are there any U.S. coins with a crown?

The Rosa Americana pieces struck by William Wood, including the halfpenny, penny, and twopence, have a crowned rose on the reverse, dated 1722 and 1723, and patterns dated 1724 and 1733. The Virginia halfpennies of 1773-74 show a crowned shield and the American Plantations 1/24 real has four crowns on the reverse. Two more modern coins, the Isabella commemorative quarter and the Norfolk, Virginia Bicentennial commemorative half dollar, depict a crown. Dated 1936, but struck in 1937, the Norfolk design includes the royal mace of the city, which bears a reproduction of the English crown at its top.

Q: What is the source for "Miss Liberty?"

The design is traced back at least 2500 years to the Roman goddess Libertas. Her temple once served as the first public library in ancient Rome. The Liberty Cap goes back further to freed slaves in Egypt who wore a distinctive cap to show their status.

Q: Is Miss Liberty on all U.S. coins?

There are a number of older coins, including the Fugio cent of 1787, the Flying Eagle cent of 1856-58, the Lincoln cent, the two-cent, the silver three-cent, and the five-cent coins of the mid-1800s, that failed to bear the Miss Liberty design. She is also missing from the Isabella Quarter, the Columbian half dollar, and the Lafayette dollar. She is missing from most of the modern commemoratives, but shows up on both the silver and gold Eagles.

Q: It's my understanding that at one time an Ohio city used a U.S. coin as a city seal. Can you track it down?

The city of Dayton, Ohio used the obverse of a large cent, the head and 13 stars as its official seal, adopted in 1826.

Q: Do the shields used on U.S. coins follow the customs of heraldry?

They seem to be variations of the pointed Nordic and English shield, which is one of the four basic shields recognized by various heraldic rules. The other three are the round shield of Asiatic countries, the curved point shield of France and Central Europe, and the rounded shield of Spain and Portugal. One source, commenting on such variations, says, "Dozens of other shields exist, many quite impossible or pure fantasy. One is wise to leave them alone."

Q: How come a peace dollar in my collection has the spelling TRVST?

For the same reason that many public buildings have "V" instead of "U" in their inscriptions. It's a bit of artistic license, tracing back to the initial lack of a "U" in the early alphabets. The spelling was used on all the Peace dollars, as well as the Standing Liberty quarters (1916-1932), so your coin is perfectly normal, right in style. The Romans did it, but the Greeks provided the original alphabet used, so they perhaps share the responsibility. The Romans took 13 letters from the Greek alphabet, added or modified 10 of their own design, but did not have a "J," "U" or "W." For a time the Romans threw out the Greek "Z," but had to restore it. The "U" and "W" were added to the alphabet about C.E. 1000, with the "J" bringing up the rear about 1500.

Q: Why the small "O" in "of" on the reverse of the Memorial cents?

This question returns with each new class of beginning collectors. The Mint's Chief Engraver at the time, Frank Gasparro, said that it fits in artistically with the design. It was a small piece of artistic license which has attracted frequent comment over the years. Perhaps you overlooked the Franklin half dollar, first minted in 1948? Or the Walking Liberty halves of 1916-1947? Then there's the Bicentennial quarter and the Peace dollar, all with small "o." Without exception, there hasn't been a new coin design issued by the U.S. Mint that wasn't the subject of rumors of recall. The 1959 cents were just like all the rest. In this case the story got around that the government was going to pay 50 cents to $1 EACH for the errant cents in order to recover them. Ignored was the fact that the design was in effect frozen by the 25-year law.

Curiously, published criticism of the Franklin half in *Numismatic Scrapbook* at the time failed to note that the small "O" had graced the Liberty Walking halves from 1916 to 1947, so everyone should have been used to the effect, especially since it had been used on the "popular" Peace dollar from 1921 to 1935 as well. Criticism fell on John R. Sinnock for doing it on the Franklin half, just as on Adolph Weinman for the Walking Liberty halves of 1916-1947. Gasparro broke the chain by using the same size O on the Kennedy half. Other coins with the small "o" include the Pratt $2.50 and $5 gold. Commemoratives include the 1918 Illinois, 1920 Maine, 1925 Lexington, 1925 California, 1928 Hawaii, 1935 Hudson, 1936 Long Island, and 1982 George Washington half.

Q: I have five 1964 Kennedy halves, and on every one of them LIBERTY is spelled LIBFRTY. How could such a mistake happen?

It is not a mistake, although collectors persist in challenging the right of the designer to balance his subject by covering parts of the letters. It is a relatively frequent occurrence—just check the Mercury dime, which has the E similarly obscured, and part of the design over the O in OF on the reverse. The Barber quarter has similar overlaps on both sides, as does the Barber half. Look at the Walking Liberty half obverse and the Peace dollar obverse and reverse among others.

Q: Was James B. Longacre's daughter Sara the model for the Indian cent?

There is some new and convincing evidence that she was the model. However, this is a reversal of generally accepted information, including Longacre's statement that he used a Greco-Roman statue of Venus, as borne out by the mature features of the coin design. The information on the use of Sara as the model can be traced to William Brimelow, known as "Bill the Coin Man." In the 1930s he did a weekly radio program on coins, as well as writing articles for publication in the coin magazines of the day. One of the stories he wrote cited the "Indian chief and the headdress" story, indicating that the story stemmed from a direct descendant of the Longacre family who lived in the same city where Brimelow broadcast from. The discrediting of the story was based at least in part on an incorrect date for Sara's birth. She was much younger than the "30 years old" generally ascribed to the time period when the model was made.

Q: Two different women are reputed to have been the models for the Standing Liberty on the 1916 quarters. Which was the real model?

For many years it was reported that one Dora Doscher (Baum), who later acted in silent films with the stage name of Doris Doree, was the model used by Hermon A. MacNeil for the quarter. This information was carried in the *Numismatist* in May 1917. Dora Doscher of NY as a child was a semi invalid, but served in the Red Cross in World War I. Prior to that she was a lecturer and writer. She posed for the Pulitzer Memorial Fountain in New York City, and for the Diana in the Metropolitan Museum of Art, sculpted by Karl Bitter. She died March 9, 1970. In 1972, a newspaper account quoting Broadway actress Irene MacDowell was published, in which she admitted being the secret model for the design. The deliberate coverup was instituted because MacDowell's husband was strongly opposed to her involvement with the artist, a common attitude of the day.

Q: Why did we switch from six pointed to five pointed stars on some of our coins in 1892?

This is a confusing problem, as the 1892 dimes, quarters, and half dollars have six pointed stars on one side and five on the other. The apparent source of the change was the adaption of the reverse with five point stars from the Great Seal, while the earlier six point stars date back to English and French heraldry. The Great Seal and the Presidential Seal both have five point stars, while that of the House of Representatives uses six point stars. No specific reason has surfaced in Mint records.

Q: Is the Jefferson nickel design a copy of a foreign coin?

It's quite unlikely, although there is an Austrian 1932 commemorative 2 schilling piece with a bust of Haydn which bears an interesting resemblance to Jefferson, complete to the "pigtail" queue and the large rectangular patch collar on the coat.

Q: Please settle an argument for us. Are there any U.S. coins that depict the American Flag?

You'll probably need an uncirculated specimen to see it, but the Walking Liberty half dollars, struck from 1916 to 1947, have the flag draped over Miss Liberty's robe.

Q: How does one know which star is meant when it says "the first (or the fifth) star?"

The stars are usually numbered in a clockwise direction, beginning with the star at the left of the date, or with the first star at the lower edge left of the upright center line of the coin. Where there is an irregular star design in the field, the description has to be more detailed.

Q: Are there more than 13 stars on any of our coins?

Lots of them: there are dimes with 14 and 16 stars; the 1796 quarter had 15; the 1794 and 1796 halves each had 16; and the Gobrecht 1836 dollars had 26. The 1796-1807 $2.50 had 13 stars on each side; a variety of the 1804 had a 14-star reverse; and the 1879 $4 Stella had 13 on the obverse and one large star on the reverse. The $20 gold had 46 stars around the edge from 1907-11, and 48 on the edge from 1912-1933, plus three stars separating E PLURIBUS UNUM. The $10 gold had 46 on the edge from 1907-11, and a 48-star edge from 1912-1933, plus 13 on obverse. The Kennedy half dollar has them all beat, with 63 stars on the reverse.

Q: Would you please explain the T-1, T-2, and T-3 abbreviations in the double eagle gold listings in your price charts?

The T-1, or Type 1, Coronet Head double eagle is the one without the motto on the reverse, struck from 1849 to 1866. In the latter year the "In God We Trust" motto was added on the reverse to make it the T-2, which was minted until 1876. For the T-3, or Type 3, the "Twenty D." denomination beginning in 1877 was spelled out as "Twenty Dollars." In 1907 production ended and the switch was made to the St. Gaudens design.

Q: Isn't there a unique feature about the Apollo 11 eagle?

If memory serves me correctly, this is the only depiction of an eagle on a U.S. coin which bears two olive branches in its talons rather than a branch and a sheaf of arrows. This of course excludes those eagles such as the Peace Dollar design which carry neither. The olive branch is a traditional symbol of peace, so a pair of branches and the elimination of the arrows was intended to show the peaceful intent of the United States.

Q: What is the difference between PAF and SAF designs on the 1878 Morgan dollars?

The PAF abbreviation stands for "Parallel Arrow Feathers" while SAF stands for "Slanted Arrow Feathers." The PAF or parallel arrow feather variety includes the first (8 tail feather) design as well as the 2nd (7 tail feather) design. The SAF is the third reverse design used for the new coins.

Q: I was disappointed when the SBA dollar appeared and Susan B. Anthony's name didn't appear on it. Why not?

Think a minute and you'll realize that nobody has their name on any U.S. coin which depicts a real person, other than some of the commemoratives. It's a matter of law that the names appear on our paper money, but tradition, based on a desire to avoid the appearance of being a "regal" currency, led to the absence of any names on coins.

Q: At one time or another I've seen the SBA dollar listed as having 10, 11, or 12 sides. Please clear up the confusion.

The final coin was round, with an 11-sided inner rim, which I helped confuse with an early reference to it as being 12-sided. One of the original patterns for the coin, with a bust of Martha Washington, had a 10-sided edge. Gasparro's original design—the "fright wig" Liberty facing the viewer's left—was round with a round inner rim. Hopefully, an end to the confusion.

Q: In examining some of the older coins in my collection I noticed that there is a mistake on the Ike dollars, because the motto slants down to the right. Isn't that sort of obvious?

It would be, if it were a mistake. However, it was designed that way. The problem is that Ike's bust was modelled leaning slightly forward, so when the coin is placed in a holder with the bust upright, the motto tilts downward at the end. If the coin is put in the holder with the bust tipped forward as designed, then the motto is perfectly normal. Every Ike dollar has this feature, so it has no effect on the value of the coins.

Q: Has any living foreigner appeared on a U.S. coin?

Philippine President Quezon joined President Roosevelt on the 1936 Philippine Commemorative 1 peso. The coin was technically a U.S. coin, and Quezon technically was a resident of a U.S. possession, so that's as close as we can come. Mintage was 10,000, struck at the Manila Mint.

Q: Who did the flying eagle design used on the Gobrecht dollars and later on the Flying Eagle cent?

The design was created in 1836 by Titian Peale II, a top naturalist of his day, and a skilled artist.

Q: Are there any U.S. coins with the same design on different denominations?

One would be the Grant gold commemorative dollar and half dollar. Also, the 20-cent piece has the same reverse as the trade dollar. This similarity isn't often spotted, but it's correct. Missing from the 20-cent coin is the motto, "E PLURIBUS UNUM," and the statement of the silver fineness that is added to the trade dollar, but the rest is the same.

1836 Gobrecht silver dollar.

Q: Was the bust of Columbus on the Columbian Exposition commemorative half dollar modeled after a picture of the explorer?

The original intent was to use a medal struck in 1512 as a model, but a copy was not available in time, and Charles Barber used some other depiction of Columbus for the coin.

Q: Was the Ike dollar the first to depict a living person? Ike died in 1969.

It was the first circulating dollar to depict a specific person, but actually the 1900 Lafayette commemorative dollar was first, depicting both Washington and Lafayette.

Q: Is there any U.S. coin which carries a cross as part of the design?

Despite that the word "GOD" appears on all our relatively recent coins, the only three U.S. coins which clearly show a cross in the design are the York County, Maine 1936 commemorative half dollar, which shows the county seal (a shield quartered by a large cross), and the 1934 Maryland Commemorative half, which has two crosses in the reverse design. The Shield nickel also has a stylized cross at the top of the shield.

Q: What was the point of using two different threes for the 1873 coins?

The first dies made for that year had closed threes in the date, which prompted an official complaint from the Chief Coiner that the closed 3 would easily be confused with an 8. As a result new punches with an open three were prepared and used for the rest of the year. This letter was discovered and publicized by Harry X. Boosel in the 1950s, but even after the information became generally known in the hobby there were still instances of the closed 3 coins being sold as 1878 dates. The "closed" 3 isn't really closed, but the ball serifs at the tips of the 3 are much larger and closer together than those on the "open" 3, giving rise to the names.

Q: I've seen the wheat ears design used on the Lincoln cent through 1958 described as a "wreath design." It doesn't look like much of a wreath to me.

A logical observation, although coin design is not always logical. U.S. coins featured a wreath as part of the design from their inception in 1792 almost continuously until 1921 when the last true wreath disappeared from the silver dollar. The wheat ears design, since the ears are curved and resemble the old wreaths, is considered a "symbolic" wreath.

Q: What is the purpose of the large "C" in the design of the silver 3-cent piece?

It was added as an abbreviation of "cents" to distinguish the denomination. Curiously, while U.S. coins have sometimes been considered to be copies of French designs, the French seem to have borrowed that big "C" for their small denomination coins of the World War I era.

The large "C" in the design of the silver 3-cent piece is an abbreviation of "cents" to distinguish the denomination.

Q: Where did the suggestion come from to put Lincoln on the cent in 1909?

There is a letter preserved in the Library of Congress which answers that question. The initial proposal, or at least the first one to come to public attention was the letter, written by Jerome Sivia of Springfield, Illinois, to President Teddy Roosevelt. In it he suggested that the switch would be an appropriate memorial of the 100th anniversary of Lincoln's birth.

Q: Why is there so much difference in the appearance of the 1968 and 1969 cent obverses?

The master die was changed in 1969, reverting back to Brenner's original 1909 design. Over the years the old master dies had gradually spread until many of the details were lost, and the lettering was pushed against the rim. Such changes are fairly frequent, although not generally as noticeable as the 1969 revision.

The usual cause of the motto extending into the rim is that the hub used to make the die had expanded from the repeated pressure, enlarging it to the point where the design is pushed outward. This would have happened to a number of dies and all the coins struck by those dies, so it would be too high a mintage to have any significant value. This was happening with great frequency by 1968, and in 1969 they revamped the cent design to correct the problem.

Q: Was there a contest for the reverse design of the Lincoln cent in 1959?

The competition was an internal affair, with a total of 23 designs submitted by the staff engravers at the Philadelphia Mint. No "outside" designs were solicited or considered. Frank Gasparro's design was chosen by Treasury Secretary Anderson and Mint Director W.H. Brett and was presented to the Lincoln Sesquicentennial Committee.

Q: Do you think the Mint will get around to changing the Lincoln cent design for the 200th anniversary of his birth in 2009?

The Mint did make a change to the memorial reverse for the 150th anniversary in 1959, so—if we are still using coins—it's quite likely they might do something with the cent to mark the event, since it will also be the 100th anniversary of the introduction of the Lincoln design.

Q: Is the bust on the Lincoln cent an accurate reproduction?

Brenner took liberties with Lincoln's hair, giving it the 1909 version of a permanent wave, as all contemporary photos show Lincoln with straight hair. Look at the coin and the hair is curly, especially if you look at a 1909 date. But, look at a photograph, and you'll note his hair was relatively straight. It was a case of artistic license again, as Brenner felt the curls would add "depth" to the design. To prove him right, compare with the smooth locks of Ben Franklin, and the bald pate of Eisenhower.

Q: The statement is made that the Lincoln cent was the first U.S. coin to depict the same person on both obverse and reverse. Is this correct?

It is the second, rather than the first. The Lafayette dollar of 1900, predating the Lincoln cent memorial reverse by 59 years, has Lafayette on both obverse and reverse.

Q: Who do I write to urge a P mint mark on the cent? Who would I write to with some suggestions for our coinage?

I'd suggest the following: Director, U.S. Mint, Washington, DC 20220. Secretary of the Treasury, Department of the Treasury, 15th and Pennsylvania Ave. NW, Washington, DC 20220. Chairman, House Subcommittee on Consumer Affairs and Coinage, 1740 Longworth, Washington, DC 20515-0534.

Send us a copy of your letters and we'll consider them for publication as well.

Q: Why hasn't the $ sign been used on our coins?

No reason other than tradition. On our early coins it was probably left off to avoid possible confusion with the peso symbol, which by the late 1700s was similar to the $ sign.

Q: Why is it that published pictures of coins sometimes look like the design was incuse, rather than in relief?

You have run afoul of an optical illusion. There are several ways of correcting this, but one of the simplest is to turn the picture upside down. This will usually change the perspective enough so that the design will "snap" back into place.

Q: When was the Commission of Fine Arts formed?

It was created by an Act of Congress, signed by President William Howard Taft on May 17, 1910. The original purpose was to "Advise on the location of statues, fountains and monuments in the public squares, streets and parks in the District of Columbia." The scope was broadened in the same year by an Executive Order and again in 1913 by President Woodrow Wilson. President Harding added coins in 1921, also medals and insignia. Congress added more duties for the seven members in 1930.

Q: Didn't Ben Franklin once propose a pretty radical idea for the designs of the first U.S. coinage?

Franklin was active in attempts to get the English firm of Bridges and Waller to strike our first coins. In a letter to the company he urged that the new coins should be graced with a variety of different slogans, such as "A penny saved is a penny got," "Early to bed, early to rise...." and others of a similar nature, making the point that a single slogan would quickly become boring.

Q: Is there any specific rule or regulation as to which way the bust has to face on U.S. coins?

The facing direction is more a matter of tradition than anything else, based in some small part on the custom in England of reversing direction with each new ruler. There is no law or regulation, so it is strictly a matter of the artist's choice.

Q: Which way is left and right on a coin?

Sounds simple, but there are two opposing schools, and a lot of confusion. The general rule is that the directions should be the viewer's left and right. To be safe, I usually spell it out when describing a coin.

Q: What did coin collectors do before there were cameras?

Collecting today without seeing the hundreds of coin pictures at every turn would be something like it was prior to the mid-1800s when photography came into its own. Before that collectors had to depend on engravings or simple line drawings of the design. Many of the engravings show more detail that a photograph, and are used even today to illustrate such things as coins from an ancient horde that are too worn or discolored to photograph well. Many early day numismatists were skilled engravers out of necessity.

Q: On the Lincoln cent, Brenner's VDB initials are incuse, but Felix Schlag's initials on the Jefferson nickel are in relief. Why?

It's just a matter of choice by the artist. The Fraser "F" is incuse on the Buffalo nickel, MacNeil's "M" is incuse on the Standing Liberty quarter, but Weinmann's AAW is in relief, as are Gilroy Robert's, John Sinnock's, and Frank Gasparro's initials.

Chapter 25

DESIGNERS, ENGRAVERS

The men and women who designed our coins are usually well known by name, at least. In answering questions about them I ran across a number of interesting pieces of information that didn't always make it into the history books.

Q: What was the real name of Victor D. Brenner?

Brenner was born Victoras Barnauskas. He was born in Lithuania of Jewish parents. He changed his name when he immigrated to the U.S. in 1890.

1861 Confederate cent.

Q: What is the significance of the incuse "L" on the cotton bale on the reverse of the Confederate cent?

The L is the designer's initial, for Robert Lovett, Jr., who designed and made the dies, and struck the 12 originals.

Q: Please settle our argument - did James Longacre or Franklin Peale design the 3-cent silver coin?

The design for the issue coin was Longacre's, but Peale is credited with an 1850 3-cent pattern copied from the pattern by Gobrecht for an 1836 gold dollar. While checking this I note that many writers tend to gloss over the differences between patterns and actual issue coins, which may have been the root cause for your difference of opinion.

Q: Who was the designer of the coins struck for the Philippines under the U.S. administration?

We have to exert a bit of care here as several sources have some incorrect information about the artist. His name was Melecio Figueroa, and he was a native of the Philippines, not California. He was trained in Spain and worked at the Manila Mint under Spain, later designing the coins which were put in circulation in 1903. Figueroa's wife was the model for the silver coin obverse.

Q: Was there an American engraver by the name of Eue?

Your man is Francis Eue, also known as Franz or Hans Eue. He worked for the Medallic Art firm in the 1930s. Reportedly, he was so prolific that his output was mistaken by historians for that of an entire company. Research by D. Wayne Johnson in the *TAMS Journal* proved he was just one man.

Chapter 26

FAMOUS PEOPLE AND COLLECTIONS

Q: What happened to Robert Morris after he paved the way for our first Mint?

He was Pennsylvania's first Senator in the first U.S. Congress, but in 1798 suffered financial reverses, went bankrupt, and spent over three years in debtor's prison, dying in poverty in 1806.

Q: Didn't Abraham Lincoln have something to say on the topic of return postage, which seems to be one of your pet peeves?

Indeed! The story is told that a woman autograph collector wrote to Lincoln for a "sentiment." In reply she got a letter which read, "Dear Madam: When you ask of a stranger that which is of use only to yourself, always enclose a stamp. There's your sentiment, and here's your autograph.—A. Lincoln."

Q: Wasn't Paul Volker one of the proponents of doing away with the cent?

The former Chairman of the Federal Reserve System was Undersecretary of the Treasury in the 1970s, and was in fact one of the leaders in the effort to get production of the cent halted.

Q: Aren't those who oppose the abolition of the one cent coin using a rather "dated" argument?

Perhaps a bit out of context, yes, but the very same argument was advanced in the late 1700s by no less a personage than Alexander Hamilton, who argued for the introduction of the half cent denomination by citing the very real possibility that merchants, for lack of a half cent, would round prices up to a full cent. If this sounds familiar it's because it's exactly the argument used today, that prices would be rounded up to the nearest nickel, but this ignores that a four cent rounding today is a small fraction of the value of a half cent in Hamilton's day. The point is perhaps moot, however, because the half cent was as unpopular in its day as the Anthony dollar is now.

Q: Did the same Robert Patterson who defeated the first proposal for the 2-cent piece as Director of the Mint later make the suggestion that it be adopted?

Same name, different generation. Robert Patterson, Director of the Mint in 1806, strenuously opposed a Senate bill for the coin. Robert M. Patterson, his son, proposed the successful bill, which passed and was made into law Dec. 12, 1836. The coin was to have been 90% copper, 10% silver, but for unknown reasons it was never produced for circulation.

Q: Was President Franklin D. Roosevelt a coin collector?

Roosevelt was much better known as a stamp collector, but he did collect coins as well, and his collection was sold several years after his death.

Q: Leonardo da Vinci is credited with inventing the coin press. Is his machine still in existence?

Leonardo da Vinci is one claimant for the title of inventor of the coin press. His sketches for a coin stamper were used some years ago to construct a working model that is now in the ANA Museum. However, da Vinci only sketched his idea and did not actually construct a press.

Q: Which president was also a Mint director?

Elias Boudinot, third director of the U.S. Mint, was president of the Confederation which preceded the United States, in 1783.

Q: Is there some sort of story connected with the magician, Harry Houdini, who used real gold coins in his act?

One source that we found says that Houdini, in a World War I version of the USO tours, entertained American troops by first filling a fishbowl with half dollars and then went into the audience and began pulling gold $5 half eagles out of the ears and hair of his audience. He would cap this by tossing the coin to some lucky soldier. By the end of the war he reportedly had given away some $7,000 in gold coins in this fashion.

Q: Is it true that all the 1794 silver dollars once belonged to a single owner?

David Rittenhouse, the Mint Director, deposited the silver and the coins were paid to him.

Q: Who was the first coin dealer in the United States?

That title is generally awarded to Edward Cogan who came to Philadelphia in 1853, at the age of 50, from England. He began selling coins on a part time basis in 1856. He held a private bid sale on November 1, 1858, which is considered to be one of the first, if not the first such sale of coins. At this sale he sold 77 lots to a total of 19 buyers for $128.68. When you consider that this was an average of $1.67 a lot for large cents, it seems minuscule compared to today's million dollar sales, but it was a major landmark at the time. His son was George Cogan.

Q: When did B. Max Mehl issue his first catalog?

The famous coin dealer issued his first fixed price catalog in 1904, and his first coin circular a year earlier.

Q: There's a story connected with Farran Zerbe that had to do with a large collection he saved from the "first" San Francisco earthquake. Do you have any details?

Zerbe was in San Francisco the day before the earthquake of April 18, 1906, and wanted to see the J.C. Lighthouse collection of Roman and Greek coins. Lighthouse reluctantly agreed and removed the coins from a safe at the Palace of Art and took it to his home for Zerbe to view.

By the time Zerbe was finished it was too late to return the collection to the Palace of Art. The next morning the earthquake destroyed the Palace and the safe and all its contents. Lighthouse's home was badly damaged, but the collection escaped unscathed, thanks to Zerbe's visit.

Q: In an old numismatic reference I found mention of a planned sale by Parke-Bernet Galleries of New York of the Josiah K. Lilly coin collection. Did the sale ever come off?

Actually the "planned" sale was a ploy to get Congress to act on a bill which had been submitted to relieve the Lilly estate of a $5.5 million tax bill. Part of the agreement was that the superb collection go to the Smithsonian Institution. The estate was pushing, claiming it was costing $1,000 a day to keep the collection, but Congress procrastinated until May, 1968. President Lyndon Johnson signed the bill into law on June 4, 1968 and within two weeks the coins were delivered to the Smithsonian.

Q: What was the Chase Manhattan Money Museum?

It was a popular tourist attraction in New York City, a museum operated by the Chase Manhattan Bank, centered around the collection of Farran Zerbe, who was the first curator. The Museum was in operation from 1929 to 1973. Gene Hessler was the curator when the exhibit closed. The money collection (more than 24,000 pieces), which was exhibited by the bank beginning in 1929, was donated to the Smithsonian Institution in 1978, except for pieces which had earlier been given to the American Numismatic Society.

Q: How many coins are in the Smithsonian collection?

A decades old figure of 850,000 was the best I could find. The collection began sometime before 1825. It is undoubtedly much larger by now. It compares with the half million coins in the Royal Dutch collection in The Hague, and the same size collection in the Vienna Kunst Museum. The Hermitage Museum in Leningrad has a collection of 1.4 million coins.

Chapter 27

GRADING, GRADING SERVICES

The ability to correctly grade a coin has become a skill that is mandatory for the collector. While the grading services have virtually overturned the old grading standards, there still are many gaps where the collector needs to know more than the average about the coin he is buying or selling.

Q: I have several U.S. commemorative coins which obviously have been in circulation. Isn't that unusual?

It was not at all unusual for the commemorative issues to circulate, all the way back to the Columbian Expo 1892 and 1893 pieces, which were placed in circulation when they didn't sell. If not then, certainly during the Depression when only a favored few could afford to hang onto collector coins. To the public they were just another coin with a stated value. The commemorative programs got a lot of bad press at the time because of the many abuses by the promoters.

Q: Please explain all the grading terms, and how I would go about learning to grade a coin.

Sorry, but it would take a book, and the book is the 4th Edition of the *ANA Grading Standards for United States Coins*. It contains all the information you want, and is available from almost any coin dealer, or directly from the American Numismatic Association. It's detailed enough so that the seemingly impossible task of learning how to grade becomes relatively easy. This book should be one of your first purchases when you get into the hobby. The best advice is to buy the book before you buy—or sell—a coin.

Q: Exactly what grade is "average circulated?"

There is no strict definition, and this is not a grading standard or a grading term. It is often applied to coins sold in bulk, and the buyer is likely to find that most, if not all, are at the very lowest end of the grading scale. It's best to check a sample of a lot offered in that fashion to determine the seller's version of the term. A group of Barber dimes is likely to contain a high percentage of "slicks" or well worn coins, while a group of current cents might include an AU or two.

Q: How do I tell whether my Buffalo nickel is a "full horn" or "1/4 horn?" Is this some kind of grade like "full steps?"

It is not a grade but a visual check of the condition of the coin, or a key area to check for wear. To determine the amount of horn remaining you either need an uncirculated coin or a good picture of one to compare the amount of horn detail or outline remaining. An uncirculated, fully struck coin will have a "full" horn, with the entire outline showing. As the coin wears, the left portion (the tip) of the horn is the first to disappear, until only the base is left on a well worn coin. It's a good "marker" for grading, but by no means the only one, so get a grading guide and study all of the parts that are affected by wear, not just the horn.

Q: What is a "full step" nickel?

This is a term applied to a very well struck Jefferson nickel, which will show the complete outlines of the six steps on Monticello on the reverse. Because of striking problems and worn dies, very few such coins are known for most dates, and some, like the 1954-S, apparently do not exist, or are excessively rare. Some of the prices paid for five and six step Jeffersons are real eye openers. It is not new, but it does seem to be part of a pattern of increasing interest in the best available strikes, as witness the interest in "full split band" Mercury dimes and Franklin halves with "full bell lines." Oddly enough, full step strikes for even the rarest dates are found on coins struck off center. There are six complete steps (steps and risers) in the center of the Monticello building front. To be classed as a full step, each must clearly show an unbroken line from end to end. If some of the steps are "broken," the unbroken quarters of each step are added together to determine the step "grade." This applies only to the central steps, not those on each end, outside the pillars.

Q: Is there a difference between "split bands" and "full split bands" for the Mercury dime series? I always understood that the "bands" on the Mercury dime were the diagonal strips surrounding the rods, but now I'm not sure.

The definitions are not "official," but one explanation of the difference is that split bands mean the bands are separated, but flatly struck, while the "full split bands" have both bands fully rounded as well as separated. The usual reference to bands is to the pairs of horizontal bands at top, center, and bottom, and the "full split bands" designation refers to the groove between these parallel strips.

Q: At a recent coin show I was surprised to see some silver dollars in slabs being offered for $30. The coin alone was worth that much or more, so what was going on?

The reason why you find lower grade coins in slabs is that they are mistakes. Someone had the coin, thought he knew how to grade it, and sent it in to get it slabbed. When it came back a lower grade than he expected, he had little recourse but to put it on the market at a bargain price in order to get rid of it. Few, if any, collectors would willingly or intentionally pay to have a low grade, low value coin slabbed.

Q: Is a CC dollar in a GSA case more valuable?

Probably not, as the coins were not graded accurately. Only a very small percentage of them would grade above MS-60 by present grading standards, as most of them had bag marks from being handled, and quite a few had been in circulation anyway. Your coins would have to be graded to determine their current status for two reasons. To begin with, the coins sold by the General Services Administration were not graded by experts, and in the meantime, grading standards have changed substantially—usually more stringent—so the coins may not meet today's standards even for MS-60. The coins would have to be removed from their original packing, but the coin is the part of the package which is to be graded to establish its value, not the case. It is a well known fact that some uncirculated coins were sold as "mixed" grades, and coins of lower grade were included among the uncirculated offerings. Tarnished coins in top condition also got "mixed." The coins were not assigned specific grades, but were merely sorted between circulated and uncirculated specimens.

Q: I have a rare coin I want authenticated and graded. Is there any place nearby where I can take it, as I will not let the coin out of my sight, because they might steal it, or switch coins.

This sort of fear is not only unreasonable, it is a phobia which will undoubtedly cost you dearly before you are done. All it takes is one substantiated charge of malpractice to put a legitimate grading service out of business, so they are not about to pull any stunts like that. Ironically, the majority of the grading services would not let you be in the room where they are working with coins—for THEIR security! They probably handle coins totaling thousands of times what your coin is worth every day. A coin which has not been authenticated and graded is worth only face value, and if you wait, sooner or later some sharpie is going to accept your "dare" and relieve you of your coin right under your nose. It's smart to be careful, but it's pure foolishness to establish unreasonable and unnecessary barriers around your coin.

Q: Are there any low grade coins rarer than the top grade of the same denomination and mint? For example, are all of the known 1876-CC 20-cent pieces in museums?

The 1876-CC 20-cent has 14 survivors, one in a low grade. This one coin is rarer, in its grade, but it is not more valuable. Most of them are in museums, but two of the pieces were sold at auction in 1983, one bringing $66,000 in uncirculated, and the other $52,500 in AU. The original 1876-CC mintage is estimated at 10 to 14, possibly as assay pieces. It's the same for low grade 1931-S cents, as most of that date are uncirculated.

Q: Are the diamonds important in grading Indian head cents?

The four diamonds on the hair ribbon are the first point to show wear. The wear points should be the second place you look on any coin you examine. Of course the date and any mint mark are first.

1901 Indian Head cent. Note the four diamonds on the hair ribbon.

Q: What is the dollar increment for the numbers in the numerical grading system?

The numbers apply only to the exact amount of wear, and not to the value. You are confusing the present system with the old one designed by Dr. William Sheldon. In that system, a coin worth $1 in grade 1 was worth $70 in grade 70. It's impossible to apply such a system to the present grading standards and coin market.

Q: Didn't Numismatic News once use a grading system which had "fair" as the lowest grade?

It did, and defined it as: "A badly worn coin with only part of the lettering showing. Usually the coin has no numismatic value, but in the case of a rare coin is used as a filler." "Fa" was used for the abbreviation, but the general use of "about good" for the same low grade won out.

Q: Isn't showing a coin to a dealer to grade it a waste of time? Most just glance at it and hand it back.

In many cases an experienced coin dealer can literally tell at a glance what the approximate grade of a coin is, especially if it is a circulated coin. It's when we get into the rarified 60+++ grades that more time (should be) is spent on the finer points of the coin. If you doubt an "instant" grade, check the same coin with several dealers and "average" the results.

Q: How many grades does a hole drop a coin?

Despite frequent "graded" descriptions of holed coins, as a practical matter, a punched hole will drop a coin into the filler or cull class, although this doesn't stop collectors from going after a rarity. An exception is the coin on a defective planchet, often worth substantially more than its numismatic grade value.

Q: How can I be sure I'm getting accurately graded coins when I buy them from a dealer?

There is one secret method which beats all the rest hollow. Simply buy yourself a copy of the *ANA Grading Standards for United States Coins, 4th Edition*, and learn how to grade coins yourself. Then you'll know exactly what you are getting and won't have to depend on others. Beyond that, the next best is to buy those coins that have been graded and slabbed by the third party grading services. In general, these are likely to be more accurately graded than other coins.

Q: If I buy a roll of uncirculated coins will they all be MS-65, or have the dealers picked out all the high relief pieces?

The grades have nothing at all to do with the relief of the coin, they are entirely based on the amount of wear—the more wear, the lower the grade. Uncirculated coins direct from the mint may grade anywhere up and down the scale due to poor strikes, damage in transit, etc. Again, this has nothing to do with anybody sorting through the coins.

Q: Why don't the grading services put a value on the coins they handle? I was very disappointed to pay a large fee and then get the coin back without a hint of what it really is worth.

Apparently you have a misunderstanding as to what a grading or authentication service provides. Their purpose is solely to determine that the coin is genuine, and to furnish you with an indication of the amount of wear the coin has suffered, placing it on a numerical scale somewhere between a perfect coin and a completely worn piece. Even though value is the first, and most often asked question about a coin, it is not one that the grading service can or will answer for you, as the price depends on what the coin might bring on the open market, a figure which can change drastically from day to day, especially in the higher grades. Once your coin has been graded you can pick up almost any current coin price guide and determine the approximate value for yourself.

Chapter 28

HISTORY

For the scholar, the history behind our coins is often more important than the coin itself. A very common question that accompanies many queries that I receive is, "What's the history or background of this coin?

Q: What's the legend about the disappearance of the 1847 Hawaii cents?

The reverse design of the coin showed a wreath of ohelo leaves and berries. The plant grows on the slopes of Kilauea volcano. The coins were popular as a substitute sacrifice to Pele, goddess of fire, so large quantities were thrown into the volcano. The stories are probably half right, according to one writer, who points out that while the coins were unpopular with the natives, they were an opportune source of scarce metal on the islands, and probably were hammered into fishhooks, which were then "thrown in the sea."

Q: What was the purpose of issuing both silver and copper-nickel five-cent coins at the same time after the Civil War?

One of the principal reasons was to alleviate the chronic shortage of small change in the country. The silver coins were still being produced but were frequently shipped overseas by profiteers.

Q: What can you tell me about the "Great Coin Shortage?"

Early in 1962, the Federal Reserve Banks in Boston, New York, and Philadelphia began rationing coins. This triggered a mini-panic and the public began hoarding coins, making the situation worse. The Treasury Department falsely blamed coin collectors for the problem, suspended making proof coins in 1965, and took away mint marks.

Q: Something was said that there were less than two dozen coin dealers in the United States at the turn of the century. Is that figure accurate?

Narrowing it down even further, my source says there were "21 coin dealers in the United States in 1900." Looking at today's multitudes, one would have to call it a growing hobby.

Q: In <u>World Coin News</u> you mentioned a Roman coin called a "two hundredth." Wasn't that the original name for the U.S. half cent?

The reference was to a coin issued to mark the end of a sales tax of a two hundredth in 49 C.E. by Caligula. Some of the Latin scholars among our forefathers may have known of the reference, because the cent was originally titled the hundredth, and the half cent the two hundredth. This was the work of the Grand Committee, with one representative from each of the 13 states, meeting in May 1785. The plan, submitted to the Board of Treasury, was amended by the two member Board so that the two hundredth became the half cent and the hundredth the cent, although that recommendation was not acted on until 1791.

Q: Is it true that there have been times when Canadian banks refused to accept U.S. coins?

This happened several times between the U.S. Civil War and World War I. So many U.S. silver coins were shipped to Canada during the Civil War that the banks refused them because the Canadian dollar was worth more than the U.S. dollar.

Q: A long time ago I read something to the effect that the nation's coins, back when they were silver, tended to congregate in certain cities. Any facts on that?

Curiously, they really did. A report from the Federal Reserve Bank showed that prior to the switch to clad coins, the half dollars collected in New York City and Atlantic City, cents in Pittsburgh and Dallas, quarters in San Antonio, Little Rock, and Cincinnati, and both dimes and nickels headed for home in Baltimore, Louisville, and Nashville. These cities were the ones most likely to return coins to the Fed, rather than just drawing them, and the pattern had repeated for many years.

Q: Is it true that a substantial number of proof sets were lost in the mail back in the 1960s?

The year was 1964, and according to published reports 36,086 sets failed to reach the address they were supposed to be sent to. Since this apparently was a perennial problem, the Mint had a reserve of 20,000 sets, both to cover mail losses and sets with imperfect, damaged, or missing coins, but the replacement supply was quickly exhausted and some 16,000 collectors got refunds instead of the sets they had ordered. I suspect that this incident led to the overkill practice that went on for a number of years, sending collector sets by registered mail, adding substantially and needlessly to the cost of sets.

Q: There have been several unpopular new coin issues, but were there any that were popular?

About the only really popular coin was the nickel. It was introduced in 1866 as a temporary measure, but the public liked it, and the half dime was dropped instead.

Q: Were the silver dollars popular only in the West in the latter part of the 1800s?

A point often overlooked in the annals of this unloved and mostly unwanted coin was that it did enjoy a period of popularity after the Civil War in the South for at least two reasons. Most of the emancipated slaves were illiterate and on that account refused paper money in any form. The memory of the worthless paper money of the Confederacy was still fresh in the minds of everyone, so the metal dollars took on a special importance, but one which would not last.

Q: I'm told that the Kennedy half was one of the speediest pieces of government action in history. Can you review the time span?

President Kennedy was assassinated on November 22, 1963. President Johnson proposed the coin to Congress December 10th, and on Dec. 13th the first trial strikes reached Washington. According to the record it took 20 days for Congress to authorize the Kennedy half dollar from Dec. 10th to Dec. 30th, 1963. Proof dies were ready Jan. 2nd, 1964, the first circulating coin was struck at Denver Jan. 30th, and joint ceremonies were held to mark the first strikes at Denver and Philadelphia on Feb. 11th. The first 26 million were shipped to the Federal Reserve on March 24th, and released to the public in the following days. However, the modern Congress is a turtle compared to the all-time record set in 1865, not for a new design, but a new denomination. The copper-nickel 3-cent coin bill was passed into law by both Houses the same day it was introduced.

Q: During the early 1970s the Mint deliberately mixed "S" mint coins in with those from Denver and Philadelphia to foil speculators who were buying bags of the coins. Were there any earlier instances of the Mint moving coins around the country?

One instance that was not directly connected was during the coin shortage in the central part of the U.S. in late 1940. Despite that the Denver Mint was running three shifts, 24 hours a day, it could not keep up with the demand, and in November, 1940 a total of 173 tons of "S" mint coins were moved from San Francisco to the Chicago Federal Reserve Bank to help fill the gap. This supposedly was the first time that San Francisco coins had ever been moved that far east in bulk. The San Francisco Mint wound up striking over 112 million cents that year, more than twice the 1939 production. Nickel production increased by more than six times, dime production doubled, quarter production tripled, and half dollar numbers almost doubled.

Q: Wasn't there also a Mint of North America?

There was, and there was also a Bank of North America, and in both cases Robert Morris had a hand in their establishment, one of the reasons he is suspected of playing a role in the Treasury seal design. He also owned a business, titled the North America Land Company. The Mint of North America was established Feb. 21, 1782 and struck the Nova Constellation silver patterns of 1783, but apparently had no connection with the North American Token of 1781, which instead came from Ireland at a much later date.

Q: What is the oldest U.S. coin struck in aluminum?

One candidate for that particular record would be the 1855 half dollar struck on an aluminum planchet, belonging to Princeton University. The piece was originally offered for sale in a George W. Cogan auction in 1883, selling to T. Harrison Garrett for $32. There is some question as to whether the coin was actually struck in 1855, or during the 1860s when the Mint was conducting official experiments with aluminum. The evidence suggests the coin came to one John Allen directly from the Mint, and Cogan described it as "struck in 1855 for the owner of the collection," tentatively identified as Allen.

Q: Supposedly there was a famous incident back during the early days of World War II when a large quantity of gold was brought to the U.S. Assay Office in New York in a cab. Do you have any information about it?

The incident may not have been famous enough to make the history books, but it did cause a stir at the time. A British ship, the Biafra, carrying half a million dollars in gold, showed up in New York harbor in 1941, but could not discharge the cargo because the armored car drivers were on strike. The nine boxes of gold bars were loaded into taxis, escorted by police cars, and driven to the front door of the Assay Office. I wonder if they left a tip.

Q: How much gold was there per capita before it was recalled in 1933?

Perhaps not as much as you might think. According to U.S. Treasury statistics, there were just over $7 per person in Gold Certificates and slightly over $3 in gold coin and bullion for each person in the United States. At the time there were about 125 million people in the U.S. This compared with nearly $21 per person in Federal Reserve Notes and another $5 worth of National Bank Notes.

Q: I've been told that Hawaii was once the richest country in the world. How could that be?

Someone once said, "Statistics can prove anything." This seems to be a case in point. Just before the turn of the century, the official estimate of the gold stock in Hawaii was $4 million. With the population at that time estimated at 100,000, this gave a per capita figure of $40, which was, and probably still is the largest per capita amount of gold for a country that has been reported.

Q: Was the process of dredging for gold—using a dredge on an artificial pond—first used in California?

30 years before the first such dredge appeared on a California stream in 1895, the process was first used in the New Zealand gold fields in 1865. California is associated with dredging because so much gold was recovered in the state by that method.

Q: Didn't the U.S. Government institute gold restrictions before the famous 1933 date?

One that escapes many historians is the curtailment of gold coin production and of payments in gold in 1917, during World War I. The Government feared that otherwise our gold reserves would be depleted by the war, leaving nothing to back our paper money.

As it turned out, we did such a brisk war material business with the Allies that gold reserves by the end of the war had reached the $3 billion mark, and in the next several years added another $1.25 billion.

Q: Why were so many gold coins struck in U.S. between 1922 and 1928?

The high volume was due to the demand in other countries for U.S. gold to back their currency.

Q: Did anyone ever try to corner the gold market in the U.S.?

Jay Gould tried it in 1869. The Treasury responded to the threat and dumped $5 million in gold on the market to end the danger of financial collapse.

Q: Some years ago there was a rumor that much of the gold stored at Ft. Knox had been secretly sold. Who was responsible for the claim?

A Dr. Peter David Beter made the claim in a national "scandal" weekly, precipitating a Congressional investigation culminated by a visit by members of Congress and the press to Ft. Knox on Sept. 23, 1974. Dr. Beter was a lawyer, and author of several books on monetary subjects. His claims proved to be completely unfounded, and were considered to be a publicity stunt to promote sales of his books.

Q: I'm told that at one time the half dime and dime were depicted on mail as postage. Is there any truth to the story?

You might be surprised to learn that both designs in the form of hand stamps were in fact used to show postage had been paid, and in addition the 3-cent silver coins were in a few rare cases glued to the envelope as prepayment, and at least one post office used a hand stamp with the 3-cent design including the word "PAID." Prepayment of postage became universal in the U.S. in 1855.

Q: Is there any record of the first Morgan dollar, struck in 1878?

The coin was located in the Rutherford B. Hayes Library and Museum in Freemont, Ohio. Silver dollar experts Leroy Van Allen and Pete Bishal found the certificate in 1980 in the library files among correspondence from Chief Coiner O.C. Bosbyshell, indicating the coin had been struck March 11, 1878. The second went to Treasury Secretary John Sherman, and the third of 10 proofs struck went to James Pollock, Director of the Mint.

Q: What are the facts on the big display of silver dollars at the Seattle World's Fair in 1962?

One million silver dollars were displayed. A Nebraska corn crib manufacturer, Behlen Manufacturing Co., filled a crib with the coins. There were 800,000 bagged Morgans dated 1904 and earlier, and 200,000 Peace dollars, weighing 30 tons. They were shipped from the Philadelphia Mint in two trucks. If stacked, the coins would have made 14-1/2 piles as high as the 600-ft. space needle. The coins were apparently sold after the Fair.

Q: Didn't the post offices and the Army get involved in trying to make the SBA dollars circulate?

The post offices across the country were enlisted, and passed out large quantities of the coins, but the effort only delayed the inevitable trip back to the bank. The Defense Department tried to force service personnel stationed in Europe to use the coins in place of paper dollars, but the experiment collapsed because most foreign countries will not exchange their currencies for coins.

Q: I understand that the down payment for the Panama Canal was made in silver dollars. How many were involved?

You have about half the story. In 1904 the U.S. Government made the down payment on the Panama Canal, paying out $10 million, but only half of that was silver dollars. Even so, this was a significant drain on the stocks of silver dollars, and it is uncertain if very many of them found their way back to the States. The result of the transaction was that the silver coins became the backbone of the Panama economy for many years afterward. This may be part of the explanation of why there are so few uncirculated 1903 and 1904 dollars.

Q: We know of attempts to get the turkey on our coins by Ben Franklin, but wasn't there a duel fought over a proposal to put a goose on the first dollar?

A challenge, but no duel. Congressman Matthew Lyon opposed putting the eagle on the coin, and in response Judge Thatcher proposed the goose, commenting that "the goslings would fit on the dime." The resulting laughter angered Lyon, who issued the challenge, but Thatcher refused it, saying Lyon knew he was a coward or he wouldn't have offered to fight. The two made up and became good friends, but the eagle won.

Q: Is there any logical explanation for the fairly frequent appearance of holed dollars of the very early years?

One credible reason given is that the coins were used as "teethers" for babies, since they were too large to be readily swallowed. A rather expensive "toy" back in the days when a dollar was a dollar.

Example of a holed dollar believed to have been used as a baby teether.

Q: From all the accounts it would seem that newspapers carried a lot more weight a century ago than they do now, as for example, the ability of a newspaper story to get the Mint to change the location of Gobrecht's name on the dollar. Why the difference?

At that time newspapers were the principal news source, leading to the axiom "If it ain't in the newspaper, it didn't happen." Today a story like that, even on TV, probably would be ignored by the Mint.

Q: How many U.S. Presidents have been honored on a coin within a short time after their deaths?

Some may stall out after listing Kennedy, but there are two others. President Franklin D. Roosevelt was put on the dime in February 1946, 10 months after his death. Dwight D. Eisenhower went on the dollar 18 months after he died, and John F. Kennedy was added to the half dollar five months after he was assassinated.

President Franklin D. Roosevelt's profile was put on the dime in February, 1946, ten months after his death.

Q: Please explain the difference between the old and new date calendars?

The English calendar differed from other countries, especially between 1582-1752. The formula for new dates is to add 10 days to dates between 1582-1700, 11 days for dates in the 1700s. Washington's birthday was moved from Feb. 11 to Feb. 22. The Gregorian calendar was introduced in 1582 by Pope Gregory XIII. The old calendar had lost 11 days, so Friday Oct. 4, 1582 was followed by Saturday, Oct. 15th. England and its colonies waited until 1752 to change, so by that time the difference was up to 12 days, so Sept. 2nd was followed by Sept. 14th.

Q: How many times did the Liberty Bell crack?

It came originally from a British firm in Whitechapel. It was cast in 1752, cracking on the first stroke after arriving at Independence Hall. Pass and Stowe recast it in 1753, adding 1.5 ounces of copper per pound of bell weight. It cracked a second time three months later. It cracked the third time July 8, 1835, tolling the death of Chief Justice John Marshall. It was tapped with a rubber mallet for a D-day broadcast, June 6, 1944, the last time it has been rung.

Q: Why did the Mint stop striking circulation S mint cents after 1974?

The claims were that speculators had disrupted normal circulation of the 1973-S cents. The 1974-S cents were shipped cross country and mixed with Philadelphia and Denver issues before being released to the public.

Q: What ever happened to that 1793 large cent that went to the moon?

There is some confusion on the coin, as it went into space on the Gemini VII for 14 days in December 1965, but not to the moon. NASA investigated the smuggling, but dropped the case without taking any action. The piece was later sold for $5,000 in cash and a plot of land worth $10,000. It was sold later for $17,500 but has since dropped from sight.

Q: Was the term penny used before cent to designate a coin?

The penny predated cent by 1,000 years, dating from the 8th century. Cent, as used for a coin, dates to 1782 when it was suggested as a silver coin for the United States. The centime of France was not introduced until 1794, one year after our half cent and cent.

Q: Is it true that a coin flip decided the name of Portland, Oregon?

It was the best two out of three, and Portland won over Boston, when two Yankees flipped a large cent over their favorite name in 1835. Of the two owners of the town site, Lovejoy of Massachusetts wanted Boston, Pettygrove from Maine wanted Portland. The flipped coin was an 1835 large cent. Pettygrove, and later his son, carried it as a pocket piece.

Q: Why was the Indian Head 1877 cent used on the experimental small size 13-cent stamp in 1978?

It was specifically noted that the reason was unknown. Possibly it was because of the work on the bicentennial, and the 100th anniversary of the coin when the stamp was worked on in 1977.

Q: In past issues of Numismatic News there have been stories or references to the "Lost Dutchman" mine. Is it still lost?

The missing mine, somewhere in the Superstition Mountains of Arizona near Phoenix, continues to elude searchers.

Q: Was there actually a serious attempt to make George Washington King of the United States?

The act was plotted by men including some of Washington's own staff, such as Alexander Hamilton, William Morris, and others, who wanted to overthrow Congress (which refused a half pay pension for war veterans) and install Washington as King. Washington was aware of the plan, but managed to dissuade the ringleaders from going ahead with it.

Q: What is the Society of the Cincinnati?

It is an hereditary order, founded in 1783 by officers of the Continental Army, with George Washington as its first President. Membership is currently limited to the eldest male descendants.

Q: With so many coins handled in rolls, why all the fuss about whether or not some of the earlier high relief coins would "stack?"

Back in the period before World War II, few coins were handled in rolls, and the standard practice in banks was to stack coins to count them, especially the bigger ones. If the stacks wouldn't stand without help, they caused problems, and the banks were quick to complain. I suspect that much the same problem existed within the mint, as I think the automatic counting machines didn't come along until later. Most references slight the operations after the coin is struck.

Q: Who was the actor who became famous during the 1930s playing the role of George Washington?

Background information is sketchy, but the person you are thinking of was not famous as a professional actor, at not least until he began playing Washington. In 1932, when plans were being made for the Bicentennial of Washington's birth, a nationwide search for a "double" turned up Laurance H. Hart, nephew of Albert Bushnell Hart, a Harvard historian and professor. The professor wrote a series of pamphlets on Washington for the bicentennial, which aroused his nephew's interest, and started his career. In the next decade he spent much of his time dressed in an authentic costume, antique sword, watch, and spectacles, addressing groups all over the country. He was a featured attraction at the 10th anniversary celebration of the Chase Bank Money Exhibit in July, 1939, where he appeared "for the 3,149th time" in his role of Washington, talking to groups of young coin collectors.

Q: In a story about the Navajo Indians, there is a mention of paying "four bits and a green," and later, "six bits and a yellow." What did the colors refer to?

The Navajo word for a nickel translates roughly as "yellow," and the word for a dime as "green," so the references are to nickels and dimes. Six bits and a yellow would be 80 cents, and four bits and a green would be 60 cents. The yellow traces to the first issue 5-cent postage notes which were printed on yellow paper. The green comes from the 10-cent note which was printed with green ink.

Q: What was the final fate of "Old Abe," the eagle that was the mascot of the 8th Wisconsin Regiment?

Old Abe was taken from a nest by Indians, who traded him for a bag of corn, and was presented to the Eau Clair Badgers, a volunteer group which became Company C of the 8th. After participating in more than 40 Civil War battles, he was pensioned at the state capitol at Madison, but travelled to veterans' conventions, the Republican convention that nominated Grant for President and other events, dying in 1881. The bird was stuffed and placed in a position of honor in the Capitol, but was destroyed when the building burned in 1904. The Central States Numismatic Society issued a medal for their Milwaukee convention in 1962 carrying Old Abe and the date 1862.

Q: Will the year 2000 be a "leap" year?

The rule, often misquoted, is that century years that are exactly divisible by 400 (1200, 1600, 2000) are leap years and will have the extra February day. The rule was laid down by Pope Gregory XIII. Now, if we could settle the argument as to whether 2000 or 2001 is the first year of the new century, we'd be in clover.

Q: Are there two Independence Halls in the U.S.?

Anyone with a Bicentennial half dollar has seen the original Independence Hall in Philadelphia. Ed Rochette is my source for the information that there is a second, identical Independence Hall in Buena Park, California, complete with an original copy of the Declaration of Independence. Built by Walter Knott at Knott's Berry Farm, it also has a replica of the Liberty Bell. This is authentic right down to the crack, created by freezing the bell in dry ice and then applying the intense heat of a heliarc welding torch. In 1951 I lived within "earshot" of Knott's Berry Farm, able to hear each Indian attack on the antique train on the grounds.

Q: When did Europe adopt the "Arabic" numerals?

This makes an interesting story, as it has to do with the eventual switch from "Roman" numerals to what are commonly called "Arabic" numerals, but which actually originated in India sometime before 773 C.E., when the Arabs borrowed the Hindu system. The first record of its use in Europe dates to 970 C.E. when the man who would become Pope Silvester II brought them to Italy. Their first appearance in print was in a manuscript dated 976 C.E. There were only nine numbers (no zero) in this new system, which at first was called algorithms, and its use did not spread rapidly until the 1200s, when someone finally invented the zero. It is perhaps a comment of the general level of education at the time, but there is ample evidence that die cutters had only the vaguest understanding of the use of the zero for the next two or three centuries, causing some major die varieties in the early 1500s, including dates such as 1502 for 1520, and even five digit dates such as 15105 for 1515.

It's perhaps ironic that the current use of the term algorithm, which depends in great part on the use of 0 and 1, stems from a system which didn't even have the 0.

Q: How long have people been tossing coins to bet or make decisions?

No doubt from the day the first coin with a distinctive obverse and reverse was struck. Dudley L. McClure has traced the practice at least to the Romans, who flipped a coin with Janus on one side and a ship on the other. The heads and tails were known as "Capita aut Navia." The Capita referred to the two headed Janus on the As coins. Navia was the ship, or ship's bow, which appeared on the reverse of the As. The term was used for a "tossup" long after the big copper coins were history.

Chapter 29

COIN HOARDS, HOARDING, TREASURE

History is replete with stories of hoards of all sizes found throughout the world. Buried treasure has its own mystique which attracts the interest—and the envy—of nearly every collector. While not all coin hoards are buried, they still are of interest.

Q: I've heard that there were some large hoards of U.S. gold coins that came onto the market after World War II. What was the source of all these coins?

Perhaps not well known to collectors is that in Europe the banks were the principal coin dealers, besides holding large stocks of bullion coins as backing for their financial dealings. After World War II, some huge hoards of gold coins found their way onto the market from banks in Switzerland, France, and England. Thanks to relentless shopping by U.S. coin dealers, most of these sources have now dried up, but many of the coins are still there. I know of one Frankfurt, Germany bank that could lay out roll after roll of any given date or mint of U.S. gold.

Q: What can you tell me about the Rapp hoard of coins? I believe it was found in Pennsylvania.

The Rapp hoard was buried in July, 1863 when General George Morgan and his Confederate raiders headed toward western Pennsylvania. Rapp apparently left the coins buried until 1878. All of the pieces dated back to prior to 1837, as they were part of a $150,000 cash payment received in that era by Rapp. It included 117,000 half dollars, including 150 dated 1794; 3,708 silver dollars dated up to 1803; and 400 quarters dated from 1818 to 1828.

Q: Do you have any information on the "Prudential" hoard of 1957 proof sets?

The insurance company reportedly "invested" in 100,000 of the 1957 sets at the time of issue, when they cost $2.10 each. While this was less than 10% of the 1,247,952 sets produced, it was a large enough group to sour the market, and within a short time they were being offered for as little as $1.60. The 1957 proof set was the first with a million plus mintage.

Q: What can you tell me about the West Hoard of silver dollars?

James M. West of Houston, Texas died in 1957 at the age of 54. A multi-millionaire, he had begun coin collecting, or at least accumulating, in the early 1920s. Following his death it was discovered that he had some eight tons of silver dollars in his cellar, an early-day version of the Redfield Hoard. According to contemporary accounts, there were something over 271,000 silver dollars. Most of them were Peace dollars, beginning with the 1922 issues.

Q: Wasn't there a large hoard of the 1935 California- Pacific International Exposition commemorative half dollars which turned up in 1966?

A hoard of 31,050 of the 1935-S coins was saved by one of the Exposition officials, and was inherited by his granddaughter in 1966, to be dispersed shortly afterward. At the time, the pieces were selling for about $20 each. Anthony Swiatek reports in his book on the commemoratives that a bag of 1,000 of the 1936-D version exists in an estate. My source indicates that a Mrs. Hamren inherited the coins, which were about 31% of the total (1935-S and 1936-D) mintage. Supposedly the entire batch was purchased by a single coin dealer.

Q: What is the story on the Randall hoard of large cents?

A wooden keg of large cents, dated 1816 to 1820, was found after the Civil War under a railway station platform in Georgia. The keg was shipped north in payment for merchandise, and eventually wound up at a firm in Norwich, New York where they were given out to customers as promotional premiums. They were unpopular because the Indian Head cent was already on the scene, and a Norwich collector, John S. Randall was able to purchase the majority of them for 90 cents a hundred. It was estimated that the keg held a total of 14,000 coins. The large cent was a good seller in small quantities. It was useful in trade, but there are a number of reported incidents in the period between 1841 and 1853 in the New York area when large cents were literally a drag on the market, and they were in fact being sold by the keg at a discount.

Q: Somewhere I read about a huge hoard of early Indian Head cents. Any help in locating the item?

For sheer size the holdings of Aaron White of Connecticut would probably rank high. He bought them in bulk in the 1862-1864 period, and his estate included 60,000 copper (large) cents and another 60,000 of the copper-nickel Indian Head cents, along with 5,000 of the 1864 two cent pieces.

Q: We read a lot of early hoards of coins. Any listings of modern U.S. coins in hoards?

Walter Breen at one time listed several: the Scharlack hoard of 1931-S cents, the Friedberg hoard of 1955-S cents, the Milwaukee hoard of 1950-D nickels, and the Prudential Insurance Co. hoard of 1957 proof sets. In each case the hoards were large enough to affect the coin market, unusual in itself.

Q: Has the Treasury ever made a serious effort to make the Kennedy half a circulating coin?

Mint policy was to flood the country to discourage hoarding, but it encouraged it instead. After striking over 400 million in its first year, the Treasury tried again in 1971, striking 460 million of the copper nickel clad version, but in the interim Treasury officials admitted that it would take an estimated 800-900 million to saturate the coin supply enough to allow the coin to circulate freely. Since 1971, the mintages exceeded a quarter million in only three years (1974 and 1975-76) and after that have not exceeded the 100 million mark.

Q: Wasn't there a hoard of the $4 gold Stellas that was discovered in the Mint vaults sometime after 1879?

Through connections at the Mint, a coin dealer named S. K. Harzfeld discovered in 1880 that 150 of the 1879 coins had not been distributed. The Mint hoard was dispersed to collectors for $15 per coin, an unusual price for the time.

1880 Flowing Hair Stella.

Chapter 30

LEGAL MATTERS

(COINAGE ACTS, BILLS, PRESIDENTIAL PROCLAMATIONS, TAXES, EXECUTIVE ORDERS)

Since our coinage is controlled by Congress, there are numerous Coinage Acts and other legalities connected with the coins we collect. Questions are numerous and often the information buried in the old law books is a fascinating commentary on both the times and the coins they produced.

Q: Did our early laws make a distinction between counterfeit coins and altered coins?

The attitude of the early lawmakers seemed to be that any spurious pieces of whatever ilk were bad. Accordingly, the law as laid down in Massachusetts in 1786, described the coloring or gilding of coins to make silver coins look gold, or copper coins look either silver or gold by whatever means, subjected the maker to the full limit of the law as a counterfeiter and forger. This could get unpleasant, as the counterfeiter if convicted faced a fine, an hour in the pillory, the loss of an ear, an hour on the gallows with a rope around his neck, 40 lashes, and a further seven years in prison at hard labor. And that was when hard meant a 12 or 14 hour day of real work.

Q: Is it true that a Mint employee could be put to death for debasing a gold or silver coin?

A casual reference to this popular fate for early counterfeiters sent me on a search through the reference library. Although the law is no longer on the books (apparently rescinded in 1806), it did at the time provide the death penalty. Section 19 of the Act of April 2, 1792 states in part, "That if any of the gold or silver coins which shall be struck or coined at the Mint shall be debased or made worse as to the proportion of fine gold or fine silver therein contained,...through the default or with the connivance of any of the officers or persons employed at the Mint, for the purpose of profit or gain,...every such officer or person shall be deemed guilty of felony and shall suffer death." Later the penalty was reduced to a maximum of ten years in prison and a $10,000 fine, which probably is still on the books.

Q: How did the U.S. Government arrive at weight standards for our earliest coins?

The Act of April 2, 1792 established standards for our coinage, expressing the weights in grains. To accurately weigh something there has to be some sort of standard weight for comparison, but nothing is said about what standard was used until the passage of the Act of May 19, 1828. That act specifies that the standard weight is to be the brass troy pound that was obtained in England in 1827, copied from the standard pound used by the Royal Mint. The act prescribed that weights were to be made up based on that standard ranging from one hundredth of a grain up to 25 troy pounds.

Q: Several patterns for U.S. coins are known with holes in the center, but we've never had a holed coin. Any special reason for this?

Trace it to the Coinage Act of 1792, which specified: "a device emblematic of liberty." Since there was no room on a holed coin for such a device, Congress never approved a holed coin.

Q: Please settle an argument. Is the "eagle" a real denomination for U.S. coins?

The Act of April 2, 1792 established standards for the eagle, half eagle, and quarter eagle denominations. The Act of March 3, 1849 authorized the double eagle. The gold dollar, three dollar, and 50 dollar coins were never officially named other than their denomination.

Q: Technically, all our early proof coins are medals, or are they?

Let's say legally, since they were struck outside the parameters of the applicable Coinage Act of 1792, with the exception of the Gobrecht dollar proofs. There are several instances of this, including the subterfuge of selling the Trade dollar proofs as medals to get around the Treasury Department order halting production of the Trade Dollar in 1878.

Q: Hasn't the value of the dollar as a money of account fluctuated substantially over the years?

The 1792 Mint Act defined it as 24.057 grams of silver or 1.604 grams of gold. The 1837 act made it worth 21.1147 grams of silver or 1.5406 grams of gold. In 1934 and 1944 it was defined as 1/35 ounce of gold, or 0.88866 gram. In 1971 it was defined as 1/38.8 ounce of gold, or 0.8016 gram of gold. In 1973 it was changed to 1/42.22 ounce, or 0.7367 gram of gold.

The original monetary system was based on a gold dollar containing 24.75 grains of pure gold. It was changed in 1834 to 23.20 grains. This was merely an accounting, or money of account figure. In 1837 the gold figure was raised to 23.22 grains.

Q: I know the disme and half disme started out with that spelling, but when was it changed to "dime?"

The patterns of 1792 were described with the disme spelling, and the term was used in the Coinage Act of 1792, but somewhere on the way to the public the "S" got lost, although "disme" was used in official Mint correspondence up until the 1830s. The word "DIME" didn't appear on either coin until the 1837 issue, when the current spelling was made official.

1792 half disme.

Q: Are all of the changes in our coinage documented in laws passed by Congress?

In the history of our coinage there are at least a couple of instances where changes were made by Presidential Proclamation, rather than by Congress. The first major change in the cent came about in that way, when President Washington issued a proclamation on Jan. 26, 1796, retroactive to Dec. 27, 1795 to reduce the weight of the cent by 40 grains and the half cent by 20 grains. This was done because the price of copper had shot up to the point where it was costing the Mint $1.22 to strike one hundred cents. The Mint continued to strike cents dated 1795 on the lighter planchets during the first three months of 1796, producing more than half a million in the period.

Q: When did Congress rescind the Executive Order of 1806 by President Thomas Jefferson prohibiting the production of silver dollars?

According to Bob Julian, Congress didn't have anything to do with the suspension of the order, as it was officially revoked—again by Executive Order—by President Andrew Jackson in April, 1831. The information is contained in a letter from Mint Director S.D. Ingham to the Superintendent of the Philadelphia Mint, Samuel Moore.

Q: When did the U.S. go on a gold standard?

The Coinage Act of 1853 made silver a subsidiary metal, putting the U.S. on a de facto gold standard. The standard was adopted in 1896, but became official with the Gold Standard Act of 1900.

Q: In 1857 when the government ended the circulation of foreign coins in the U.S., the Spanish dollars were redeemed, but did they pay full value for them?

The coins from a variety of countries, but mostly Spanish reales, including the 8 reales, or Spanish dollars, were redeemed at post offices, land offices, and at the U.S. Treasury, but only for about 80 cents to the dollar. This in part was due to many of the coins having been worn smooth from years of hard usage.

Q: When did it become law that United States coins must bear the date of the year in which they are struck?

The first statute requiring the corresponding date was passed in 1869. Exceptions are the 1976 Bicentennial coins struck in 1974 and 75, and the 1964 and 1965 coins, struck into 1966 under special laws.

Q: Wasn't there something about the Morgan dollar design that was illegal?

The Coinage Act of 1873 specified that the legend, E PLURIBUS UNUM, be on the reverse of all coins struck after that date. On the Morgan dollar it appears on the obverse, above the head. The same problem occurred with the design of the Liberty Head, or V Nickel. In this case the switch was made after patterns had been struck with it correctly on the reverse. The Act of Feb. 28, 1878 specified that the devices be those of the Act of Jan. 18, 1837, which omits any reference to E Pluribus Unum. There was no special law authorizing the change to the Liberty Head design in 1883.

Q: On some of our coins it is difficult to determine which side is the obverse, and which the reverse. Is there any hard and fast rule covering which is which?

There ought to be a law.... and there is. The coinage act of 1873 specifically designates the side of the coin with the date as the obverse, so for all coins struck since that year we have a good answer. However, it adds to the confusion, because two coins which were struck before and after 1873—the gold dollar and the gold $3 coins—have the date on what would normally be the reverse, so for those coins the two sides switch places. The gold $1 and $3 are usually incorrectly listed.

Q: What was the authority for ending two-cent production?

The two-cent, and both three-cent coins died ignored. The Coinage Act of 1873 terminated them by not listing them as authorized coins.

Q: What foreign coins were the first struck at the U.S. Mint?

By 1874 law, the first officially struck were for Venezuela in 1875-76. The 1833 Liberia cent tokens were struck "in U.S." but not specifically at Philadelphia. The 1847 Hawaiian cent was struck at Philadelphia, from dies made in Boston. A specimen set of Peruvian coins was made in 1855 to demonstrate U.S. minting machines. That set is now in the Smithsonian.

Q: It's my understanding that President Hayes didn't want the Morgan dollar struck. Is that correct?

Hayes vetoed the bill ordering the striking of the coin in 1878, but Congress passed it over his veto, and then rubbed it in by having the first coin struck presented to the unwilling President.

Q: How many of our coins have failed to meet the 25-year minimum law for design?

The Standing Liberty quarter 1916-30, the Franklin half 1948-1963, and the Ike dollar 1971-1978 are the only examples. The law specifies a 25-year tenure for a design, but Congress has the power at any time to override the law by passing a special law with an exemption.

Q: Wasn't the Board of Lady Managers, who were responsible for the Isabella commemorative quarter struck for the 1892 Columbian Exposition, unique in other ways?

The claim was made in an article written by the head of the board, Mrs. Potter Palmer, in the June 1892 Ladies Home Journal, that this was the first time in history that a body of women had been legally appointed to act in a national capacity for a government anywhere in the world.

Notice "Board of Lady Managers" inscribed upon the 1893 Isabella quarter.

Q: Weren't the Morgan dollars of 1898 minted under a new law?

The War Revenue Act of 1898 was used as authorization for the striking of about 109 million silver dollars to pay for the Spanish American War.

Q: Why didn't the branch mints strike any of the minor coins in the early days? Certainly there must have been a demand for the small coins.

The demand was there, as evidenced by the multitude of tokens introduced during the Civil War to alleviate the small coin shortage, but the coinage of the cent and nickel (plus the two and three cent nickel) was the exclusive province of the Philadelphia Mint.

It would not change until 1908 when the first Indian Head cents were struck at San Francisco, and Denver didn't get going on small change until 1911 when it struck the first "V" nickels. The changes were authorized by the Coinage Act of April 24, 1906.

Q: Could you please give me the name and date of the legislation which authorized the production of the Peace dollar?

This is likely to come as something of a surprise to many collectors, but there never was a specific law passed to authorize the Peace dollar. A bill was introduced in 1920, but it was killed when it was discovered that the provisions of the Pittman Act of April 23, 1918 still applied, and the design change could be made based on approval by the Commission of Fine Arts and the President.

Q: For a number of years I have been trying to find any official notice of the different weights of the 1943 cent. Some of them supposedly weighed 41.5 grains, and some 42.5 grains. Do you have an official citation?

As with many coin specifications, the parameters frequently never appeared in published form; they were based instead on internal memoranda between officials of the Treasury Department and the Mint. The weight of the steel cent was set in an order of the Secretary of the Treasury, dated Dec. 23, 1942 at 41.5 grains. Those cents struck between February 23rd (when the first steel cents were struck) and an uncertain date in May, 1943 were at that weight, which was then changed (apparently by a further order of the Treasury Secretary) to the 42.5 grain figure. The 42.5 grain standard is given in the 1943 Mint Report, but there is no mention of the earlier 41.5 grain standard, or why the change was made.

Q: Are there any "blue laws" still on the books relating to coins?

Probably not too many, although the state of New Hampshire, (where I grew up) didn't get around to repealing one coinage matter until 1950. The repealed item was a clause in the State Constitution which required that money matters were to be computed in shillings and pence.

Q: What authority did President Franklin D. Roosevelt have to close the banks, prohibit the sale or export of gold, and stop the minting of U.S. gold coins in 1933?

None, very little, or lots, depending on who you talked to at the time. Authorities on Constitutional Law claimed that there was little if any legal precedent for his actions and that they were quite probably unconstitutional. The point was moot, because in a rare burst of speed in a single day (March 9, 1933) Congress passed the Emergency Banking Act which retroactively gave him the legal power to do what had already been accomplished. The bill was introduced in the House shortly after noon, passed by that body at 4:30, by the Senate at 7:30 and signed by Roosevelt at 8:30 p.m.

Q: How effective was the withdrawal of gold from the public in 1933?

Like many government programs, it was something of a flop. Approximately $40 million in bullion, gold coins, and gold certificates was returned to the Treasury. Later the Treasury estimated that the public still held some $311 million in coins and $217.4 million in gold certificates, so only about seven percent was actually turned in.

Q: President Roosevelt did actually veto one of the commemorative coins in 1938. Do you know which one it was?

Finding this particular bill was one of those proverbial "needle in a haystack" affairs. This was primarily because the bill was submitted originally in 1937, so it didn't show up on the list of more than 60 bills submitted in 1938. Passed at the last moment before adjournment, the bill called for 100,000 halves to commemorate the 400th anniversary of the exploration by Coronado in the Southwest. Roosevelt wrote a two page letter explaining his reasons for the veto.

Q: When was the U.S. ban lifted on owning the Canadian 1967 $20 gold?

It expired at midnight, Dec. 30, 1974. It was part of severe restrictions on ownership of most modern gold, but many gold coins were smuggled in anyway.

Q: Is it true that the Mint could resume striking the Ike dollars?

Unless an amendment or revocation has escaped me, the Mint still has authority under the Coinage Act of 1978 to resume production of the Ike dollar, but only the 40% silver version. At least as late as 1980 the Mint still had authority to resume striking the billon Ikes. I'm not sure whether that authority has expired or not, but it would make an interesting project for collectors. Whether a battle cry of "Give us back our silver dollars!" would work is another matter.

Q: How can I avoid excessive tax on my coins when I sell them?

Collect receipts as avidly as you collect coins. For tax purposes you need to know (and be able to prove) exactly what you paid for a coin. Otherwise the tax man will be happy to charge you on the difference between the sale price and the face value of the coin. Keep your coin records as a permanent file, separate from the three-year records that you usually need to satisfy the IRS.

Q: How do merchants get away with these promotions where they offer to sell items at "prewar" prices or some such gimmick, if payment is made in 90% silver coins? I thought the coins were still legal tender.

They are, and the merchants aren't breaking any law, just taking advantage of the current value of the bullion content of the silver pieces.

Q: You've mentioned several times that it is legal to make such things as elongated coins and even coin jewelry. But is this true for gold coins?

At one time it was illegal, but current law generally ignores the question of whether or not a coin contains any bullion, the prohibitions centering upon "fraudulent" alteration of the coin. This is why you can see large gold coins made into watches or soldered into jewelry. The Secret Service in 1971 announced that it was illegal to mutilate gold, whether soldered, holed, trimmed, or altered. However, the ruling did not apply to foreign imports, so it was unworkable.

Q: Was there ever a time when Federal law permitted the alteration of dates and mint marks on coins?

In 1962, legal council for the U.S. Treasury took the position that since such alterations did not affect the "face" value of the coin for purposes of circulation, it was not a violation of Federal law. An adverse court decision and further research into the intent of the law resulted in a reversal of that position a year later. Since such opinions are not binding, and there was no change in the law, the alterations technically were never legal.

Q: Is it legal to cut out a coin design, or roll an elongated coin?

The law was repealed in 1909 which prohibited defacing coins, especially gold or silver. Sect. 331, Title 18, U.S. Code, says anything goes, as long as you don't alter the date or mint mark with intent to defraud. The last prohibition to be dropped was gold plating coins.

I'm neither a lawyer or a judge, but a lay reading of the law says that you can do as you please with a U.S. coin; cut, scrape, bend, plate (yes, even gold), roll, or whatever, and it is legal, so long as you do not attempt to alter the denomination or mint mark or otherwise attempt to increase its value. Section 331 covers the mutilation of coins, but limits its application to "fraudulent alteration, defacing or mutilation." In practice, this is generally limited to changes in the date or mint mark intended to improve the value of the coin to a collector.

Q: I thought when they restored the mint marks to U.S. coins back in 1968 that it was mandatory. How come the Mint didn't use the "S" and "W" on all coins struck at those mints—or for that matter on the cents from Philadelphia?

The law rescinding the five year ban on mint marks beginning in 1965 gave the Mint the "discretion" of restoring the mint marks, rather than making it mandatory. That's a loophole any bureaucrat can drive a tank through.

Q: I hope this won't start an argument, but does a coin become money at the instant it is struck with the design by the dies?

This is a point which probably has slipped by most of us, but a coin is nothing more than a piece of struck metal, like a nut or a bolt or a car fender, until it has been counted and formally turned over to the Superintendent of the Mint by the coiner. In the case of gold and silver coins both a count and weight are required.

Q: I thought the Constitution prohibited anyone but the Federal Government from minting coins. How did private mints like those in California get away with violating the law?

The prohibition in the Constitution is worded to prevent the States from coining money, but since nobody happened to think of private mints, the point was overlooked in the original document, and remained legal until it was outlawed later.

Q: In the reports of the gold cargo on the S.S. Central America it was mentioned several times that the gold, regardless of form, was intended ultimately for the Philadelphia Mint for coinage. Was this the case for gold coins of other countries too?

Under federal law, any gold coins from another country which were deposited at one of the mints or assay offices had to be melted down and coined into U.S. coinage. This put a substantial burden on the Mint, as any time there was a request for gold to export, it was of necessity U.S. coins or gold bars. This was a bone of contention between the Secretary of the Treasury and the Congress for many years, and the subject of numerous official complaints.

Q: Can you cite the law which authorized the "W" mint mark on the 1984 proof $10 gold Olympic coins?

You might expect it to be incorporated in the original law which authorized the 1983-84 Olympic Commemorative coins, but that is not the case. Actually there was no special law passed to place the "W" on the coins. It was a decision of the Mint Director, Donna Pope, and was contained in an interim memorandum signed by her in January 1983. It's only one of many important decisions by the Treasury Department or the U.S. Mint which are virtually impossible to document later on.

Q: Is there any record of who was responsible for putting George Washington on the quarter in 1932?

Representative Randolph Perkins of New Jersey apparently was the first to submit a bill in early 1931, which was passed by Congress on April 4, 1931. This resulted in the Washington "commemorative" of 1932.

Q: Wasn't it illegal at one time to photograph U.S. coins?

Up until 1951, photographing coins was just as illegal as photographing paper money. It could be done, but you had to have specific permission from the Chief of the Secret Service. That provision was removed for coins by the July 16, 1951 amendment to Title 18, section 489 of the U.S. Code. The requirement for requesting permission to photograph paper money remained on the books for a while longer, and it is still illegal to make machine copies or photographs of U.S. currency except in certain specific sizes for educational purposes. The majority of the public is totally unaware of this law and my mail includes at least one violation a week by some unsuspecting correspondent who could find himself in serious trouble.

Q: Wasn't there at one time a tax on silver bullion sales?

There was a silver tax that was in effect from 1934 to 1963. While it sounds like a confiscatory tax, it really wasn't. The tax amounted to 50 percent of the net profit on the transfer of silver bullion. But, it affected only those dealers selling bullion and since bullion prices were fixed, profits on the sales were minuscule at best.

Q: Is the surcharge on the Olympic coins tax deductible?

No. A direct donation is, but not the purchase of coins. This applies to all of the modern commemoratives since 1982.

Q: Didn't the U.S. Olympic Committee have to pay for the lobbying done by the two private firms that attempted to take over distribution of the 1983-84 Olympic coins?

It was not the U.S.O.C. that got stuck for the lobbying fees, but the Los Angeles Olympic Organizing Committee, which agreed to pay the lobbying costs incurred by Oxidental Petroleum and Lazard Freres. Just how much they wound up paying for a losing cause is unclear, but it must have been a substantial amount, as the two firms made a full-scale, but unsuccessful, effort to win the distribution rights for a 29-coin program. Congress shot the plan down and the U.S. Mint wound up with the job, which they carried out successfully to the tune of a $73.4 million check to the U.S.O.C. The two firms stood to make a $100 million profit if they had been successful in winning the contract.

Q: Please explain why the seven year statute of limitations doesn't apply to ownership of such coins as the 1913 nickel, the 1933 $20, and the 1964-D Peace dollar?

Although never tested in court to my knowledge, the Treasury Department's legal position is that the pieces were never legally issued, and thus remain the property of the government, subject to confiscation, to which a time limit does not apply.

Q: The legal piracy of the early days of our country is well documented. If I read the Constitution correctly, it sounds as if it would still be legal.

The founding fathers included two specific weapons in the Constitution, the Letter of Marque and the Letter of Reprisal, which were used in several cases to turn our ships into pirates working within the letter of the law. If you would care to apply for such papers for your gunboat, check Article 1, section 8, paragraph 11 and the first paragraph of section 10.

Q: What is the earliest known instance of piracy involving the Spanish galleons carrying gold and silver back to Spain from the Americas?

The earliest mention I can find is that of a successful raid by a French buccaneer in the Gulf of Mexico in 1520. Once the word got around it became open season on the ships, which were forced to travel in convoys for protection.

Chapter 31

LEGAL TENDER

The legal tender status of our coins is often a very confusing matter, frequently with conflicting laws. Keeping up with the provisions covering legal tender generates many questions from readers, including these samples.

Q: Were U.S. gold coins legal tender at one time in Canada?

When the U.S. and Canadian dollar were equal in value in the period prior to World War I, the U.S. gold was accepted as legal tender in Canada.

Q: What are the current statutory limits on the number of coins that can be accepted as legal tender?

The current law makes all U.S. coins legal tender, but is silent on any limit. The catch is that there is no provision in the law which requires anyone to accept the tender. In a recent case, the Miami post office had refused to accept $100 notes by posting a sign to that effect. In theory at least, anyone can demand to be paid only in paper money, only a certain denomination, etc. As a practical matter, however, most merchants would hesitate to place restrictions on their sales in this manner.

Q: I recently found a proof-only coin in circulation. Is that legal?

U.S. proof coins are considered legal tender, and may be used for any commercial transaction, a status which is not necessarily true of proofs or non-circulating legal tender coins in some other countries. Since proofs are sold at a premium, the frequent reason for finding one in circulation is that it was stolen or pilfered from a collector, or that a dealer dumped defective coins from broken up proof sets. It's designated as legal tender, the same as any other coin, so if you are willing to take the loss in value there is no other prohibition or reason not to spend a proof coin.

Q: Were the U.S. gold coins always legal tender at face value?

This is something of a trick question, as the answer is that they were not. Full weight gold coins were legal tender at full face value, including coins which had not exceeded the allowable wear for the number of years they had been in circulation. However, if a coin was worn to the point of weighing less than the allowable, then it was accounted to be legal tender only "in proportion to their actual weight."

Q: Are the new golden and silver Eagles legal tender coins?

Technically, yes, although one would be foolish to redeem them for face value.

Q: Have all the Ike dollars been withdrawn? I can't find a bank that has any.

Both the Ike dollars and the Anthony dollars remain legal tender and have not been withdrawn by the Treasury Department. This means that they are still technically legal tender circulating coins, although as a practical matter the Ikes ceased what little circulation they enjoyed with the advent of the Anthony dollars in 1979. The irony of that was that the Anthonys followed the most direct route from the bank to the public and back to the banks, so with minor exceptions, the Anthony never seriously circulated either. Keep trying and you may find a bank which isn't populated by coin collectors and has a stock of the two coins still on hand.

Q: Which one of the Coinage Acts eliminated the legal tender status of the Trade dollar?

The Trade dollar was authorized under the provisions of the Coinage Act of 1873, which gave them legal tender status to the sum of $5. They were included in the revised statutes under the law of June 22, 1874, Section 3586 of the Revised Statutes, which restricted legal tender status of "all" silver coins to not more than five dollars. Some sources consider this inclusion of the trade dollar as "inadvertent." The next act affecting it was a joint resolution of the Congress, dated July 22, 1876, which eliminated the legal tender status and empowered the Secretary of the Treasury to limit mintage to those needed to supply demands for export. Coinage was officially discontinued under the act of Feb. 19, 1887. The legal tender status of the Trade dollar was "accidentally" restored by the Congress in 1933 and confirmed by the Coinage Act of 1965.

Example of an 1876 trade dollar.

Chapter 32

MELTS

The laws of supply and demand would dictate that melting large quantities of coins would raise the collector value of the remaining coins. Surprise! It doesn't work that way. Why? It's anybody's guess.

Q: How much silver did the Mint recover from coins after 1964?

As of 1970 when the primary phase ended, the Mint had recovered 212.3 million ounces from 563,882,690 quarters and 1,552,903,056 dimes. That sounds like a lot until you note that Denver struck 1.357 billion dimes in 1964, plus another 933 million at Philadelphia, so the Mint didn't even recover the last year of production. Quarter recovery was almost exactly the 1964 Philadelphia mintage of 564,341,247.

Q: Somewhere I read that tons of silver coins were melted down during World War II and the silver was used in defense plants. What possible use would they have had for coin silver?

The U.S. Treasury loaned 16,300 tons of silver in 1942 to the Defense Plant Corporation. The silver was used to alleviate a critical shortage of copper, needed for war materials. In many cases it was cast into heavy bars known as "bus bars," used to connect heavy electrical equipment. More of the silver was used to make wire, which was used in the windings of the electrical motors. Silver was ideal for the purpose, as there was little need for it as a war material, and it was nearly as good a conductor of electricity as the copper it replaced. Nearly all of the silver was returned to the Treasury after the war.

Q: When will your price charts start reflecting the tremendous melts of silver coins in 1980?

The charts follow the market, and so far the market has shown no indication or inclination to scale prices significantly upward because of the 1980 melt, or the many previous major melts of history. Relative rarity of the various issues remains much the same, and prices continue to reflect this, because demand has not yet exceeded the supply of coins that escaped the melting pot.

Q: Were any of the 1883 "No Cents" nickels melted?

An unsubstantiated source said "the greater portion" were never issued, implying they were melted. However, this source used a mintage of 2 million. The actual mintage was 5.4 million. This could mean that 3.4 million were never issued, but this is unsubstantiated.

Q: Weren't most of the white cents melted down?

The coins struck between 1856 and early 1864 were an alloy of 88% copper and 12% nickel, and the government did actively withdraw them to be melted down. One source indicates that about half of those struck were melted between 1871 and 1900. The impetus was the Act of 1871, which authorized redemption of nickel alloy and bronze coins for "lawful money" (paper money). One estimate puts the total melted between 1871 and 1900 at about 40% of those struck. 200,772,000 were issued, so that would mean that about 80,308,000 were melted. This doesn't rate as "most" of them, but it is one of the higher percentages of an issue to be withdrawn and melted.

Q: Wasn't there a major melt in 1834 of gold coins?

It's believed that this is the primary cause for the scarcity of many earlier dated issues. The Coinage Act of 1834 set new weight and fineness standards, and made each $100 in face value of the old coins worth $106.60. Much of the inflated mintage of half eagles in 1834 and the next several years can be traced to old coins sent in by banks and melted down for the new issues.

*Q: Is there a dollar value placed on the gold coins which were surrendered to the Trea-
    sury following their recall in 1933?*

Mint figures show that $1,933,809,000 in gold coins were withdrawn and melted under the provisions of the various regulations established in 1933. This included $1.329 billion face value in double eagles and $177.3 million in eagles, the rest the smaller denominations.

Q: How detailed are Mint records of gold coins melted?

Since 1914 they are detailed, but prior to that only the bulk totals of all gold coins were recorded. Unfortunately, prior to 1914 the Mint melted by weight, rather than by denomination, so records prior to that year show only the total amounts melted, without giving a breakdown of the individual denominations. It doesn't help even for coins minted after that, because the denomination breakdowns still included older coins. From a numismatic standpoint it would have been ideal if they had kept a record of each date and mint melted, but they didn't, so we have to make do with a lot of estimating.

Q: With all the melts, just how many silver dollars are still in circulation?

While technically in circulation, just about all are now in the hands of hoarders, dealers, or collectors. The last figure I can find indicated that the Treasury considered that about 480 million of the 90% silver dollars still were out there somewhere. At least a small percentage of that figure has to fall in the "lost, strayed, or stolen" or melted class, so a good guess might be that about 350 million are still in existence. When the 1964-D Peace Dollars were melted at Denver, I'm told they were melted by weight and not by date, so the suspicion remains that some of them were replaced with other date silver dollars to satisfy the weight requirements.

*Q: In all the stories about the quantities of silver dollars melted for shipment to India
    in 1918, there is nothing said about how all that valuable metal was transported.
    Any information?*

The silver was melted into $1,000 bars weighing about 62 pounds. 5,000 to 10,000 of these bars at a time were loaded onto special trains, consisting of five express cars guarded by armed men for the trip from Philadelphia to San Francisco. A total of 18 of the special trains were involved in the transfer. The bars were loaded onto ships at San Francisco for the trip to India.

Q: Why are the silver three-cent pieces from the latter part of the production so rare?

According to Harry X Boosel, the U.S. Mint in 1873 ordered the melting of any old standard coins then on hand. The branch mints began melting them down in April, including unsold proofs and business strikes. The main Mint at Philadelphia began its melts in July of that year. Included in the melt were virtually all of the silver three-cent pieces struck from 1863 through 1872. In the other silver denominations, this decimated the supply of 1872 and 1873 issues without the arrows at the date.

Q: Any statistics on the number of two-cent pieces that were melted down over the years?

A total of 45,601,000 two-cent pieces were minted. Of that total, more than 17,000,000 were melted down by the Mint.

Q: I'm told that the U.S. Mint waited until the 1930s to melt down its stocks of 20-cent pieces. Why didn't they sell them to collectors like they did with the CC dollars in the 1970s?

With the cheapest 20-cent piece (the 1875-S) today at a "mere" $500 in MS-60, it seems hard to imagine any mint official callous enough to melt down a hoard of 360,000 of the unloved and unwanted coins that had been struck in limited quantities way back in the 1870s. It did happen, and while I'm sure that none of the participants are still around to bemoan their lack of foresight, the problem in 1933 was that the bags of useless 20-cent pieces were cluttering up vault space, so they were flung in the furnace.

Q: Are there any figures available on the number of large cents melted down after the small cent was introduced?

Two figures are available. In 1871, the Mint melted down about one million large cents that had been traded in for the new coins, and in 1872, it melted 1.5 million during a combined period of about 10 months. One source gives a total melt estimate of about 25% of the original mintage.

Q: How did the Mint dispose of the 1,093,838,670 steel 1943 cents when they were removed from circulation?

The Mint began the withdrawal in 1945. In 20 years they retrieved 163 million, or about 14.9% of the steel cents in circulation. Some 900,000,000 are still out there. Apparently the recovered coins were turned over to private smelters to be melted down. One instance of this was reported in 1959 when the Philadelphia Mint disposed of 1,250,000 of the steelies by giving them to a steel company which melted them down in exchange for the steel content. Using a weight of 2.7 grams, it figures out to 168 steel cents to the pound, or 7,440.5 pounds. The official word was that they were not being withdrawn, and it wasn't until nearly 15% of them had been removed from circulation that it was admitted. The coverup apparently was a futile attempt to inhibit "hoarding" of the coins. The coins were removed from bulk quantities of cents as they passed through the Federal Reserve Banks.

Q: How much would copper have to rise in price in order to profit from melting cents?

One pound of copper would make 154 of the 95% copper cents produced up through the beginning of 1982. Thus, copper would have to reach $1.55 a pound before it would equal the face value of enough cents to contain that amount, assuming a loss to worn coins and in the smelting process. Then you have to add labor, storage, transportation, and smelting costs, which would probably raise the break-even level to $2 or even $2.50. Then you have to figure out how to get tons and tons of coins to melt. Remember, you're working with pounds of copper, not the ounces of precious metals like gold and silver. If you make one cent a pound profit, that means you would make all of $20 on a ton of cents.

Q: Weren't a large quantity of the large cents used to make bells?

According to a quote from a Troy, New York coin dealer, a firm in Watervliet, New York contracted with the Mint to purchase all the recalled large cents, and used the metal to cast bells. The stories connected with the firm indicate that at times there were barrels of the coins sitting in the yard waiting to be sent to the foundry. Another source cites kegs of large cents melted down to make stove parts (water tank liners) at the Glenwood Range Co. in Taunton, Massachusetts.

Q: Speaking of bells made of cents, what about the Liberty Bell made for the Chicago World's Fair in 1893?

That's a real mystery item. According to sketchy information available, patriotic children across the country contributed 250,000 cents which were melted down and cast into a replica of the Liberty Bell by the Daughters of the American Revolution. It had been planned to tour the country with the bell, but when the Fair closed, the bell disappeared, and was never found. A quick check shows that the cents would have produced just over 1,700 pounds of bell metal.

Q: I know that over the centuries a lot of bells were melted down and turned into coins, and that there have been instances in the past of coins being melted down to cast as bells, but have there been any recent instances of bells made of coin metal?

One of the more recent instances is the Peace Bell, presented to the United Nations in 1954. The bell was cast from coins donated by the delegates from some 60 countries who attended the 13th general conference of the U.N. associations in Paris in 1951. The bell is hung in the U.N. headquarters in New York.

Chapter 33

MEXICO

The exciting early history of the Mexican mints, right down to the modern coins of our neighbor to the south, all make interesting reading. Some of the silver statistics are staggering.

Q: Are there any early examples of coins which had mintage figures in the billions?

One figure from close to home, the Mexico City Mint, struck over 1.5 billion 8 reales in the period from 1580 to 1967.

Q: Please explain the Mexican fineness indications on their coins.

Two terms, or abbreviations, are used: dineros and granos. 12 dineros silver is pure silver. Each dinero equals 24 granos, so the markings on the coin show the fineness. Each dinero equals .083, so 10 dineros silver would be .833 fine. Each grano equals .0003, so 12 granos would equal .0415 fineness.

Q: How many different mints have there been in Mexico?

One source gives a figure of 23, although there is some question as to whether both the old and new Mexico City mints are included in that figure.

Q: I ran across a vague reference to a Mexican Mint at San Francisco. Was this something that occurred while California was still part of Mexico?

The so-called Mexican Mint at San Francisco was from a much later time period, actually coming into discussion in early 1861, when a schemer by the name of William Churchwell proposed to the New York firm of Duncan, Sherman & Co. that for $500 he would obtain a concession from Mexico to mint Mexican pesos in San Francisco for shipment to the Orient. He obtained a contract with the Mexican government, but included his own name, at which Duncan, Sherman & Co. balked, and refused to sign the agreement. The Mexican Congress repudiated the contract in September, 1861, ending the scheme which would have added San Francisco to the lengthy list of Mexican mints.

Q: Did Mexico issue any proof coins in the 1800s?

Apparently not very many. However, I do have a listing which mentions a "complete set of proof coins for 1869 for all the gold, silver, and copper coins, a total of 20 coins, presented to Secretary of State William Henry Seward as a gift from the Mexican Mint." It would be extremely interesting to learn the fate of that particular proof set—and its current value! A similar set of 1879 Mexican coins is described in Buttrey and Hubbard's *Guidebook of Mexican Coins Fifth Edition*. This was given by the Mexican Mint to the wife of the American Ambassador. It sold in a Henry Christensen sale in 1977 for $15,000, but it only contained 11 coins, all circulation strikes, six of which were overdates. Five of the coins were dated prior to 1879, as far back as 1872. This would suggest that in that era the Mexican Mint may have given out other similar sets.

Q: Is there, or was there a "world" mint?

You no doubt are referring to the title that the Mexico City Mint was given in the 1700s. Because of the millions of coins and the sheer tonnage of silver produced and struck into coinage, the Mexico City Mint was dubbed "La Casa de Moeda del Mundo." This translates from the Spanish as "The Mint of the World."

Q: Didn't Mexico cause some problems a few years ago with one of their coins that was the same size as one of the U.S. coins?

Beginning in 1984, Mexico began striking a stainless steel one peso coin which is identical in dimensions to the U.S. quarter. Almost immediately it was discovered that the pieces would operate vending machines along the border. Since the Mexican coin was worth only a fraction of a cent they quickly started moving into the U.S. in quantity. Mexico continued to strike the pieces through 1988. This is a common problem in European countries where coins move readily across national boundaries.

Q: I have an old Mexican coin which has a raised design which looks like a very large "S" on top of the regular design. Is this a special countermark of some kind?

From the appearance, it looks like this is the remains of some silver solder, used to make the coin into a button. This was a very common practice in the last two centuries, all over the world. Almost all countermarks and counterstamps are added to the coin after it was minted and are incuse, or into the surface. You should always be suspicious of any added relief design like this.

Chapter 34

THE MINT

(U.S. MINTS, BRANCH MINTS, TREASURY DEPARTMENT, PRIVATE MINTS)

Q: Does the government make a profit on the circulating coins that the U.S. Mint strikes?

All coins make a profit for the government. It's been a close call a couple of times when the price of copper rose, but it didn't exceed the limit, so the Mint kept on making cents. The profit is known as seigniorage. In a few countries of the world the lowest denomination coins cost more to produce than their face value, which puts a lot of pressure on the government to eliminate the coin.

Q: How did the Mint count its coins before the invention of the mechanical counting machines?

Mechanical counting machines were not introduced at the Mint until some time after the turn of the century. Before that it was strictly a hand counting job, with the help of what was called a counting board. This was a flat board made for each denomination, with copper partitions separated by the diameter of the coin. The boards were designed so that when each row was filled, the total would be some even amount. Some of the counting boards, according to early drawings, apparently were decorated with copies of the intended coin to ensure they were used properly. An experienced counter using the counting board could accurately count $25 in nickels in less than 60 seconds.

Q: I still don't understand why that coin press that General Motors designed back in the 1960s wasn't used to avert the coin shortages of that era. Shouldn't anything that could strike 10,000 coins a minute be in use?

The development of the roller coin press ran into several fatal flaws. While it was true that the press, by using over a hundred pairs of dies, could strike 10,000 coins per minute, it was unable to sustain that speed for more than about 10 minutes at a time. By then most of the dies were worn out, and usually several would have failed, breaking apart, cracking or chipping, resulting in defective coins which had to be hand separated from the good ones. It took 2 hours and 30 minutes to replace the full set of dies, so that in an eight hour shift average production was limited to about 360,000 coins. While this was an improvement over the 288,000 from a regular coin press, it required substantially more work and expense for a relatively minor increase in production. Instead of installing six of the presses at the new Philadelphia Mint, it was necessary to crowd in 132 standard coin presses to strike coins there.

Q: I know that some of the coin presses now in use in the various mints are capable of striking two coins at a time. Do you have any information on when the Mint began using this kind of press?

The dual coin press is mentioned in the 1945 Annual Report of the Director of the Mint, crediting Superintendent of Coining Joseph Steel and machinist William P. Kruse of the San Francisco Mint as the creators of the attachment which was added to the old single coin presses. The report does not give an actual date, but indicates that the device must have been invented and installed prior to June 30, 1944, as it is credited with making possible the large number of domestic and foreign coins struck during the fiscal year

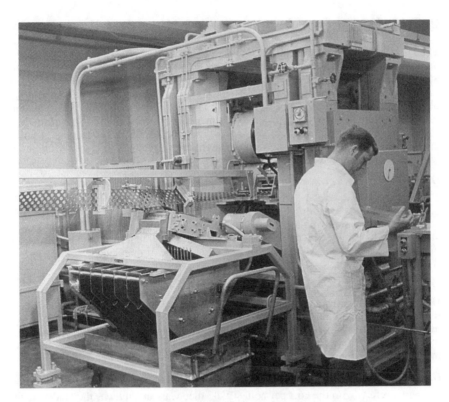

A 1960s roller coin press designed by General Motors.

beginning July 1, 1945. The device was credited with increasing production by 90 percent. Still later, the concept was broadened to construct "quad" presses which could
strike four coins at a time.

Q: What was the striking rate of the old screw presses?

Two men and a boy could strike up to 150 coins per hour, or slightly more than two a
minute. Steam operated presses upped the rate by more than 50 times, or about 120 a
minute.

Q: How accurate were the old scales that you see on display at the Mint?

These tremendous balance beam scales were made right in the Mint tool shop by old-
time skilled craftsmen who took pride in their work. I have seen demonstrated that a
scale which can handle hundreds of pounds of coins can also show the weight of a single
digit written on a sheet of paper. Almost all of them were made "in house" by expert
craftsmen on the mint payroll, with several dating back well into the 1800s.

Q: Were all dates punched into U.S. dies with four digit logo punches?

The number of digits on the logo punches varied from two to four. Examination of
various coins of the mid and late 1800s show evidence of the different number of digits
from the placement and style of the numbers. The use of logo punches began with either
engraver Franklin Peale or Christian Gobrecht.

Q: Did the U.S. Mint ever make its own coin presses? I know they made their own scales to weigh bullion and coins.

The Philadelphia Mint did manufacture some of its own coin presses. In 1940 a total of nine presses were built at a cost of $8,500 each, with the notation that this was about $1,000 cheaper than bids from an outside press manufacturer. At the time, they joined some of the old Carson City coin presses which were still operating at Philadelphia. The oldest of that group was a coin press made in a railroad machine shop in 1867. The same source mentions an item appropriate to the recent uproar in Congress about the Mint using foreign equipment, because it lists four French-made coin presses in use (built to metric scale), along with presses from such American manufacturers as Morgan and Orr, and Waterbury and Farrel, long since gone from the scene.

Q: An old book on the U.S. Mint mentions the job of "whitener." What did a whitener do?

The whitener was the wash "lady" of the old mint, and actually the job still is performed in today's minting operations. The whitener washed the planchets in a solution of borax, soap, and water to remove the grease and dirt, brightening them up for striking. The job also involved cleaning silver planchets with sulfuric acid to remove tarnish before striking, which leached some of the copper from the surface of the planchets, making them whiter.

Q: Is the master die ever used to strike coins?

Under normal circumstances it would not be used, since the master die is intended as a model from which to make the working hubs and then the working dies. However, the master die often was used to make trial strikes, to demonstrate what the proposed coin would look like. In world coinage there are instances where the master die has been used in an emergency for coinage.

Q: Which of the mints operating in the 1890s was the most expensive to operate?

If you are referring to the cost per coin struck, then Carson City was the leader, with a cost of 5.6 cents per coin for the gold and silver coins struck there in 1891. The Philadelphia cost was 1.75 cents for gold and silver coins. By including the minor coins, Philly costs dropped to just over half a cent per coin. San Francisco and New Orleans costs were slightly over 2 cents per coin.

Q: How much did it cost to strike an Anthony dollar, compared to a paper dollar?

The Bureau of Engraving and Printing's production cost figures showed that paper money costs ran about 1.5 cents in 1980, 1.8 cents in 1985, later 2.3, and later up to 2.6 cents per note. One point on this is that it costs just as much to print a $100 note, or any other denomination, as it does to print a dollar note. The SBA dollars cost 3 cents each to strike in 1979-81. Many collectors wonder why the Treasury doesn't just melt down the coins to save storage costs, but to do so would destroy the 97 cents in profit, or seigniorage, earned by minting them.

Q: Aren't some of the Carson City silver dollars supposed to have been below standards for fineness?

In one of the rare instances when the Assay Commission found something wrong during their annual meetings, the 1881 body discovered that about 3000 CC dollars had been struck in 1880 from an alloy that assayed .892 fine rather than the normal .900 fineness. It is unclear from Mint records as to whether the coins were recovered and melted.

Q: Did the Carson City Mint strike coins after 1893?

Only medals. A dollar coin press used at Denver in the 1960s coin shortage was returned to Carson City and used in 1975 to strike the Nevada ARBC medals. The same reverse die used for the Nevada 1876 centennial medal was used to strike the 1976 dated medals in gold, silver, bronze, and copper.

1880 Morgan dollar struck at the Carson City Mint.

Q: Can you give any details on the "gold plated potatoes" which played a part in the Carson City Mint scandals?

During the trial of James Heney, an ex-Mint employee accused of stealing $25,000 worth of bullion, the defense claimed that gold was washed out of the vats and into a nearby potato patch. Assays showed that the dirt contained $9 in gold per ton. The newspapers reporting the trial coined the "gold plated potato" on the basis of that evidence, which the prosecution proved was the result of the potato patch being "salted" with gold. Heney was ultimately convicted.

Q: Is it true that silver proof coins were once smuggled out of the San Francisco Assay Office?

The story is true, as three men were arrested in 1973 for smuggling 23 silver proof Ike dollars out of the building by holding them in their mouths, and later "spending" them. Quite a mouthful of a story!

Q: Not long after the new San Francisco Mint was built, a couple of teenagers got into the building. Do you have any of the facts on this event?

An embarrassment for the officials at the mint, certainly. Two fifteen-year-old boys got into the San Francisco Mint in broad daylight in December, 1938. Perhaps attracted by a partially open window on the second floor, the two scaled the wall, inched along a ledge to the window, and got in unobserved, despite that a guard tower at the corner had an unobstructed view of the wall. The two were able to wander around inside, picked up a piece of bronze strip for cent blanks, and tossed it out the window before starting to make their exit. The incident at the year-old mint drew front page attention in the newspapers of the day. The Mint spent $10,000 for an outside wall, floodlights, and other security measures as a result.

Q: Why were so many coins minted at San Francisco during World War II?

Although Philadelphia set most of the production records during the war years, San Francisco outproduced Denver in many instances because of the large military payrolls and the concentration of defense industry on the West Coast, which increased the demand for coins.

Q: The San Francisco Assay Office struck coins beginning in 1968, but have there been any of the other Assay Offices that struck coins?

San Francisco holds the distinction of having had two different official Assay Offices which struck coins, the only one of the Assay Offices to do so. The San Francisco Assay Office of Gold (its then title) also struck gold $10, $20, and $50 coins in 1853-54.

Q: When was the old New York Assay office built?

The rather imposing five story building was constructed in 1931-32, and went into operation in the latter part of 1932. It was built on the East River waterfront at what was known as "Old Slip." The building was 142 by 195 feet and had a 160 foot smokestack to carry off the smelting fumes.

Q: When did they start storing our gold at Ft. Knox, Kentucky?

The Ft. Knox Gold Depository was constructed in 1935-36. The contract for the construction was awarded October 10, 1935. The first shipments from New York and Philadelphia left on the evening of January 10, 1937, but the facility was not actually completed until January 13. Some 50 armored trains traveled only at night, and the first phase of the transfer of the gold was completed by June with $5.5 billion in gold moved. The high security surrounding the trains effectively deterred any thought of robbing them, but two of the trains were stalled for a time by flood waters that left 400,000 people homeless in the Ohio River valley.

Q: Is it possible to visit Ft. Knox, and see all our gold?

The gold repository at Ft. Knox, Kentucky, about 30 miles southwest of Louisville, is strictly off limits: No Visitors.

Q: Was it still possible to buy individual circulation strike coins from the Treasury after World War II?

The Treasury sold them until 1946 with a limit of two of any denomination and mint, but beginning with the 1947 coins the full set was the minimum that could be ordered.

Q: Whatever happened to the Bureau of the Mint?

It really hasn't been that long, but the long-standing title of Bureau of the Mint was discarded officially on January 25, 1984 in favor of the new title, United States Mint. The Bureau was established by the Coinage Act of 1873 as one of the departments of the U.S. Treasury. Most collectors and hobby publications at least informally referred to the Bureau as the "Mint," or "U.S. Mint," so the change was more in line with popular usage.

Q: Has the Mint been involved in promotion campaigns for coins prior to the well-known drum beating for the Ike and SBA dollars?

I ran across a Mint press release from November 1962, quoting Director Eva Adams as announcing that "the silver dollar is gaining in popularity ....now a greater demand throughout the entire country." This is just one example from a long list, stretching back to the early 1800s. On a somewhat smaller scale, the Treasury resorted to several gimmicks to promote circulation of the Peace dollar, which wasn't all that popular either, especially in the East. One of the schemes tried was to put a silver dollar into the pay envelopes of each of the 5,000 Treasury employees. Before admitting defeat the Treasury had managed to "push" $10,000,000 into circulation, but in a matter of months they were back in the vaults. Sale of the original Ike dollars in 1971 was pushed hard. The theme of the Mint campaign was that every American who wanted to own a (silver) Ike dollar could. To that purpose, some 50 million order blanks were printed. The mintage figure of only 6,868,530 for the 40 percent silver special uncirculated coins for 1971 tells the story.

Q: Were the silver dollars which were sold by the Treasury Department in the 1960s the subject of a previous count and settlement by the Mint?

The Mint uses the term "settlement" to cover the results of physical inventory of such items as bullion, bars, and struck coins. Way back in fiscal 1897, the Philadelphia Mint concluded a count of 50 million silver dollars in the main vault. The count had been precipitated by the discovery that many of the original bags had rotted, and there were silver dollars lying loose on the floor of the vault. When the count was concluded, the coins were rebagged and placed in wooden boxes. At a cost of $13,000 for labor and materials, the count was determined to be 47,782,104 "perfect pieces," and 2,217,000 "rusty pieces," leaving a shortage of 896 pieces. Those 896 coins must have been the topic of some creative bookkeeping, because the annual settlement made no mention of them and reported officially that "All of the coin .... was on hand that the Superintendent was charged with."

Q: Did the Treasury issue any of the silver dollars that were in the vaults prior to the run in the 1960s?

Three million were released for Christmas, 1954, mostly coins of the 1880s. Uncirculated 1889 dollars that were found in the bags sold for $16. Other newspaper stories cited values to $17. One bank in Montana got a bag of 1,000 1893-CC dollars.

Q: Didn't the U.S. Mint issue a flat statement that no more dollars would ever be produced?

Mint Director George E. Roberts is quoted as saying on June 30, 1904, "There will never be another silver dollar minted in this country."

Q: Did the Treasury Department resist striking the Morgan dollars?

Many times, but the silver lobby was too powerful. Secretary of the Treasury Charles T. Fairchild said in his 1887 annual report, "It is a waste to coin and store any more silver dollars at present. There is no function which those that are coined after this time will probably ever perform, except to lie in Government vaults and be a basis upon which Silver Certificates can be issued. The five, two and one dollar certificates furnish a convenient currency, and it is evident that the future use of the silver dollar will be almost exclusively in that form."

Q: Is it true that the "power plant" cost more than the first coin press that was used in the U.S. Mint?

This is fairly well documented, and true. The U.S. Mint bought its first coin press for $47.44 in 1792. Then they bought a pair of oxen for $60 to power the press. The oxen didn't work out very well, so they were almost immediately replaced with horses, but as stated your question was correct.

Q: Wasn't the original plan to have the first U.S. Mint in New York City?

The original bill in Congress would have placed the Mint in the capital city of the United States. Since New York was serving as the capital, that would have put the U.S. Mint there. However, after deciding to create the District of Columbia as the capital, it was determined in 1790 that it would be several years before it would be ready, so Philadelphia was picked as the temporary capital and as a result got the U.S. Mint. At the time Philadelphia was the largest city in the United States (45,000 people), even larger than New York.

Q: Wasn't the Mint involved in one of the first efforts to use a camera to take pictures in America?

The oldest surviving photo taken in the United States was taken from the window of the United States Mint in Philadelphia, in October 1839. Joseph Saxton read an article in a newspaper and constructed a camera from a cigar box and a lens from a burning glass.

He was able to successfully take a photo of the school across the street. The interesting part to numismatists is that the "film" that he used was a strip of highly polished silver coin metal. The photo is in the possession of the Historical Society of Pennsylvania.

Q: Why do the Tiffany mosaics in the Philadelphia Mint depict children performing the duties of the minting process?

The design is based on an early painting of the 1st Century C.E. found at Pompeii, which showed winged cherubs doing the mint work.

Q: Do you have a list of the items that were placed in the cornerstone of the current Philadelphia Mint?

The cornerstone was laid September 18, 1968. Placed in a box in the cornerstone were the following items: a set of uncirculated 1962 coins; 1968-dated cents from Philadelphia, Denver, and San Francisco; a 1968-D and a 1968-S nickel; 1968 and 1968-D dimes; 1968 and 1968-D quarters and a 1968-D half; a 1967 special mint set; a 1963 and 1968 proof set; an 1891-CC dollar; a .77 ounce package of silver granules; 1967 Assay Commission Medal and Mint Medals for Lyndon Johnson, Henry H. Fowler, and Eva Adams; a copy of the Coinage Act of 1965; a "Mint Story" booklet; a copy of Secretary Fowler's speech at the ceremony; copies of several coin publications; and other documents. Apparently there was no special ceremony and no cornerstone for the first Mint. The cornerstone of the second Mint was laid July 4, 1829, but there is no record of anything placed in the cornerstone. The story for the third Mint, completed in 1901, is the same, with no record of anything special going into the cornerstone.

Q: Are there official records of four 1854-C gold dollars being struck? I don't find them listed in the catalogs, but there are old references to them.

Walter Breen reported that the figure is the result of a dummy bookkeeping entry that was in turn the basis of the Mint reports listing them. The pieces eventually were identified and determined to be assay samples of the 1853-C dollars, stolen in transit to the Philadelphia Mint, along with eight 1953-C half eagles.

Q: I read somewhere that the introduction of the clad coins in 1965 had a significant effect on the cost of building the Philadelphia Mint. How could that have made a difference?

The switch more than doubled the estimated cost of building the Philadelphia Mint, jumping the estimate from $16.5 million to $37.7 million, principally due to the expensive technology needed to produce clad coinage strip. In the first year of the new clad coins, the Mint paid more than twice the previous total coin manufacturing cost just for fabrication of the clad coins, which accounted for less than half of total coin production. The clad strip line has recently been removed from the Mint, and the work is being contracted to private manufacturers.

Q: Did the big robbery in 1923 at the Denver Mint have any numismatic repercussions?

Two that are of note; one a far reaching change, the other temporary. As a result of the robbery, the Mint decided to remove the Mint Cabinet of coins from the Philadelphia Mint to the National Museum in Washington. The other was the closing of the mints to all visitors for a time.

Q: Were there any coins minted at the Denver "mint" after it was purchased from Clark, Gruber and Company?

One of the original purposes of the purchase by the U.S. Government was a face-saving method of putting Clark, Gruber out of business as a mint. The firm had minted $2.50, $5, $10, and $20 gold pieces, most of which were of finer gold than the U.S. Mint product. However, the firm was considered to be a direct competitor to the U.S. Mint by the Philadelphia Mint director, James Pollock, so it was bought out in 1861 for $25,000. The remainder of an appropriation of $75,000 was apparently wasted rather than being used to upgrade the facility, and the Clark, Gruber building reverted to the status of an assay office, with not a single coin struck there after its transfer to the Treasury Department. It would not be until 1906 that coins were officially struck in Denver.

1860 $5 gold piece minted at the Clark, Gruber and Company mint in Denver, Colorado. Notice "Clark & Co." on cornet.

Q: Wasn't there a metal Great Seal set in the vestibule floor at the Denver Mint at one time?

Until 1961 the metal version was part of the floor, but by 1961 it had become so worn that it was replaced with a mosaic, and the original was moved to the numismatic sales room for display.

Q: Wasn't there some kind of a mysterious fire at the New Orleans Mint in 1893?

A fire occured in the cashier's vault at the New Orleans Mint while it was closed for the weekend in June, 1893. The cashier, J.M. Dowling, claimed that $25,000 in paper money was destroyed. A government expert identified $1,182 in charred currency. The belief was that the cashier had set the fire to hide a shortage in his funds, but when he was arrested and tried, he was acquitted of embezzlement.

Q: What special distinction does the 1851-O 3-cent silver coin struck at New Orleans have?

It was the first and only U.S. coin with a value of five cents or less struck in the 1800s with a mint mark. Several readers questioned this answer, citing various coins. The half dime, dime, silver three-cent, and all other silver coins except the silver war nickels were classed as "subsidiary" coinage, while the copper-nickel 5-cent, 3-cent, two-cent, cent, and half-cent were all classed as "minor" coinage.

Q: Did anyone ever find a way of distinguishing the cents struck at West Point from those struck at Philadelphia?

To the best of my knowledge nobody has ever discovered any distinguishing marks on West Point coins, since the dies are made with the same hubs used for the Philadelphia dies. The only coins directly traceable to the West Point Mint prior to the introduction of the W mint mark were some Panamanian pieces struck there, as I recall, sometime in the late 1970s.

Q: How did they get around the law which prohibited striking coins anywhere except at Philadelphia, Denver, and San Francisco? I'm thinking specifically of West Point.

West Point fell under the control of the New York Assay Office, which was singled out specifically in the law and prohibited from striking any coins. Congress changed one part of the law in 1974 to permit any facility to strike coins, but left the prohibition on New York in another part of the law. To get around this provision without having to go back to Congress for still another change, the Mint transferred control of West Point from the New York Assay Office to the Philadelphia Mint.

Q: Did they try to get a mint at Chicago?

At least two concerted efforts were made to secure a mint for the Windy City. The first was made in 1896, but was unsuccessful. Representative Frank Annunzio introduced a Chicago Mint bill in 1972, but remodelling of the San Francisco Mint scuttled the proposal.

Q: Were the 1920, 1921, and 1922 Philippine coins without mint marks struck at Philadelphia?

The Manila Mint began striking coins in 1920, but did not use a mint mark until 1923, so the coins all came from the Manila Mint. The Manila Mint operated as a branch of the U.S. Mint from July 16, 1920 until the Philippines were granted independence in 1946. The last U.S. coins struck with the M mint mark were the 1941 issues.

Q: I thought the U.S. Mint destroyed dies as soon as they were outdated, or worn out. Wasn't the Manila Mint still using 1929 dated dies to strike coins in 1936?

A reader makes that rather startling claim, telling us that visitors to the Manila Mint in 1936 were allowed to strike, and then buy 1929-M 20 centavos coins, one of the very rare instances of any world mint allowing visitors to strike a circulating coin. U.S. coinage dies are normally destroyed by, or at the end of the year of production. At the time, the Manila Mint was a branch mint of the U. S. Mint.

Q: How long has the Franklin Mint been striking foreign coins?

The first were the 1969 1 dinar silver coins struck for Tunisia. The original order was 20,000, but eventually they struck 35,000.

Q: Do you have a list of the private mints in the U.S.?

Unfortunately there is no complete listing of the private mints that I am aware of. Hundreds of mints sprang up during the silver art bar boom in the 1970s, but most closed their doors when the boom broke. It would have been helpful if you had indicated what your interest was, as I could possibly have steered you to some specific mints that would fit your requirements. If anyone has a list you might send it along as we can always use it to refer to. We get one or two letters a month asking for private mint information.

Q: In a discussion with a friend the question came up as to what happens to coins after they have been in circulation for a while. For example, are all of the 1965 dated quarters still in circulation, or has the Treasury taken some of them out of the hands of the public?

Attrition takes its toll, but the only coins actually officially removed from circulation (other than bullion coins) are those which have been damaged or mutilated to the point where they no longer can be used as coins. Coins are supplied by the U.S. Mint to the Federal Reserve Banks, and through them to local banks as demanded. Collectors pull coins from circulation, but the number is a very small fraction of the total number produced in any given year.

Q: I'm told that the U.S. Treasury at one time was ready to conduct a coin "census" among collectors and dealers to determine how many coins they were holding. Do you have any information?

A joint committee of the Treasury and the Federal Reserve Board did in fact recommend that an outside group be hired by the Treasury to conduct just such a survey, to determine exactly how many coins were being "hoarded." The report was entered into the records of the House Government Operations Subcommittee on Legal and Monetary Affairs in early 1966, along with testimony from Mint Director Eva Adams.

Q: Just how many coin collectors are there?

"And how many angels can dance on the head of a pin?....." A lot of different figures have been offered, but nobody really knows. A popular quote in the past has been 8 million. Some use the Mint's mailing list, somewhat less than three million, as an indicator. The only reasonably accurate survey that I am aware of is one run at the Epcot Center in Florida in January, 1986 for the U.S. Mint. Some 12,000 people were asked a number of questions about their use of coins, and finally whether they collected coins, or held them as an investment. A total of 33 percent of the adults indicated they collected for fun or profit, as did an even larger number of those under 18. If we used the lesser figure, a third of our 245 million population would equal 80 million collectors! Even if we had some reason to seriously doubt the accuracy of the poll and cut the figure in half it would still total 40 million collectors, far more than any other source has ever estimated. Many people who have coins don't consider themselves collectors and many others who have only a few coins claim to be collectors, so these two factors would tend to even out. The figures will not sit well with some, and certainly will be controversial, but there they are for you to take a shot at, if you like.

Chapter 35

MINTAGE FIGURES, STATISTICS

Mintage statistics are frequently frustrating and often generate more than their fair share of questions. This is especially true with readers until they understand that "official" government mintage figures from the early days were often inaccurate, incomplete, or simply missing. Also causing problems is the totally different purpose of government mintage figures, based on totals, rather than specifying varieties.

Q: In a question you mentioned that the Indian Head and Lincoln cents were struck at the same time in 1909. Weren't the Buffalo nickels and Jefferson nickels both struck in 1938?

As nearly as I can find out, the last Buffalo nickels were struck at Denver in early 1938, legally completing the 25-year requirement. Schlag's design for the Jefferson nickel was not accepted until late July, so production would not have started until later in the year, so the two did not overlap. Philadelphia switched to the new Jefferson design, proofs, and circulation strikes in 1938, Denver switched later in the year.

Q: I was given a roll of 1970-S nickels, but when I tried to sell them I was told they weren't proofs. How can this be?

The San Francisco Assay Office was reopened in 1968, with the principal function of striking proof coins, but it also struck circulation coins in various years with an S mint mark, including the SBA dollars as well as cents, nickels, and dimes. Your 70-S nickels are normal circulation strikes.

Q: Are there any statistics on the number of silver coins in circulation when the switch was made to the clad coins in 1965?

One estimate I found was that there were approximately 12 billion silver coins still in circulation or in bank vaults as the change to clad coinage was made. The Government got several billion of them out of circulation, and many more were melted down.

Q: Was the fire at the Mint the cause of the 1815 gap in cent production?

The real cause was a serious shortage of copper. The fire actually wasn't until January 1816, and only damaged part of the rolling mill operation. The War of 1812 caused the shortage of copper. When cent production was suspended in 1815, it was the only year they hadn't been coined since 1793. This gap led to numerous fantasy counterfeits, dated 1815.

Q: Weren't our copper-plated zinc cents originally planned for earlier than their 1982 issue?

The Mint schedule originally was to start striking 1981 dated zinc cents on July 1, 1981 at the beginning of the fiscal year, but by the time various delays had occured, the production didn't begin until after the 1982 date was authorized.

Q: When did the U.S. Mints finally satisfy the country's demand for coins?

It may come as a surprise, but it wasn't until the 1870s that production caught up with demand. The statement is made that the Mint produced less than 50% of the country's needs up to 1853, the balance being foreign coins which circulated freely until 1857.

Q: Why was there such a long delay in resuming proof coin production after World War II?

One reason, which probably has not received much publicity, was that the Philadelphia Mint was tied up for several years after the war striking the millions of medals that had been authorized for veterans of the war. On the average, each man or woman who had served in the armed forces was entitled to three medals. The Mint Director, Mrs. Nellie Tayloe Ross, officially blamed the war medal production for the delay in a letter written in early 1948, but it wasn't until 1950 that proof production was resumed.

Q: Were there 1000 proof 1878 Morgan dollars struck, or only 500?

Robert Julian presents excellent Mint record evidence that only 500 were struck and delivered—100 each on March 12th, 15th, and 18th, and a final delivery of 200 on March 26th, 1878. He also makes a good argument that the rare 7 tail feather proofs were not officially struck, but were under the counter "specials." To top it off, of the 500 officially struck, 16 were placed in circulation at the end of the year.

Q: What is the largest U.S. proof set in number of coins?

That honor would have to go to the proof coins of 1873, although it bears some explanation. Although there were some 25 "complete" proof sets delivered in early 1873 which contained all of the coins then currently being struck, from the cent to the $20 gold, most of the proof coins were issued as part of individual sets, such as the minor sets or gold sets. Later in the year, proofs were made of the silver coins with arrows at date. Walter Breen listed one so-called "double set," presented by the Mint to Charles A. Whitney, which included specimens of both the with- and without-arrows silver coins of that year. In all, 20 different coins were struck as proofs in 1873. The Whitney set contained two specimens of each coin to show the obverse and reverse.

Q: Did Carson City strike any proof dollars in 1883?

Wayte Raymond quoted a mintage of 12, apparently at a ceremony marking the closing of the Mint. Walter Breen listed two that have been authenticated, and two other possible examples known.

Q: Did the U.S. Mint make any special provisions for the 1964 proof sets with the first Kennedy coin?

As a special concession to small collectors, the Mint cut bulk orders back to 75 sets and reopened the ordering period, only for those wanting just one or two sets. This made 384,737 sets available, but orders "far exceeded" that number, and many got their money returned. The price was $2.10 a set.

Q: Some sources list the 1827 quarters as regular issues, some as proofs, including the one sold in the Garrett sale. Can you please clear this up?

Mint records list a mintage of 4,000, but R. W. Julian believes these were struck with 1825 dates. Walter Breen, in his book on proofs, estimated "12 1827 proofs," and lists the pedigrees for nine of them. The Garrett piece, sold for $190,000, is one of the four proofs obtained by Joseph J. Mickley directly from the Mint in 1827. Julian mentions "one known" 1827 circulation strike, and elsewhere describes the (proofs) as "technically and legally ... medals struck with coinage dies."

Q: Old-timers tell me that the U.S. Mint sold its entire production of proof sets in 1969 in just six days. How could that have happened?

Those were the good old days: B.C., or before computers. At that time, collectors could order up to a maximum of 20 sets. With production moved to San Francisco in 1968 after a three-year hiatus, collectors and dealers were quick to jump on the bandwagon and there were a lot of people who submitted multiple order blanks, each for the maximum. That the 1968 mint sets had "sold out" in a month undoubtedly had an effect as well. At that time orders were accepted beginning November 1, with no orders post-marked earlier being accepted. By November 6 the number of orders already received had exceeded the estimated 3 million sets the Mint felt it could produce. The sales wound up at 2,934,631 sets. The Mint did make an effort to spread the sets around by searching for and eliminating duplicate orders, but many of those who procrastinated about getting their orders in failed to receive sets that year.

Q: Which will last longer, a die for a small coin, or a die for a large coin?

There's conflicting evidence on this point, so it's not a matter of saying one or the other. For example, the cent is our second smallest coin, with a die life that has in the past exceeded a million strikes per die, and currently is averaging in the area of 750,000 strikes. Our smallest coin, the dime, has a much lower die life due to the highly abrasive copper-nickel alloy used. As a general rule, the larger coins have a lower die life because of the additional pressure needed to get a decent strike. The specific alloy used, the pressure, and even the design all have a bearing on die life. Statistics from other mints even show that silver coin dies have a shorter life than those used to strike nickel coins, but I suspect another factor, namely the discarding of the silver coin dies at the first sign of serious wear, in contrast to the practice of using an abrasive to hide the wear and lengthen die life for the base metal coins.

Q: Is it true that the Mint was getting very poor die life with the first Shield nickels?

R. W. Julian, who has extensively researched the Mint archives, estimates that for the 1866 and early 1867 nickel production, before the design was changed, the die life was averaging about 10,000 strikes per pair, or only slightly more than the Mint is getting from its proof dies today. This statistic points up both that the design was not the easiest to strike and that nickel alloy planchets were extremely difficult to handle with the then current technology. This extremely low number of strikes per die also explains why there are literally hundreds of die varieties for the early Shield nickels, with production of the coin probably tying up most of the efforts of the die department for a number of years. By 1880 the average was 26,000 coins per die; current is about 250,000.

1881 Shield nickel.

Q: What kind of die life did the Mint get with the Morgan dollar dies?

As is usually the case, they got better with practice. With all the startup problems, they got an average of 83,400 strikes per die pair in 1878. By the following year die life jumped to 137,700, by 1884 to 234,000, and by the 1890s it had increased to 350,000 to 400,000. Die life for the Peace dollars was in the 500,000 area.

Q: Next to the Lincoln cent (86 years), what U.S. coin designs have remained in production the longest?

It may surprise you, but the longevity records were held by four gold coins. A second place tie goes to the coronet eagle, struck from 1838 to 1907 and the coronet half eagle 1839-1908 (69 years). Fourth goes to the coronet quarter eagle made from 1840 to 1907 (67 years), and fifth to the coronet double eagle struck from 1849 to 1907 (58 years). The large cent was struck over a 65 year period, but with several types.

Q: Has anyone compiled percentages of existing examples of old series of coins?

Walter Breen cited a few figures: an estimated 3 to 6% of the large cents surviving, 4-8% of the early silver, and 0.02 to 2% of the half cents. Any such figures have to be classed as estimates as there is no known way of determining exact numbers. Population listings by grading services are a help.

Q: Who, or what official body, keeps track of the number of coins of any given issue that have survived?

There is no such body, as there are too many factors involved to keep anything approaching accurate records. In fact, most official meltings of coins are by weight, without regard to date or mint.

Q: What were the actual stopping dates for striking silver coins?

STOP: Silver dimes—Philadelphia, November 1965; Denver, Feb 14, 1966.

START: Clad dimes—Philadelphia, December 1965; Denver, March, 1966.

STOP: Silver quarters—Philadelphia, July 1965; Denver, November 1965, San Francisco, (No mint mark) January 1966.

START: Clad quarters—Philadelphia, August 1965; Denver, December 1965.

STOP: 90% Silver halves—Philadelphia, April 1966; Denver, December 1965.

START: Clad (40% silver) halves—Philadelphia, May 1966; Denver, December 30, 1965.

Q: I can't find a listing for a 1975 dated quarter. Didn't they make any quarters that year?

No quarters, halves, or dollars with 1975 dates were minted because they were already striking the three denominations with 1976 dates for the Bicentennial. The 1975 proof and mint sets were issued with the cent, nickel, and dime with 1975 dates and the other coins with the 1976 date. For 1976, all of the coins in the sets had the 1976 date.

Q: Why did the nickel and half dime circulate at the same time?

The half dime of 1794-1873 was silver. Before the Civil War many silver coins were shipped out of the country to be melted, or were hoarded during the Civil War, and for all practical purposes the half dime did not circulate then. The nickel was intended to relieve the coin shortage and was used to phase out the fractional paper.

Q: Most references list the half dime production as beginning in 1794, but there are those who claim that the 1792 dated coins are business strikes and not patterns as listed. Why the argument?

Depending on the source, either 1500 or 2000 pieces were struck in 1792. Many saw circulation and are heavily worn. Those who argue that they were intended to circulate cite Washington's letter in which he states: "There has been a small beginning in the coinage of half dimes, the want of small coins in circulation calling the first attention to them." The purists argue that because they weren't struck at the Mint, they don't count as coins.

Q: What's the story on the "rare" 1950-D nickel? The mintage figures don't indicate it is worth the premium asked.

2,630,030 nickels were minted at Denver that year, which marked the start of the Korean War. Production was geared to a peacetime economy and its needs. Quite a few were hoarded, but it wasn't until the speculation boom of the mid-1960s that the price was run up far above where it is now.

Q: Why are there gaps in coin production for several denominations during the 1920s and 30s? I thought the Mint had to strike coins every year.

There in no requirement that the Mint strike every coin, every year. The gaps in production of any given denomination, especially in the 1920s and 30s, were due either to a lack of demand or stocks of unused coins struck in previous years. The demand for coins dropped sharply at the end of World War I, and then even further in the Depression in the 30s. Coins are struck either on demand from the Federal Reserve System, or in anticipation of the demand. The Mint keeps a reserve stock of coins on hand to meet changes in demand.

Q: Can you give me some statistics about coin production? When did the United States Mint first strike a million dollars worth of coins in a single year?

The million dollar mark was surpassed in 1807. This included $437,495 in gold coin, $597,448 in silver coin, and $9,652 in minor coins. The $10 million figure was reached in 1843, and $100 million in 1881.

The old record for a single year was set in 1904, when a total of $250,800,000 in face value was struck, including $233,400,000 in gold. In 1964, that mark was eclipsed by quarter production alone, which amounted to $318,100,000. In regards to cents struck in a single year, in 1907 the Mint had its first million dollar cent year with $1,081,386.18, and it passed the $10 million mark in 1941 with 1.108 billion cents.

The all time record for the smallest production of coins was set in 1815, with a total value of $20,483.

Q: Do you happen to have the total value for all of the coins struck at Carson City?

Just happened to have these at my fingertips ... Actually it took a little searching.

Double eagles - $16,689,680	Half dollars - $2,654,313.50	Quarters - $2,579,198
Eagles - $2,822,780	Silver dollars - $12,660,288	20-cents - $28,658
Half eagles - $3,279,085	Trade dollars - $4,211,400	Dimes - $2,090,110.80

In total, there was $22,791,545 struck in gold, $24,223,968.30 in silver, and a grand total of $47,015,513.30 in face value.

Q: Back in the days of visual inspection of struck coins, what percentages of gold and silver coins were rejected?

One set of figures I found shows that at Philadelphia just over 90 percent of the double eagles passed inspection, and the figure for the Peace dollars was just under 90 percent. However, from the ingot to the struck coin the rejection rate was much higher, only 32.4 percent of the gold coins, 36 percent of the subsidiary silver, and 51 percent of the silver dollars passing muster. The high rejection rate reflects the return of below standard weight planchets to be melted down and recast into ingots.

Q: Why can't I find an exact figure for the mintage of the 1823 large cents? You show it included in the 1824 mintage.

In all our publications and catalogs, we use the same inclusive figure as are found in most reference works for 1824, which includes all 1823 dated mintage, as this is the best available figure based on extensive research into the mint records. The early records were frequently confused, including two or even three years of production, or including coins struck with dies for any of several years, so it is impossible to go beyond the generally accepted figures.

Q: When did one of the mints first exceed the billion mark for a single coin?

In 1944 Philadelphia struck 1.098 billion cents.

Q: I suppose this might be considered a trivia question, but I recall years ago seeing some astronomical figure as to how many cents the copper in the Bingham, Utah mine would make. Any hope of finding it?

I'm in luck on this, and not too trivial a figure at that. In 1938 the Kennecott copper reserves at Bingham were said to be enough to make 2.102 trillion cents, or enough to "last for the next 11,427 years." Where the latter figure came from is anyone's guess, as only 50 years later we are consuming well over 10 billion cents a year, which would eat up that two trillion pretty fast.

Q: Is there an accurate accounting of the total number of large cents struck between 1793 and 1857?

Given the rather erratic bookkeeping of the early years, one of the best figures available comes from the Early American Coppers publication, *Penny-Wise*. They account for approximately 156,844,474 large cents. Of that number, the Mint lists 118 million as still on the books, or unredeemed. Undoubtedly a large percentage of that figure represents coins that were melted down for their copper in the early 1800s. In 1916, the three mints struck 190 million cents in a single year, more than enough to replace every large cent struck.

Q: How many of the 35 percent silver nickels were struck during the 1942-45 period?

The statistics for the silver war nickels show that a total of 869,923,700 were struck over the four year period, a large percentage of them at the Philadelphia Mint. The big P mint mark that appeared on them to distinguish them from the prewar alloy was billed as the "first use" of a mint mark at Philadelphia, but it had already appeared on several foreign coins and a few medals. The full "PHILADELPHIA" and an abbreviation were used even earlier on some foreign coins struck there. Curiously, more steel cents were struck in a single year (1,093,838,670 in 1943) than the total for the silver nickels.

1943-P Jefferson war nickel.

Q: Wasn't there some question about the 1893-CC dollars struck at Carson City?

No satisfactory explanation was ever made for 80,000 of the coins which turned up in the vaults of the Nevada State Treasury, despite a statement from the U.S. Treasury that none existed outside the Treasury vaults. Evidence showed that a number were poorly struck, evidently in haste to avoid their illicit manufacture being discovered.

Q: What's the story on the controversy surrounding the mintage figures for the 1899 Morgan dollar?

The coin seems to have run afoul of dealer competition, or possibly honest differences of opinion, with one side claiming that the 330,000 mintage for Philadelphia is correct, while others claim that substantial quantities were struck in 1900 with surplus 1899 dies and included in the 1900 mintage figures. There is little hard evidence to work with.

Q: I read a story in another publication about the "rare" 1981 SBA dollars. Just how rare are they?

It's a bit difficult to associate the term "rare" with a coin which had a mintage of more than 3 million at each of three mints. The proof mintage is over 4 million, so any way you look at it, the coin is not rare, even if it may be hard to find.

Q: How many of the three-coin sets of 1979 and 1980 PD&S Anthony dollars were made by the Mint?

This is a recurring question, and one that I have referred several times to the Mint without being able to get an answer.

Q: Is the 1845-O gold quarter eagle a legitimate coin? I've heard that it was not listed in the Mint reports.

Supposedly the piece was discovered by B. Max Mehl in the early 1900s, and up to that time no record of the issue had been found in the Mint reports. Later it was determined that 4000 of the coins had been minted that year at New Orleans.

The coin was not listed originally in the Director's report because it was struck in January of 1846, and included with the coins of that year. A search of the Mint archives discovered a delivery by the coiner of 4,000 of the pieces on Jan. 22, 1846, which happened to be two days before the 1846 dies arrived from Philadelphia. This was ample proof that they were dated 1845. The coin was apparently unknown until B. Max Mehl gave it some publicity after worn specimens turned up in the 1950s.

Q: Is there any coin which was struck at all the principal mints?

There is only one coin which fills the bill: the $5 gold half eagle. It was struck at Philadelphia, Carson City, Charlotte, Dahlonega, Denver, New Orleans, and San Francisco. Actually, since West Point has struck both the 1988-W Olympics half eagle and the 1989-W Congress half eagle, the technical point stands, now for a total of eight mints.

Q: Why didn't the U.S. Mint strike any $20 gold coins until 1849?

To put it into perspective, let me ask a question. How much use would you have today for a $2,000 coin? That's about the situation that the Mint faced back in the early 1800s. There simply was no need for that large a coin in an era when a day's wages were counted in cents rather than dollars. A $20 coin would have been equal to several month's wages for most people, so there was no point in making them. Even when the economy reached the point where the coin had some practical purpose, that purpose was merely to provide banks with an easy to handle bulk coin which could be stored to serve as a reserve to back the business. Even in the heyday of the $20 gold piece there were few people who could afford, or needed, to carry even one or two of the coins in their pocket.

Q: In the very old catalogs there are no listings for the 1907-S $10 gold eagle, yet today the mintage is shown as 210,500. What's the story?

As is often the case, Mint records are not always accurate, and for some reason no mintage figure for that date at San Francisco was listed. To add to the confusion, a private list put out by Ben Green listed the approximate mintage (210,000), but for the Indian Head eagles. Collectors who had 1907-S eagles which had survived the 1934 massacre began asking questions and the correct mintage figure finally was dredged up.

Q: If there are only "four known" 1804 $10 gold pieces, why aren't they more valuable than the "15 known" 1804 silver dollar?

There are many similar puzzles throughout numismatics, and the simple answer in many cases is publicity. The 1804 dollar has been in the spotlight for so long that reaching for the checkbook is a reflex action when one is mentioned. The rarity of the $10 gold of 1804 just hasn't had enough publicity to catch the public fancy.

1804 $10 gold piece.

Chapter 36
MINTING VARIETIES

Minting varieties, which include, but are not limited to "errors," are some of the most popular collectible coins, simply because, unlike regular coins, they have instant value, with no century-long waiting period. The heavy volume of questions and the public interest in coins like the 1995 doubled-die cent attest to their collectible status.

Q: When was the gold 1854-S quarter eagle first discovered?

It turned up in 1911 and was one of the reasons why coin dealers began paying serious attention to mint marks. Until that time, it was assumed that all of the first year's production at San Francisco had been lost, melted, or never minted.

Q: Why is the mint mark on the Silver Eagles on the reverse? I thought it was the law that they had to be on the obverse.

There was no actual law changing the mint marks all to the obverse of our circulating coins, merely an internal decision at the Mint to standardize the position. While the official comment at the time the Silver Eagles were first struck was that the S "looked better" on the reverse, it apparently was a throwback to the traditional position for the S mint mark for the coins, which had an obverse that was copied from the old Walking Liberty halves.

Q: I have a 1918-SM quarter. Why the SM mint mark?

The S is the San Francisco mint mark. The M which appears on the Standing Liberty quarters is the designer's initial, for Hermon A. MacNeil.

Q: I've noticed that the "S" mint mark on my proof dimes is different than the "S" on the other proof coins. Is this unusual?

This bears a little explanation as well. The original announcement from the Mint in 1985 implied that the mint mark was being added to the master die, but this was not technically correct. In actuality, the mint mark was added to the model used to make the reduction for the master die. Thus each denomination had its own model, and literally, its own mint mark. This is readily apparent if you compare the S mint mark on a proof dime with that on any of the other proof coins. The dime mint mark is a thin double curve with fully open centers while the other coins have thicker and more closed loops.

Q: Why don't they go back to large mint marks like the ones on the war nickels, so a collector doesn't have to have a microscope to see where a coin came from?

A good thought, but one that is not likely to get much support from the Mint. As far as they are concerned, the mint mark is tolerated as a means of identifying or tracing a coin to its origin, and it has been only under extreme pressure from collectors that they have retained the tiny letters in use. The monsters used on the 1942-45 nickels were among the largest in the history of world coinage.

Q: Why didn't early U.S. collectors pay any attention to mint marks?

Living in an era where information on every aspect of coin collecting is at our fingertips, it is hard to picture the primitive conditions under which early-day collectors labored. Mintage figures were unavailable and the Philadelphia Mint dominated the interest of collectors; the other mints, while of local interest, rarely influenced collecting in any way. From what I can find, there was almost no interest in mint marks until the Civil War period and afterward. The collector of the day wanted a coin of the year, regardless of where it was minted, perhaps because little or no mintage information was available. As a result, collectors went strictly by date on coins in hand, guessing as to relative rarity. The turning point came with the publication by Augustus C. Heaton of "A Treatise on the Coinage of the United States Branch Mints" in 1893. Heaton listed 17 reasons for collecting mint marked coins, and the race was on.

Even then the mint mark concept didn't catch on universally. Coin dealer B. Max Mehl is quoted as saying that in 1903-04, when he began dealing in coins, he looked only at the date side of a coin before making an offer for it. Unthinkable today, but not back then. Curiously, the same attitude applied as recently as 1972 in Germany, when collectors first showed interest in mint marks because of the Olympic coins of that year from the four German mints.

Q: Please list the mint marks used by the U.S. Mint.

C—Charlotte, CC—Carson City, D—Dahlonega and Denver, M—Manila, O—New Orleans, P—Philadelphia, S—San Francisco, W—West Point.

Q: Wasn't there a move by the government to repeat the 1965-67 ban on mint marks in the 1970s?

The Mint has never been particularly famous for learning from history, so it's not surprising that they were all set to repeat the anti-collector move by taking the mint marks off again. A joint study released in October, 1974 by the Treasury Department and the Federal Reserve determined to their satisfaction that the only purpose (which they labeled as "questionable") was to identify the source of production mistakes among coins already shipped out. Mint Director Mary Brooks was exerting considerable pressure, enough to remove the mint mark from circulation cents struck at San Francisco. She had been angered enough by ads offering S Mint cents for sale to go to the expensive move of shipping the coins to Denver and Philadelphia to mix them with strikes from those two mints. Fortunately, the coin shortage eased and collector pressure for mint marks caused abandonment of the idea, at least for the time being. Vestiges of that viewpoint survive in the refusal of the Mint to put mint marks on Philadelphia cents and coins other than commemoratives struck at West Point.

Q: What would be the possibility of getting the Mint to issue a "starter set" of current cents, each with the mint mark of the different mints?

This has been suggested in the past without success, since Philadelphia, San Francisco, and West Point are, or were, striking circulation cents without mint marks. Who knows, maybe this time it will find a receptive ear. Given that such a set would contain three coins unavailable from circulation, it would find a ready (and profitable) market.

Q: I have a 1921 Morgan dollar which must have been struck at the Manila Mint as it has a large M on the neck. Why isn't it listed?

Usually some overzealous copywriter at one of the pseudo mints is to blame for confusing the M with a mint mark. It's the designer's initial (for George T. Morgan), but in this case, while Manila was a U.S. Mint, and used the M for a mint mark, none of the Morgan dollars were ever struck there. It remains Morgan's initial.

Q: With all the interest in mint marks sparked by the 1990 no-S proof cent, I'm curious as to how many different mint marks were used on the Morgan dollars.

Leroy Van Allen, one of the top dollar experts, lists five variations for the CC, six for the S, four for the O, and a normal and "micro" D. There are two different S mint marks and three for the D on the Peace dollars. In several instances more than one was used in the same year.

Q: Please explain the two types of mint marks on the 1979- and 1981-S mint proof coins.

The two varieties of mint marks occur on all six coins in the sets, although you may see only mention of those on the SBA dollar.

1979 Type I

1979 Type II

1981 Type I

1981 Type II

In both 1979 and 1981, the letter punch used to punch the mint marks into the dies broke. As a result it was necessary to make new punches, which did not match the previous ones, so two different style "S" mint marks show on coins for both years. The punches were used for all six coins in the sets, so it isn't just the Anthony dollars that were affected. In both years the Type II mint marks are the rarer and more valuable.

For convenience we list the prices for a set with all six of one of the two types of mint marks, but the approximate value of a mixed set can be determined by adding up the values of the individual coins which are usually listed in our classified ads. You will require a magnifier in order to be able to see the exact differences on the coins.

Q: Do you have any idea how many of the 1979-S and 1981-S proof coins were struck with the variety II mint marks?

The official U.S. Mint estimates for the Variety II "S" mint mark proof coins for 1979 and 1981 are:

Denomination	1979-S Mintage	1981-S Mintage
Cent	829,000	599,000
Nickel	668,000	498,000
Dime	737,000	623,000
Quarter	624,000	922,000
Half Dollar	428,000	314,000
Dollar	425,000	330,000

Q: Just how rare is the 1916-D dime with repunched mint mark?

As with almost any minting variety, there are no exact numbers to work with, so estimates have to be made based on the numbers that are reported in the hobby. In this case, we do know that there are two dies with repunched mint marks for 1916-D dimes, and that there are four different reverse dies in all that have been identified, so in theory, half of the 1916-D dimes should show the repunch. Since the 1916-D dime is in itself a rarity, the two varieties with repunched mint marks are just that much rarer.

Q: Can you give me the exact numbers of the proof coins without mint marks that were minted in several different years after 1968? I've read several figures for some of them.

The only three proof coins without mint marks that there are reliable Mint estimates for are the 1970-S dimes, estimated at 2,200, the 1971-S nickels, estimated at 1,655, and the 1983-S dimes, estimated at 3,336. These figures were available because some of the coins were caught before they were shipped out, and they had the dies and die records. In the other cases, the dies had been destroyed by the time the mistake was discovered, so it was impossible to match the die with the coins. There are at least two dies involved for the 1983-S dime without mint mark.

No mintage figures are available for the 1968 and 1975 dimes, as they left the mint before the mistake was discovered. At least one dealer took advantage of this by claiming that only 25 of the 1968 no-S dimes had been struck, an obviously self-serving "estimate."

Q: Is there a gold half eagle variety similar to the 1922-D "No D" cent?

Examples of the 1916-S $5 gold half eagles exist which do not have a mint mark. So far as I know it has never been determined whether this was due to a filled die, or if they were struck with a die without a mint mark like the recent proof coins.

Q: Why is there so much stress on the "large" and "small" mint marks on the 1945-S dimes, when there are numerous other examples that are ignored?

The '45-S dimes got all the publicity, and the glory, with the nickname "micro" S dime. Collectors are human, and they head for the brightest lights and the loudest noise. If the other varieties had received the same amount of publicity, they too would be sought after.

Q: I have several coins that I bought several years ago which have tilted mint marks, and some out of the normal position (low and high, etc.) Are they worth more today?

Unless you paid face value for them, they are probably worth less, as minor tilts and mint mark locations are too common to have any collector value. If the mint mark is tilted more than 45 degrees, repunched, or touching some other part of the design, then the collectors will be interested. The mint marks are punched into the dies for circulation coins with a letter punch and a mallet, and can vary over a wide area, depending on the eye and hand of the engraver. These variations are common and high mintage, so they have no collector value. On all U.S. coins minted prior to 1983, the mint mark was added to the die by hand after the hubbing process used to make the die was completed. Since the mint mark was added later, it of course cannot be hub doubled. Beginning in 1983 with the commemoratives, and in 1985 for the proof versions of our circulating coins, the mint mark was added to the hub, so it can be hub doubled like any other part of the design on those coins. Further, in 1990 the mint mark was added to the hubs for the circulating cent and nickel, and in 1991 to the other coins, so after these dates the mint mark can be hub doubled. However, as before, the vast majority of doubling you will find is machine doubling damage, the result of die bounce after the coin was struck. This kind of doubling is worthless to collectors.

1943/1942-P nickel overdate.

Q: Is there more than one variety of the 1943/1942-P nickel overdate? I've seen pictures of some labeled as overdates that are different from the ones originally reported.

There is only one die with the overdate, so only one variety. There are several dies with somewhat similar markings that are heavy die scratches, at least one of which has been accidentally labeled as the overdate in the past. On the true overdate die, even in the lowest grades, you can identify the base of the 2 across the lower loop of the 3, as well as the clear diagonal running up toward the lower edge of the center point of the 3. The die scratch on the false overdate runs more vertically, from the lower tip of the 3 to a point in front of the center tip.

Q: What's the "reverse of 1838-O" referred to in your charts for the 1839-O dime?

I've answered this question several times in the past, quoting Kamal Ahwash that the 1838-O die can be identified by some prominent rust spots. However, Walter Breen had the correct answer in his encyclopedia. The mint mark used for the 1838-O reverse is a large round O, while that used for the 1839-O is either a tall narrow O or a small round O. The "extremely rare" 1839-O dime with the 1838 reverse shows a large round O which is 1.2 mm tall. The more common varieties have either a tall narrow O or a small round O which is only 0.8 mm tall. The rusted die is instead a variety of the 1838-O No Stars date.

Q: The mintage for the 1823/22 dime is listed at 440,000 for both overdates, but the mintage for 1822 is only 100,000. How can an overdate have a larger mintage than the total for the date?

The 1823/22 dimes are from different dies than the 1822 dimes, so there is no connection between the two mintage figures. It's simply a case of unused dies which were left over, repunched and used in 1823. The same would be true of almost any other overdate, as there are only rare instances where a die was used to strike coins and then repunched with a different date. Even then the figures are separate. These are considered to be 1823 coins, not 1822, as the 1823 is on top of the 22.

Q: Who was the discoverer of the 1880/79-CC overdate dollar?

Veteran dealer Harry Forman reportedly discovered the overdate in 1964. Since then, several dies for the date have been identified as overdates.

Q: Is the 1942/1941-D dime from the same hub as the 1942/1941-P overdate?

Two hubs were used to produce this overdate, one with the 1941 date for the first impression, and the second impression was with a hub dated 1942. However, at least one of the hubs was not the same for the Denver die, since the positioning of the overdate is different than it is on the Philadelphia die.

Q: Are there any U.S. dies which were used in one year to strike coins, and then repunched to use them in a subsequent year, producing an overdate?

Our sources list three such dies, all from the same year. In 1806 single dies for the quarter, half dollar, and quarter eagle were retained from 1805 production, and were repunched or recut for use in 1806, giving us the three overdates for that year.

Q: Please settle an argument in our local club. One side says that all overdates are "errors," while the others say that some are intentional. Who is right?

When we can get "Quantum Leap" to schedule a visit to a mint on the day and hour that a particular die was overdated, we could answer the question with some certainty. Being non-clairvoyant and unable to travel in time, we have to guess at the cause in many instances, but we can come down firmly on the side of those who cite several possible causes for overdates. There are some that are done by accident. There are others (probably most) that are done for the specific purpose of salvaging an expensive die for further use, or to press an available die into service while new ones are made. I'm afraid the proponents of the "everything's an error" theory will have to retreat in confusion on this one.

Q: Several experts in the past have stated that various overdates are "die cracks" or "die breaks." Care to comment?

In most cases these comments trace back to the days when the minting process was still a mystery even to the most knowledgeable of experts, although it was repeated by a latter day "expert," not much more than a decade ago when the 1943/1942-P nickel overdate was first discovered. Among those damned by the pundits of the day were the 1918/1917-S quarter, and even Newcomb called the 1839/6 cent a "die crack." Much more frequent though is the (still) common practice of calling overdate hubbing varieties "recut."

Q: You've said several times in response to questions that visual inspection of coins at the various U.S. mints went out in the 1960s. Does that statement still stand?

As far as I can determine it does, at least as far as the coins are concerned. The minting process now depends in great part on "riddlers," which are vibrating screens which catch the under- and oversize planchets and coins. However, at least in the early stages of the switch to the copper-plated zinc planchets in 1982, they revived the belt inspection for the unstruck planchets. 10,000 out of every 600,000 planchets coming from the private supply company were put on the belt and visually inspected.

Q: Is there any factual basis for the claim that 200 silver quarters and 60 silver dimes were minted with 1965 dates?

Absolutely none for the specific figures. However, there were a very small number of both denominations struck by accident, the so-called "transition" coins. There are probably less than a dozen of either denomination. These have typically sold for around $1,500.

Q: Did the Secret Service ever seize any of the 1943 cents struck on brass planchets?

I have been unable to find any documented instance of a seizure by the Secret Service, although threats of such action were made with considerable frequency after the first one was discovered in 1947. The Mint flatly refused at first to either admit having made a mistake or having struck anything but steel cents in 1943, part of the long running effort to convince the public that the Mint was infallible, which continued well into the 1970s. As a result of the threats, the genuine brass strikes were not publicized by their owners, allowing the con artists to produce thousands of altered date and copper plated steel coins with which to bilk the public. The first check anyone should run on a supposed brass 1943 cent is to test it with a magnet. If attracted, it is a plated steel cent, and worth only face value.

Q: Please explain the method of applying the "rolled edge" to the 1907 eagle $10 gold coins?

The coins have a beveled edge, rather than the square cornered edge with wire rim found on other gold coins. The difference is due only to the different shape of the die surface. "Rolled" is a misnomer, although over the years many attempts have been made to alter (other denomination) coins by actually rolling them through a die to round the edge.

Q: What's a "witness line?"

A witness line is a raised ridge of metal on the edge (not the rim) of the coin, at right angles to the edge. It is extruded between the segments of an edge die as a result of the pressure exerted by the dies in striking the coin. A segmented edge die is one which is separated into three or more pieces. The segments are mounted so that they can be forced against the edge of the planchet, usually by hydraulic pressure as the dies hit the planchet.

Q: I have a lettered edge early cent which has the edge lettering upside down in relation to the obverse. How could this have happened?

The planchet undoubtedly was normally processed through the Castaing machine, but at that point the planchets were dropped into a bucket or some similar container to be transported to the coin press. No special effort was made to make sure the planchets were right side up when they were struck so the appearance of the edge lettering in relation to the obverse of the coin is a random occurrence. This is true of almost all edge lettering methods other than the use of the steel ring, or the edge dies which are hydraulically pressed into the planchet as the coin is being struck by the die pair. Over the years this random relationship has repeatedly been questioned by collectors, but there never has been any proof advanced that it was other than a coincidental matter.

Q: Are there 1795 cents with reeded edges?

There are examples with part of the edge reeded, and at least six specimens are known with full reeding. They are the result of experiments at the Mint that year with the idea of reeding the coins rather than lettering the edges, using a Castaing machine.

Q: I have a 1964-D dime, which has been examined by several dealers who tell me it is a proof. Can this be true?

It is unlikely that your '64-D dime is a proof, as the information that proof coins were struck only at Philadelphia that year is correct. What you may have is a first strike from new dies, which often will have an appearance similar to a proof. Send the coin to an authentication service if you are still in doubt.

Q: Going through a lot of cents, I notice that a number have weak or missing letters in STATES OF or the E, and sometimes the dot in E PLURIBUS. What causes this?

This is a frequent question, since such defects are readily noticed. That very frequency is an indication that these coins have no value, because of the high mintages involved. The cause is poor die design, a perennial failing of U.S. coins, which allows too much metal to flow into the obverse design, not leaving enough to come up in the reverse design. If you check the wheat cents you will find the same weakness on the O in ONE on a high percentage of the coins.

STATES OF is weak on many cents because it is opposite the bust of Lincoln and there isn't enough coin metal to fill the design on both sides of the coin. The lower portion of the Lincoln bust is both the largest and deepest cavity in the die, so most of the flow is into that particular part of the die. Over the years the Mint has tinkered many times with the dies to solve this problem, by reducing the relief of the bust, changing the slope of the field, etc., but the usual result has been to move the weakly struck area around rather than correcting it. Because this is a very high mintage minting variety, they are too common to have any special collector value.

Q: Would you please describe the three dies that produced the 1922 "plain" cent?

In brief, no cents were struck at Philadelphia in 1922. At least three dies were used at Denver which produced 1922 cents with a missing "D" mint mark, or else various stages of a weak or broken "D." The authenticators at the American Numismatic Association determined that dies number 1 and 3 were quite worn when the mint mark began to disappear, going through cycles where the letter filled with dirt and grease. The hardened filling would fall out, only to reform. The filled die strikes resulted in the weak or missing "D," but on such an irregular basis that neither of these dies are recognized. The number 2 die clashed and was repaired by abrading the field in the mint mark area, cutting the field away until the D disappeared. Every coin struck by this die after the repairs is missing the mint mark. This die can be identified and authenticated because the second 2 in the date is sharper than the first 2. The letters in TRUST are sharp and WE is only slightly mushy. The reverse is sharp, because a new reverse die was matched with the repaired obverse. On both the 1 and 3 dies, the second 2 is weaker than the first 2. Die pair number 1 has a die crack down through the O in ONE and the reverse is very weak. Die pair number 3 usually has a slight rotation of the reverse die.

Q: My Washington commemorative half dollar has an S instead of an 8 in the date. What's the story?

Your coin is from a die which has been heavily abraded, taking off enough of the surface to "break" the lines of the 8 and make it appear to be an S. Like almost all abrasion varieties, the mintages are too high to have any significant value. In this and most cases of abrasion varieties, a number of dies had the same problem.

The conversion of the 8 into an S is an ideal example of what abrasion can do to a coin die. The 8 does not have the same relief all over, so when the surface of the die is abraded away, the lowest relief disappears, "breaking" the 8 and making it look like an S. This could also occur if the hub was not driven fully into the die during the die-making process. As a result there are thousands of both proof and uncirculated versions of the Washington half with 19S2 for a date.

Q: Weren't there actually three different date sizes for the 1960 cents—a small, medium, and a large date?

This is another situation akin to the problems with the different mint marks on the 1979 and 1981 proof coins. Shortly after the small date 1960 and 1960-D cents were first reported, enthusiastic collectors reported that there were three sizes, and for a time the medium dates were advertised right along with the small. Later it was conclusively proved, based on mint records, that only two different size dates were used for 1960. The so-called medium date was merely a large date die which had been heavily abraded, altering the shape and appearance of the digits. This is something that happens to a number of dies every year and is generally ignored, but it attracted attention because of the excitement over the discovery of the small dates.

Q: I've heard that there is a $1,000 reward for a certain variety of the 1964 nickels. I have one, so will you get the reward for me please?

I'm sorry to disappoint you, but I know of no variety of any kind in the minting of specifically the 1964 or 1964-D nickels that is worth $1,000, or even a significant fraction of that figure. The only one I can think of offhand is the PLURIDUS variety, attributed by the Mint to die abrasion, which is worth upward of $50 to $75, depending on the grade. I don't know of any legitimate offer of a "reward" for coin varieties either.

Q: Some time ago you mentioned that the so-called "poor man's double die" was an abrasion variety, yet at one time it brought some pretty hefty prices didn't it?

"Once upon a time" is the story of this coin. It is an abrasion variety, doubling the last 5 on a 1955 cent, sometimes both 5s, but it is no relation to the real doubled-die variety for 1955, and is too common to be worth more than a few cents. However, as you have discovered, before the real cause of the 1955 doubled-die cent was well-known, anything that faintly resembled it was sold by coin dealers for anything the market would bear. One source claims that the abrasion doubling 5/5 sold for as much as $400, but I could just about guarantee that less than a handful were ever sold at that price, even given the general lack of knowledge in the hobby. The difference in spelling is key to the difference in value—a double die is almost worthless, while a doubled-die variety may be worth hundreds or thousands of dollars.

Q: What is meant by a "Bugs Bunny" half dollar?

"Bugs Bunny" is a nickname or slang term for a die clash which appears across Benjamin Franklin's mouth on the half dollars, giving him the appearance of having buck teeth. The die clash is damage to the die from its hitting the opposing die without a planchet between them. This damage from the reverse design is then transferred onto the struck coins. It occurs on any date or mint for the Franklin halves, but the 1955 date got all the publicity.

The so-called "Bugs Bunny" 1955 Franklin half dollars were a very popular minting variety in the 1960s and at the time were selling for $10 to $20 each. Today they would probably still bring a small premium, but not too many of today's collectors are even aware of them. It's been incorrectly called everything from a die flaw to die "suction" over the years.

Q: I have a dateless Type I Standing Liberty quarter. I've been told there is a way of telling the difference between the 1916 design and the 1917 by one of the folds in Liberty's gown—but which fold?

The marker, if you like exercises in futility, is this: The 1916 has the big toe of Miss Liberty's right foot (viewer's left) protruding slightly beyond the front edge of the exergue, and the gown touches the right side of that foot (again viewer's left). The bottom fold is nearly straight, where it is curved on the 1917. On that date the gown does not touch the foot. When you are done, remember that, if dateless, the coins are worth only bullion value.

Q: In your catalog listings you mention that 1976 dated coins with minting varieties carry a premium over other dates. How about my Kennedy half with missing letters or stars under the building on the reverse?

Weak or missing letters and stars under the building on the reverse of the 1976 half dollars are due to faulty die design. Too much of the coin metal is going into the Kennedy bust on the obverse, so there isn't enough to complete the reverse design. This is a common problem with almost all 20th century U.S. coins, causing weak or missing reverse design elements. Because it is so common, it rarely has any numismatic value. The rarity factor for 1976 coins doesn't apply to the high mintage varieties like this.

Q: Will you please identify the difference in the two types of Ike dollars for 1976?

This is currently at the top of our list of most asked questions, perhaps an indication of some new interest in the last of the cartwheels. The system is very simple: the Type I Ikes have thick, round letters "O" in the reverse lettering. The Type II has tall, thin oval letters "O." There are other differences but this is the easy one to spot. All 40 percent silver are the Type I.

TYPE I   TYPE II

Examples of the Ike Dollar.
The Type I Ikes have thick, round letters "O" in the reverse lettering.
The Type II has tall, thin oval letters "O."

Q: I have several coins, some of which are greenish, and some a golden hue. Would this increase the value of the coins?

Surface discoloration in itself is not classed as a minting variety, and it has no value. If there is a marked change in color along with an indication of a division or separation between the coin metal and a different piece of metal rolled or struck into the surface, then that is a different story. I suspect the greenish hue may be due to contact with PVC, which will do permanent damage to the coins. The golden hue could be anything. Even if the coin is discolored in the mint there is no way of proving it.

Q: Is there any chance that the Mint would deliberately strike additional examples of some rare new variety after it appears? I see from your news stories that they have duplicated some of the hubbing varieties.

The duplication occurs only under test conditions in the Mint and is done only to determine exactly how a given variety occured, so that corrective measures can be taken to prevent it from recurring. There are no provisions—or intentions—for purposely issuing minting varieties.

Q: I have a coin with a partial date or missing letters. What is it worth?

This continues to be on of my most frequent questions in the incoming mail as missing design is something even the untrained eye spots readily. A filled die is the usual cause, the result of dirt, grease and metal fragments sticking to the die, plugging the incuse design in the face of the die. This "goop" will leave fairly distinct markings on a coin, but they are similar to marks associated with wear and even deliberate damage, so they are not always easy to distinguish from other causes. This is why we established two mandatory rules for filled die varieties. One is that to have value the coin must be an uncirculated, current coin and the other is that the entire design element must be missing, even under low (10X) magnification. Beyond that the value would depend on several factors, ranging from the denomination to the particular design element that is missing, as for example there would be more collector interest in a missing date digit or mint mark (such as the 1987-1994 quarters with missing mint marks) than in missing tail feathers on the eagle or a missing star. Missing design due to abrasion of the die is a completely different matter as well.

Q: Where can I get a list of minting varieties to look for?

There isn't any such list available, simply because it would cost too much to compile it and would have only a limited market. More important is learning what, rather than which, to look for, as most minting varieties repeat year after year at every mint. Once you've learned what the different varieties look like you are well on the way. The most recent listing of all of the classes and some of the values was in the latest edition of *North American Coins and Prices*. For the classics get a copy of *The Cherrypicker's Guide to Rare Die Varieties, 3rd edition*, by Bill Fivaz and J.T. Stanton, from Bill Fivaz, Box 888660, Dunwoody, GA 30338.

Q: Please explain the difference between a double strike and a doubled die?

A double strike means that the coin was struck twice by a pair of dies, and (usually) will show equal doubling on both sides of the coin. A doubled die is one die, which has part or all of the design doubled in the die making process, and imparts this doubling to one side of a coin during the (single) strike.

Most novices refer to any form of doubling as a "double strike," but there are at least 20 different forms of doubling which can occur from either a doubled die or from some sort of mis-strike, only one of those forms being a double strike.

Q: How do I tell whether I have a near or far date 1979-P SBA dollar?

To confirm which variety you have, remember that all 1979-D and 1979-S dollars have the far date, while all of the dollars from all three mints struck after 1979 have the near date. Compare the location of the date with one or the other, as rim widths not only may vary, they are easily mistaken for each other. Rim width may vary for several reasons, ranging from a spread out hub, to a weak hubbing, a worn die, or a weak or strong strike. Thus it is not a valid marker. Out of the total 79-P mintage, the Mint estimated that they struck "up to" 160,750,000 dollars with the date closer to the rim, slightly less than half the year's production. The near date variety has been scarce because nearly all of the coins are still buried in the Treasury vaults, but in recent months bag quantities of the near dates have been reported. As far as value, near date MS-60 specimens were selling in the $10 to $15 range.

The example above is a 1979 Anthony dollar near date;
on the right, a 1979 Anthony dollar far date.

Q: My 1864 two-cent piece shows about a 40-degree rotation of the reverse die. Can you tell me anything about it?

A substantial number of the 1864 two-cent coins were struck with rotated reverses, so they do not carry much of a premium. We generally quote $1 to $2 extra for lower grade coins, and $10 to $25 extra for higher grades. As a rule, rotated reverse dies are much more common in the 1800s than in the modern coins.

Q: I spotted a description of a coin as having a "completely turned" reverse. Another has "zero rotation." What did this mean?

Either someone was adept at leg pulling, or was not saying exactly what he meant. A completely turned (rotated) reverse would be right back at the starting point, in a normal position. This comes out like the "100 percent off center strike." What I think the description was supposed to mean was that the reverse was turned 180 degrees, or upside down to its normal position, but there is no way to be sure at this point.

Q: I have a 1975 proof Ike dollar with a dull surface on one side. How can this happen?

I'd been trying to answer this question for a decade, and finally found the answer by accident during my visit to the Royal Mint in England. The planchet for the coin stuck to a second one, and they went through (most of) the polishing process stuck together. It later was struck normally, with one "proof side" and one dull side.

Q: I have a current cent which has a strong raised ridge under the letters in the obverse motto. What is the cause?

Your coin has been struck with an obverse die which "sank" along the inside of the rim. This occurs when the die isn't properly heat treated, and the constant pounding pushes the die face down, leaving a corresponding raised ridge on the coin. It is technically a worn or damaged die, so has no particular value to the collector.

Q: I say that an off-center strike cent is a "one-of-a-kind" piece, thus is rare and should be worth quite a bit. Am I right?

An off-center cent is unique, with none other exactly like it. This is a characteristic of striking varieties—each one different, but there may be thousands of similar pieces. For that reason off-center strikes rarely are worth more than a few cents to a few dollars, depending on the denomination and grade of the coin. A die variety, in contrast, has hundreds or thousands of identical coins, because a die variety repeats exactly until there is some change in the die.

Q: What are Type I and II Indian Head cents?

The two varieties of the 1886 are of equal value, so there is no incentive to try to sell them, and consequently they get little publicity or notice. They depend on feather position for identification. On the Type I the last feather points between IC in AMERICA, struck from 1859 to 1886. For the Type II the last feather points between CA, found on the cents from 1886 through 1909. By comparing an earlier and a later date you can find the difference. Mintages for the two varieties in 1886 were about evenly divided, so there is no particular premium for either variety.

Q: Would you please list the varieties of the 1982 large and small date, brass and zinc cents please? I've seen conflicting lists, and I'm confused.

This is correct: There are no small date brass cents from Denver. The varieties that are found are the large and small date brass cents without mint marks, the Denver large date brass, the large and small date zinc cents without mint marks or with the D for Denver, plus the proof, which is a brass large date. This makes eight. The 1982 production began with the large date dies, and the change to the small date dies was made at differing times through the year. At Denver, there was a one week gap in production between the brass and zinc cents, and the small date dies were not introduced until the zinc production began. The brass small date was never struck, as production of brass stopped a week before small date dies were introduced. No small date 1982 brass cent with a D mint mark has ever been reported.

Q: Why isn't the 1958/7 cent overdate still listed in the popular catalogs?

I first identified it as an overdate, but after extensive research, Del Romines determined that the markings were lathe marks on the die, rather than being an overdate, so the listing has been dropped.

Q: I've noticed recently that several recent date cents seem to have little raised dots all over them. Is this normal?

For the copper plated zinc cents, yes. The official answer is that the bubbles under the plating are due to dirt or impurities on the surface of the zinc as it is being plated. The result has been that our coins have been struck on some of the best scrubbed planchets in history. The bubbles are the result of contamination on the planchet under the plating, which causes the zinc to corrode. If you open one of the bubbles you will find a whitish zinc oxide pushing the copper up. These have no collector value.

Q: I have a 1970-D quarter which appears to be much thinner than normal, and poorly struck. Any special value?

These are still turning up in circulation, after a several-year pause. They are some of the famous "dime stock" quarters struck at Denver on planchets shipped from San Francisco, which had been punched from dime thickness stock, to normal quarter diameter. The pieces will weigh about 65 grains, and an uncirculated specimen should bring around $20 these days.

Q: I have a number of supposed "small date" 1970-S cents which I found (purchased) over the years, but I still can't tell for sure whether they are the right coins. Can you help?

Many collectors and dealers find it difficult to distinguish the variety, since there is no visible difference in the size of the date. A simple pair of markers will help. The level 7 (Type of 1971) "small" date has the tip of the loop of the 9 bent sharply in toward the stem, and the left side of the stem of the 7 is straight. On the low 7 (Type of 1970) "large" date, the tip of the loop points down at about a 45-degree angle and the left side of the stem of the 7 is curved. The location, size, or shape of the mint mark has nothing to do with either variety. For direct comparison, all P&D 1970 cents have the low 7 date, and all 1971 (and later) PD&S have the level 7 date. Problems affecting the LIBERTY are NOT a valid marker for either variety.

The cent on the left is considered a "small date."
The one on the right is a "large date."

Q: Can you tell me the story behind the STATESOFAMERICA varieties of 1814 and 1820 dimes, with the three words run together?

Walter Breen describes the coins of both years as being from a single die, which later was sold for scrap. Coin dealer Robert Bashlow used the die in Scotland to strike some 536 impressions, some uniface and some with a fantasy obverse with GOD PRESERVE PHILADELPHIA AND THE LORDS PROPRIETERS 1869 M. A wide variety of metals were used, from platinum to lead. These pieces were seized by U.S. Customs and destroyed, and Treasury agents seized the dies in Scotland. The agents destroyed the historic die, assuming that it was as "counterfeit" as the fantasy pieces, despite frantic efforts by Dr. Clain-Stefanelli to obtain the die for the Smithsonian collection.

Q: Are there any examples of private gold coins struck over U.S. gold?

Not very many, but there are two Clark, Gruber & Co. pieces, both $20, struck on U.S. Mint coins. One of the 1861 $20 is on an 1857-S double eagle, and the other is struck over an 1849 $10 eagle. More examples of Territorial gold struck on U.S. coins include the Parsons & Co. $2.50, struck on an 1850-O half dime, of which there are "two or three known." There is also a Parsons $2.50 on an 1836 dime. Both were in the Kosof sale November 4-6, 1985.

Q: What is meant by a "copper wash" on a coin, as listed in a dealer's catalog?

This is a misnomer which has crept into the hobby. In the past, experts blamed the copper color sometimes appearing on nickel or even silver coins as coming from the acidic (or soapy) bath which the planchets pass through to clean them after they are annealed. However, there is no way that this could occur and affect only an occasional coin in the bath. It instead traces to bronze or brass powder which is sintered by heat onto the surface of subsequent planchets as they pass through the annealing drum, the odd planchet sticking long enough to get a coating, and in rare instances getting a measurable layer of sintered powder.

If the "wash" occurred in the bath, there would be substantial quantities of copper-colored coins, far more than are found. Another problem is that a very thin sintered layer can be duplicated with a little effort by plating the piece, requiring expensive analysis to determine if the coating was in place before the strike.

Q: It is said that the breaking of a crucible was the cause for halting the production of the Mormon gold coins. Why would this make any difference?

A crucible was a vessel made of fired clay which was used to hold the metal being smelted or alloyed, capable of withstanding the very high temperatures needed to melt the metal. It was not an item found just anywhere, especially in the West, and there was no way that it could be patched or another made.

Q: Just what year was it that the Mint struck cents in aluminum? I have several cents with different dates and all of them appear to be on some metal other than copper.

If you had an aluminum cent, you would know it, just by the weight. The Mint struck a quantity of aluminum cents on a trial basis with 1974 dates and then destroyed all but about a dozen that disappeared in the halls of Congress. Not one of the missing coins has turned up. The 1974 aluminum cents weighed about 14.5 grains, or slightly less than one gram. In contrast, the brass cents up to 1982 weighed 48.0 grains and the copper plated zinc cents from 1982 on weigh 38.6 grains. If your cents are all normal size and weight with full strikes, and round, then they undoubtedly have been plated after leaving the Mint.

Q: When did the U.S. Mint start chrome plating its dies?

The first evidence of the use of chrome plated dies at the United States Mint is back in 1928. Then, as now, the purpose was to improve the wearing qualities of the dies. However, I believe that the chroming was discontinued shortly after 1928, and not resumed until 1974 when the proof quarter, half, and dollar dies were chromed. The chrome plating work on the proof dies was done outside the Mint.

Q: Were all dies completed at Philadelphia in the early days before shipment to the branch mints, as they are now?

Before the days of mass production, the dies were shipped out in rough form, but with the design impressed. The individual mints machined the die shanks to fit their particular coin presses, and then hardened the die and polished the face. All of this work is now done at Philadelphia. Proof dies are made at Philadelphia, then polished and prepared for use at San Francisco. However, there have been times in the past when the work on some dies has been done by outside firms, including some of the commemorative coin dies.

Q: What part of the coin is the collar?

From my mail there are quite a few collectors who are confused by the different names for parts of the coin, and it's one part of a serious overall problem. The collar is not a part of the coin at all. It is a heavy steel plate with a hole in it, which is part of the coin press. It surrounds the planchet when it is struck by the die pair, forming the edge of the coin, either smooth as on the cent or nickel, or reeded as on the dime, quarter, and half dollar. Edge and rim are two parts of the coin that are frequently confused with the collar. The edge means the surface at right angles to the faces of the coin, while the rim is the raised area surrounding the faces on each side of the coin, next to the edge.

Q: Are there any coins with multiple flat edges which have edge inscriptions?
Undoubtedly there are foreign coins, but a U.S. example would be the Augustus Humbert $50 slugs which were octagonal (8 sides) with an edge inscription reading: "AUGUSTUS HUMBERT UNITED STATES ASSAYER OF GOLD 1851."

Q: What causes the narrow spots on the edge of a coin?
It's a recurring problem, as the metal goes into the design instead. It can be caused by differences in striking pressure, or the way the dies are set up in the coin press. Differences on the same coin usually trace to a part of the design (top of Lincoln's head or base of bust) being too close to the edge of the coin, so that metal intended for the edge is diverted into the central design. This is a perennial problem for the U.S. Mint and one that is often difficult to explain to the layman. Die alignment can also affect the thickness of the edge.

Q: What is a wire edge on a coin, such as is listed for some of the U.S. gold coins?
A wire edge is a raised, thin flange of coin metal at right angles to the outside edge of the rim, caused by the striking pressure squeezing it out between the edge of the die and the collar. It is also called a knife edge, but in most cases it resembles a thin piece of wire at the juncture of the rim and edge of the coin, hence the name. It is typically found on proof coins which are struck twice.

Q: What is the sequence in which the two sides and the reeded edge of a coin are formed?
There is a very common misconception that only one side of a coin is struck at a time, but to do this would violate some very basic laws of physics. Simply put, you can't strike just one side of anything. The coin is struck by a pair of dies while resting in a reeded collar, so both sides and the reeded edge are formed by the single stroke of the dies. Proof coins are struck two or more times to bring up all of the design. Paper money is a different story, as U.S. notes are printed in three separate operations, first the back, then the face, then the overprint of the seals and serial numbers.

Chapter 37

MISCELLANEOUS

Despite the number of chapters into which I separated these questions, there were a number that just didn't fit anywhere else. I guess that's what miscellaneous is all about.

Q: Somewhere I saw something about a passbook savings account that will be worth one quintillion dollars. Do you have the facts on that?

The passbook is in a helium-filled stainless steel time capsule at Amarillo, Texas. It was a $10 savings account, drawing four percent interest. The capsule is to be opened in 2968. By then the account will be worth $1,000,000,000,000,000. Congress must have this in mind, because the proceeds are payable to the U.S. Treasury, and can be used to pay off the national debt. The 1,000 year capsule is one of four to be opened at varying intervals. The 25 year capsule was scheduled to be opened in 1993.

Q: I search through a lot of circulated coins, and I have found several quarters with red paint or nail polish on them. Is there some special purpose for defacing them?

The coins you have found are known as "shill" or "house" coins, which are used to feed a jukebox to encourage customers to pick out their favorite songs. These coins normally are sorted out when the coin box is emptied and returned to the owner of the establishment, so the ones you found either were accidentally included in a bank deposit, or perhaps stolen. Some years ago in New Jersey a protest group put red paint on quarters to protest an increase in the highway toll rates. They were used by house employees in some Nevada casinos as well.

Q: What is the history of the portrait known as the "Silver Queen?"

In a tavern in Virginia City, Nevada there's a painting of a woman whose dress is decorated with 3,261 silver dollars. Her belt is made of 28 $20 gold coins, and her bracelets and necklace are silver quarters. About 900 more silver dollars are used for the border of the 8'x15' picture designed by Carroll and Ruby Easton.

Q: Can you repeat the poem about silver dollars?

I don't know the author, but here's the poem:

> "Oh give me a big silver dollar to throw on the bar with a bang.
> A dollar all creased may do in the East,
> But we like our money to clang!"

Q: I'm curious as to how many towns there are in the United States which have names having to do with coins or money?

While I doubt that this list is complete, one source lists these: Cash, in Illinois, South Carolina, and Texas; Cash Money, Florida; Cash Point, Louisiana; Cash Corner, North Carolina; Dollar, Oregon; Dollar Bay, Michigan; Dollar Junction, Alabama; and Greenback and Greenback Junction, Pennsylvania. Then there's Cash and Dollarway, Arkansas; Cashiers, North Carolina; Cashtown, Pennsylvania; Dime Box, Dollar Bay, and Dinero, all in Texas; Dollar Ranch, California; Money, Maine; Money Order Unit, in Louisiana and Pennsylvania; Pence, in Wisconsin and Indiana; and Nickelsville, Virginia.

Chapter 38

MOTTOS, INSCRIPTIONS

Mottos and inscriptions on coins have always been important, from the very first coins right down to this year's issues. For ancient coins they provided a ready means of identification. On modern coins they are an expression of a nation's pride that broadcasts a message wherever they go.

Q: Where did our "E PLURIBUS UNUM" motto come from?

Dudley McClure traced the motto to the Roman poet, Virgil (70-19 B.C.E.) who used it in "Moretum," in the line "Deperdunt propias; color est E Pluribus Unum," referring to ingredients ground up with a mortar and pestle. The term was used to describe either a stew or a salad, made as one out of many ingredients. Curiously, it was used as a masthead slogan by a number of English newspapers of the early 1700s, which may well have been the indirect source of its appearance in the Great Seal and later on our coins. The motto was adopted to signify the joining of the 13 colonies into one nation.

Q: Recently you mentioned the mottos on U.S. coins, and skirted the issue of the autho-rization for the "E PLURIBUS UNUM." Would you please cite the law authorizing this motto on our coins?

The answer is that there was no law authorizing it in the beginning, although later laws incorporated it, after the fact. This may come as a surprise, but Congress never got around to including it in the law until the Coinage Act of 1873. The first U.S. coins to carry the motto were the silver dollars and $5 gold half eagles in 1795, where the motto appeared on the scroll with the heraldic eagle. The motto was used on the reverse of the 1796 $2.50, and on some of the silver coins in 1798, then was dropped from most gold in 1834 and from the silver in 1837. Earlier the motto had appeared on the Jefferson Great Seal of 1782, the New Jersey cents of 1786, and on the 1787 Brasher doubloons as PLURIBUS E UNUM. What it boils down to is that the motto was a discretionary matter for the mint director to decide up until the Act of 1873 which prescribed it for the coinage.

Q: Why is "The" missing from the inscription, "The United States of America," on our coins?

Section 10 of the Mint Act of April 2, 1792 says, "....with this inscription, 'UNITED STATES OF AMERICA,'...." Once this tradition was established, nobody saw any need to change it. Particularly in the early days when dies were hand made, they economized in every possible way, so perhaps this was another reason for not adding the extra three letters.

Q: Trick question—what four words appear on all U.S. coins?

Easy—"United States of America." If you said "IN GOD WE TRUST," I "gotcha!" because that didn't make our coins until the 1864 2-cent piece—a long time after we started striking coins. Go forth, and win a few bar bets among your unsuspecting friends.

Chapter 39

NOT LEGALLY ISSUED COINS

The government is particular about the coins that the Mint makes. If for some reason they don't meet with official approval, they are described as "not legally issued." As such, they are subject to confiscation on sight. Presently there are four modern coins that fit this proscription, the 1913 "V" nickel, the 1933 $20 gold piece, the 1964 Peace Dollar, and the 1884-85 Trade Dollars.

Q: What is the source of the story that there are six known 1913 Liberty Head nickels? I can account for only five.

Five is the correct number. The figure of six arises because when the estate of Col. E.H.R. Green was sold, it included six 1913 nickels. It was reported in that fashion, but one of the six coins was a 1913 Buffalo nickel, struck on copper, without the F designer's initial. This was ignored, or overlooked. The wrong number was given further credence when it was reported that the special holder made for the coins had six holes, rather than five, after the coins had been removed. The five Liberty Head 1913 nickels were in the six-hole holder when they were sold to Col. E.H.R. Green by dealer August Wagner. The "missing" piece has been the source of a myriad of rumors and thousands of disappointments as collectors spent countless hours searching, only to find badly damaged coins that "might" be a 1913 date, or one of the thousands of altered-date pieces. Presently only one of the five genuine pieces, made clandestinely at the U.S. Mint, is unaccounted for. It was stolen from George O. Walton, who was killed by the thief while on the way to a coin show. Authentication by a qualified expert is mandatory. Wishful thinking will not make a genuine coin out of a badly worn piece with an illegible date, so don't waste your time on the culls.

Q: A question about the "McDermott" specimen of the 1913 "V" nickel, which is listed as "Extremely Fine, nicked and scratched." Did this coin circulate?

For all practical purposes it did, as James V. McDermott for a time carried the coin loose in his pocket, used it for barroom bets, and generally treated it as a coin rather than as a collectible.

1913 V Nickel.

Q: Is there any way that the 1933 $20 gold could be made legal to collect?

The only way would be if a proof of purchase over the counter could be found, dated during the first three months of 1933.

Chapter 40

NOVELTY COINS

The category of so-called novelty coins includes a conglomeration of altered pieces that have been changed for any of a variety of reasons, greed included. Most are too common or too dubious to collect, but sooner or later they will join the ranks of collectible pieces.

Q: I have found a "hollow" cent. It has a perfectly normal reverse, but just a thin edge, and a hollow instead of the obverse. What happened?

Some magician spent his coin rather than keeping it for his act. Your coin has been altered by hollowing out a genuine cent. This is done to use in a magic trick where a dime is inserted in the hollow so that when turned over the coin appears to change from a cent to a dime. These can be purchased for about 50 cents in almost any magic supply or novelty store. Many of these coins have a thin steel disc glued in the bottom of the hole so that the piece can be moved about with a magnet for another trick.

Q: A friend showed me a half dollar which appeared to be in three pieces, because he could bend it. How did that get out of the mint?

When it left the mint it was a normal coin. Someone sawed it into sections, and probably cut a groove around the edge so that it is tied together with a spring or rubber band. Another form of "novelty" coin and not a mint product.

Q: I have a coin with two obverses, so it has the bust of Washington on both sides. I've been told it is very valuable, so what's it worth?

I'm sorry to disappoint you, but you have an altered coin, made by hollowing out one coin and cutting down a second to fit inside it. The joint can be found along the inside edge of the rim on one side. For the record, the U.S. Mint has never struck a coin with two obverses or two reverses (two-headed or two-tailed) for circulation, as it is physically impossible to match two such dies in a coin press. Several commercial companies make these altered coins by the thousands, so they have no significant collector value. The first commercial offer of the coins at retail I can find was in early 1967. However, don't use that as a "cutoff date" as numerous older coins were altered in this fashion later on, including Morgan dollars with a Peace dollar reverse. The first regular ads for the pieces described them as magician's coins, without indicating they had been altered. A quick check found a dealer ad dated 1972 offering two-headed cents for $1, nickels for $1.50, dimes for $1.95, quarters for $2.95, and Kennedy halves for $3.95.

Q: I discovered a coin in my change, a 1982 cent, which has President Kennedy facing Lincoln. Where was this minted?

The mail on these particular coins has shown a sharp increase recently, so apparently these pieces are beginning to show up in the hands of new collectors. The coin was altered after it was minted by adding the Kennedy design. There are also half dollars with Lincoln added. You will find literally hundreds of similar designs which have been added, such as a pipe or cigar for Lincoln to smoke, state maps, etc. These are classed as "novelty" coins, and have no numismatic value, or at best only a very minor value as a collectible. They became rather popular novelty items back in the 1970s, but few firms are still making them, so it is rare to find one on a recent cent. The best known, "Kennedy Looks at Lincoln," began appearing first on 1964 cents, although there may be examples on 1963 dated pieces. The big problem is a lack of any "mintage" figures, and the relative ease with which a "scarce" piece could be copied.

Chapter 41

PACKAGING, MINT PACKAGING

Q: I'm having an argument in my local coin club about whether a proof coin loses its status if it is taken out of the original packaging. I say it doesn't, but who is right?

You win the argument. A proof coin is a proof coin is a proof coin, period. The coin is what is a proof, not the packaging. There are thousands upon thousands of proof coins which were never packaged by any issuing authority, but this would hardly deny them proof status. Proof is a condition, not a grade, and a proof coin that has circulated or been damaged is still a proof, but classed as an impaired proof. Those who argue that the packaging makes the coin are the same ones that would only buy proof sets which were still in the original sealed shipping boxes from the mint a few years back. They kept that up until somebody got smart and started filling the boxes with newspapers and rocks. If they still want to argue, ask them to show you any listing, anywhere for any holder, case, or slab which is sold as a proof, but without the coin. Final argument. The mint makes the coin. They do NOT make the package, which means that nobody but the mint can make the proof coin, but ANYBODY can make the package it comes in.

Q: Please describe the packaging methods used for the early proof and mint sets from 1936 on.

For the proof sets, the coins were issued in individual cellophane envelopes, packed in a cardboard box from 1936 through early 1955. From 1955 to 1964 the sets were in pliofilm envelopes similar to current mint set packaging. Mint set coins from 1947 through 1958 were packaged in cardboard holders which tarnished the coins. The mint sets from 1959 on have been in the pliofilm packets.

Q: I have a mint set with a quarter instead of an SBA dollar. Is this a mint "error" and does it have any value?

It is a packaging mistake. Anyone with access to a plastic sealing machine can "issue" his own set. For almost any mixup in the coins I quote a nominal $1 premium. Even with proof sets it is possible to split the hard cases open and substitute coins. One proof set with the same switch you describe is known, and classed as a "practical joke" by someone on the packaging line.

Chapter 42

PAPER MONEY

The collecting of paper money, stocks, bonds, and other paper is one of the growth areas of the hobby. It's also of interest to coin collectors, whose collecting often jumps the boundaries into topics far from coins.

Q: Have the Barr notes ever gone up in value?

This single note probably draws more questions than almost any other that comes to mind. Joseph W. Barr served as Treasurer for 23 days in 1968-1969, his signature appearing only on the 1963-B series of $1 notes. However, a total of some 484 million notes were printed with his signature, so they are not likely to become even scarce in our lifetime.

There are two different figures that have been published for the regular Barr notes from the San Francisco District. Both figures can be found in reference works. The incorrect figure first appeared in 1970 when the Donlon catalog made the original mistake. Correct is 106.4 million. There were 471,040,000 regular notes printed with Barr's signature. In addition there were star (substitute) notes printed: 3,680,000 for the New York District, 3,040,000 for the Richmond District, 2,400,000 for the Chicago District, and 3,040,000 for the San Francisco District.

I've found at least two events which undoubtedly led up to the national mania for saving the notes signed by Barr. One was a widely published statement by Leonard W. Stark, a Chicago coin dealer, who claimed the 1963-B notes were "difficult" to find. The other was a story published in a hobby publication of the day which implied that the notes were very scarce and would become valuable. The story was printed on the false assumption that notes with his signature were only printed for 23 days. Actually the plates with his signature were used for six months after he left office.

A $1 Barr note deposited in an interest bearing account in 1969 would be worth over $4 today, figuring 6 percent interest compounded annually. A circulated Barr note kept in a safety deposit box for 26 years is worth $1 today.

Q: My handwriting is bad enough, but who signed the 1875 U.S. Notes?

The signature is that of John C. New, Treasurer from June 30, 1875 to July, 1876. His scrawl would be classed as an example of cacography, the Victorian term for bad handwriting.

Q: What was the purpose of exchanging Silver Certificates for silver and when did the redemption of Silver Certificates stop?

The government offered to redeem the Silver Certificates in order to replace them with Federal Reserve Notes. Issue of the $10 Silver Certificates ended on March 14, 1962. The last $5 notes were issued on April 25, 1962. Both were the 1953-B series. The last $1 notes went out on November 6, 1963, the 1957-B series.

In 1967 the Treasury agreed to redeem Silver Certificates for bullion, granules, or bars at the official exchange rate of $1 for .77 ounce of silver. When the ceiling on silver prices was removed May 1967, it went from $1.29 an ounce to as high as $2.17 and to $2.58 in 1968. The redemption period ended June 24, 1968 with $150 million turned in. This left some $240 million still in circulation. Many people ignored the end of the redemption period and kept their notes, assuming that redemption would be renewed. As history tells us, it was not.

If you have a quantity of Silver Certificates, or even just a few pieces, by all means get them checked. Many of the circulated and worn notes carry no premium over face value, despite the big redemption. You are losing a serious amount of interest by holding them. Crisp uncirculated Silver Certificates with no folds do carry at least a small premium even in the last series so those should be retained.

A $1 Silver Certificate stating "One dollar in silver payable to the bearer on demand."

Q: Is it legal to own a printing plate for Confederate money?

Apparently not. Maurice Gould once owned a Confederate printing plate which had been made in England and was captured by the North from a blockade runner. When Gould made an inquiry about the plate it was seized by the Secret Service and never returned.

Q: What do stars in the serial numbers on a note mean? Are they worth collecting?

The star in the serial number of your note indicate that it was specially printed as a replacement note, used to replace defective notes, which are pulled out by inspectors before they are shipped from the Bureau of Engraving and Printing to the Federal Reserve Banks. A star note is also used for the final note in a 100 million note run, as the numbering machine only has eight digits. For current series there are usually large numbers of star notes. In some of the older series they command a premium over the regular notes, because only a few stars were printed.

Q: What's the story on the K-11 notes that predicted President Kennedy's assassination?

Rumors abounded after his death that the Dallas Federal Reserve District notes with K-11 on them "warned" of the impeding shooting. There is no basis in fact as the K-11 is the designation of the 11th Federal Reserve District, which has its headquarters at Dallas. The K is the letter designating the 11th District, which has appeared on Federal Reserve Notes for many decades.

Q: What's a 1976 Bicentennial $2 note worth?

They're still worth $2. Millions of them were and still are being printed. The Treasury Department has a very ample reserve of them which they'd be glad to see circulate. The note is current, the most recent issue of the denomination.

1976 Bicentennial $2 note.

Q: What can you tell me about a $1,000 promissory note on The Bank of the United States with serial number 8894?

Questions on this note beat out the Barr notes, but not by much. This is a copy, one of millions, some dating back to the Civil War. Charles Promislo, president of Historical Documents Co. of Philadelphia, discovered a process to artificially age parchment in 1942. This $1000 promisory note, which is printed on this artificial parchment, was one of his most popular reproductions. Number 8894 is one of the better known fakes, with untold thousands of copies floating around. I have one hanging on my office wall, and two more adorning the covers of the boxes that my personal checks from the bank came in. A court in Puerto Rico heard a suit attempting to collect on one of the $1,000 note copies. The plaintiffs claimed that it was worth 21 million dollars. The original, genuine Bank of the United States $1,000 note, with serial number 8894, was sold by paper money specialist Grover Criswell in 1955. As of 1967 the original was still in existence, and in the hands of Promislo. In the 1960s he was reproducing millions upon millions of copies of paper money, Confederate currency, and documents such as the Bill of Rights. Number 8894 has caused more grief for potential collectors than almost any other reproduction in history, and has resulted in a number of other court cases where owners of the copies have tried in vain to collect the interest "due."

Q: I have a key chain and a pocket calculator with reproductions of U.S. notes on them. Are they illegal?

Title 18, U.S. code prohibits any such reproductions, especially since they are in color. They are thus subject to confiscation on sight. The Secret Service will take away any that you bring to them to ask about. The calculators are printed as very close reproductions of U.S. currency and thus are in violation of the law. I've seen one of these that came from Europe which apes a $10 note and the Secret Service booth at the 1991 ANA Convention in Chicago had one printed as a $100 note. The same goes for the key chains with a set of miniature notes attached.

Q: What's the story on the balcony that was added to the White House on the 1934-C $20 notes?

In the middle of the issue a balcony was added to the 2nd floor of the White House. If you compare the two notes, the trees and shrubs are much larger on the later issue. A total of 7.4 million of both designs were printed, roughly half and half of each design. Because it was added while Harry Truman was president it became known as the "Truman Balcony." The 1934-C notes were printed between 1946 and 1953.

Q: My piece of U.S. currency doesn't have "IN GOD WE TRUST" on the back. How many were printed like that?

Literally billions of pieces, since the motto was not added to the back design until the law was signed July 11, 1955. The first $1 notes with the motto were available to the public on October 1, 1957. This is probably the third most commonly asked question about paper money. Some of the 1935-G Silver Certificates and all of the 1935-H series $1 notes carry the motto, but it was not added until the 1963 series for the $2, $5, $10, and $20 notes. It was put on the $50 and $100 notes in the 1963-A series. Even if your note is from one of these or a later series, it may well have been altered to remove the motto. It was in the late 1950s, after the 1957 series $1 notes with the motto appeared, that people began to notice that earlier notes didn't have it, and got the rumors started, still very much alive today. There are no notes that command a premium for having, or not having the motto.

Q: Is it still illegal to own one of the cancelled $10,000 gold certificates?

Still. During a fire in the Old Postoffice Building in Washington, December 13, 1935, a quantity of the cancelled certificates were dumped in the street by firemen. Hundreds were grabbed by spectators who thought they were still good. Over the years more than 250 of that number have been confiscated and recovered by the Treasury. At least one bank was victimized (paying face value for one). Others of the certificates have been sold privately over the years, but they are illegal to own, as they are Government property. If you have one turn it in, to save yourself potential problems.

Q: Would you please print something on the make of the automobile on the back of the old $10 notes?

The small size $10 notes in several series show a car in the near foreground, a subject of controversy for many years. While we have repeatedly reported the correct information it is still challenged, so perhaps repeating it will give you some ammunition to help squelch the rumors. The auto is a composite of several makes and is NOT any specific make. Our authorities are both the Treasury Department and the automobile experts who work for a sister publication here at Krause Publications, called *Old Cars Weekly News and Market-place*. The Treasury and our car experts state flatly that it is not a 1926 Hupmobile, a 1926 Maxwell, or others suggested. It has the features of several different makes.

The infamous auto on the $10 note.

Q: What is the meaning of the design on the back of the $1 notes?

It's a copy of the Great Seal of the U.S., adopted in 1782. Here is a quote from Chick O'Donnell's *Standard Handbook of United States Paper Money*: Series 1935 $1 Silver Certificates are the first to carry both the obverse and the reverse of the Great Seal. The positioning of the two sides of the seal as incorporated in the original design was the opposite to that actually adopted. The Great Seal was adopted in 1782 - even before the adoption of our Constitution. On the front is depicted an American eagle breasted by a shield with our national colors. The bird holds in its right talon an olive branch, symbolic of peace, of 13 leaves and 13 berries. In the left talon is a bundle of 13 arrows signifying the original colonies' fight for freedom. A ribbon flying from the beak carries the motto 'E Pluribus Unum' which is translated 'One out of many,' a reference to the unity of the 13 colonies. Over the eagle's head is a constellation of 13 five-pointed stars surrounded by a wreath of clouds. The reverse of the seal is also rich in symbolism. The pyramid is representative of permanence and strength. At its base in Roman numerals appears '1776,' the year of the Declaration of Independence. The structure's unfinished condition denotes that there was still work to be done to form a more perfect government and signifies the expectation that new states would be added to the Union. The eye in the triangular glory represents an all-seeing deity and with the motto 'Anuit Coeptis,' alludes to the many signal interpositions of Divine Providence in the forming of our government. The motto is translated 'He (God) has favored our undertakings.' 'Novus Ordo Seclorum' is translated as 'A new order of the ages' and in the words of the designers of the seal, signifies 'The beginning of the New American Era.'

Q: Is it legal to make a copy of a U.S. note?

It is legal to make a machine copy or photo, but there are some very strict rules you must follow. Machine copies or photos are legal ONLY if they are made on a black and white copy machine or on black and white film. It is ILLEGAL to use a color copier or color film, as you cannot make copies or photos of small size bank notes in color. It is legal to copy the old, large size notes in color, but the same size rules must be followed as for black and white copies.

When making copies, you MUST follow the rules for photographs. That is, they can only be made if the reproduced note is less than 75 percent of normal size or more than 150 percent larger than the original. If you have a color copier at your place of business, by all means post this information to keep somebody from inadvertently breaking the law. You might as well post this over the black and white machine as well, as the size rules are important there. Despite all the "old wives' tales," it DOES NOT make it legal to skirt the size requirements by writing "COPY" or "SPECIMEN" or to place a strip of paper across part of the note, or as one reader did, to cut the copy apart and recopy it with a gap between the two parts. The illegal act is making the copy or taking the photo. What you do afterward is too late to affect the fact that you have already broken the law.

We publish pictures of small size notes, but only under rigidly specified conditions as to size, and only in black and white. It is illegal to use all or any part of a bank note in any sort of ad.

Chapter 43

PATTERNS, DIE TRIALS, TRIAL STRIKES

Whenever a new coin design is made, new equipment is put into service, or new dies are used, it's necessary to test the design, the new press, or the die. The results of these tests usually go into the scrap bin, but enough get into the hands of collectors to make them highly collectible.

Q: Has the U.S. ever minted a platinum coin?

Three, to be exact, but they are patterns and not a regular issue. Three specimens struck on Russian platinum with regular 1814 half dollar dies are known. One is defaced with punch marks, one is in the Smithsonian and has a test cut, and the third is in private hands, auctioned at the Great Eastern Numismatic Association convention in September, 1974. It is not known whether the pieces were struck in 1814, or at some later date.

Q: Years ago a story appeared in <u>Numismatic News</u> about a zinc cent for some other date than the 1943 zinc plated steel cents. Do you remember anything about it?

I believe it referred to a 1942 cent struck in zinc which escaped into circulation mixed with the 1943 pieces. However, I did find a reference to the piece, which turned out to be a trial strike for the 1943 cents, dated 1942, and struck on the same zinc "coated" steel, which was the Mint's way of ducking the fact that they were about to issue their first plated coin. The piece is similar, if not identical, to the plastic cents struck in that year, with Liberty facing left on the obverse, LIBERTY and FREEDOM to the left and above. On the reverse, UNITED STATES MINT is in three lines with a wreath. Of interest is that the Liberty bust is from the 1918 Colombian 2 centavos struck at Philadelphia, and the wreath is from the 1860 U.S. $5 gold. Philadelphia Mint records show that a small quantity of experimental 1942 dated cents were made, at least one of which was lost, possibly into circulation.

Q: Are there any U.S. aluminum pattern coins?

Among the first were the 1863 patterns for the cent, two-cent, three-cent silver, half dime, dime, quarter, half, and dollar. At that time aluminum was considered to be a scarce, precious metal, costing as much as silver. In the 1890s it dropped to 50 cents a pound. There was a proposed three-cent coin in 1863, and in 1864 several additional alloys with aluminum were tried, and there was an 1867 pattern five-cent. That year aluminum and silver were of equal value.

Q: The $10 gold pattern of 1874 shows the current conversion rate into several foreign currencies, followed by the word "UBIQUE." Is this supposed to be "unique?"

Ubique might almost be considered an antonym (opposite) of "unique," as it means "everywhere" or "anywhere," an obvious reference to its intent as a universal coin, good anywhere in the world. It comes from the same Latin root as ubiquitous.

Dana Bickford had the idea of a coin denominated in several currencies: English pounds, German marks, Swedish kronen, Dutch gulden, and French francs. The Mint Director, Dr. Linderman, liked the idea and had patterns made, but Congress failed to approve the issue.

Q: Please tell me what a "Blind man's nickel" is.

It's a rarity, that's for certain. One of the pattern coins struck in 1882 was a nickel with five bars on the edge, so that the blind could identify the piece by touch. The idea was fine, but posed production problems and never went beyond the pattern stage, with just five of the pieces struck. Two 1882 pattern nickels, Judd 1683 and 1697, have five equally spaced bars on the edge. They were listed by Haseltine in a March 1, 1883 sale as designed for the use of the blind.

Q: Is it true that the U.S. Mint did not produce or design a coin with a George Washington bust until after 1850?

Contrary to some sources, Mint Director James Ross Snowden made that statement in a letter dated 1857. The first pattern of a Washington coin actually wasn't struck until 1863. It was the 1863 2-Cent pattern, Judd 305-311. The U.S. Mint did strike medals with the Washington bust prior to 1863, but no coin patterns.

Q: Why aren't there more 20th Century U.S. pattern coins around?

A change in Mint policy closed down what once was a lucrative sideline for various Mint personnel during the previous century. The Mint stopped the sale of patterns, and began destroying them instead. Beginning with the coins of 1916, it was claimed that it was illegal to own any later 20th Century patterns. However, this was later proved to be an unsubstantiated statement in a Jack Anderson column, and in a statement by pattern specialist Dr. Judd, according to Ken Bressett, editor of the *Red Book*.

Q: Many years ago the U.S. Mint destroyed a quantity of patterns, dies and hubs. When was that?

It was the so-called "Crime of 1910." Some 200 hubs, dies, and patterns, many dating to the 1830s, were melted down by the Mint on orders from the Treasury Secretary, callously ignoring their historical significance. A complete list was published at the time. It was part of the "cleanup campaign" by Secretary Frank MacVeagh, which resulted in the complete destruction of all of the models, hubs, and dies for the Morgan dollar. When production was resumed in 1921, the Mint had to start from scratch, with new models, hubs, and dies.

Chapter 44

POLICIES, RULES, TIPS

I try to provide readers with as complete service and assistance as possible. However, there are certain company policies and rules that I have to follow, so I've included questions which explain how to successfully gain the information that you want.

Q: Do you buy or sell coins? I want to buy a coin you pictured. I have a coin to sell. Will you put an ad in for me? Will you buy a coin for me, if I pay you a commission?

This is a composite of questions that come across my desk every day. Unfortunately, I can't be of help to you, since to avoid any possible conflict of interest company policy says that we do not get involved in transactions with, or between, readers and our advertisers. Afterward, if you think you got a bad deal, then we do have a consumer affairs department that may be able to help. We do not buy or sell coins. It's a matter of ethics.

Q: What would you recommend I collect?

Collecting is strictly a matter of personal interest and choice. While we may offer suggestions in our articles or columns, they are a general coverage aimed at our entire reading audience. You as an individual need to decide for yourself, reading, researching, looking at coins, and then picking out what you like, literally what "turns you on." Collect to enjoy, not to follow the leader.

Q: As a coin dealer I get a lot of questions from my customers about minting varieties, and other areas that I don't specialize in. Any objection if I refer them to you?

Glad to help, so give your customers my address, and remind them to include a loose first class stamp, and a good description of the coin, paper money, or other collectible in question (rather than sending the piece in their first letter). Quite a few people hesitate to contact us, because they are going under the mistaken assumption that I only answer letters from subscribers. Also remind them to mention that you sent them, and I'll be happy to see that they get a free sample copy of *Numismatic News*.

Q: I have a large collection of coins that I want to sell. How do I go about getting the best possible price for it?

This frequent question is one that unfortunately is impossible to fully answer, as it is the kind of advice that would have to be based on a lot more information than you have provided. A "large" collection might be several hundred rolls of cents, worth little more than face value, or it might be a bank vault full of gold coins worth millions, so obviously the advice in each case is going to be completely different. Any advice would have to be general in nature, as I have no idea of the extent, condition, scope, or potential value of your collection, all of which have a bearing on what to tell you. One common first step is to make a list of all the coins in your collection, listing the date, mint mark, denomination, and condition, or grade. A knowledgeable coin dealer can scan such a list and get a basic idea of the potential worth, and possible avenues you should follow. Ultimately, someone is going to have to examine your collection to determine its actual value, something that can't be done without seeing the coins.

Q: I live in a small town, and recently inherited a large quantity (partial list enclosed) of numismatic material. Can you tell me what it is worth?

In a case like this it is mandatory that an expert examine the material and evaluate it— something that is impossible to do from a written description. My best suggestion would be to contact an appraiser or a coin dealer (shop around) in the nearest large city, and ask his rates to appraise the material. Usually, if a coin dealer appraises and then buys the material the fee is waived, but you may wish to have an independent appraiser do the work. You will find appraisers listed in the yellow pages. Before going to the expense of a formal appraisal, check locally for a coin club whose members may be able to at least give you a general idea of the possible value of the coins. The first rule is to get more than one opinion, and NEVER dispose of any of the coins until you are certain of their value, both as individual pieces or as part of a collection. Make as complete and detailed a list as possible before you get the collection appraised.

Q: If I send you a foil pressing or a pencil rubbing of a coin can you tell me what the coin is and what it's worth?

A foil pressing or a rubbing will not tell much about doubling on a coin, but may help with other questions. This is because there are about 20 different forms of doubling which can occur in the minting process, as well as several forms of damage which can easily be confused with them, so in most cases the coin itself has to be examined. Also, most collectors who send foil rubbings fail to protect them from crushing. Unfortunately foil rubbings will not survive mailing unless they are protected from pressure in a reversed 2x2, match box, or some similar container. Pencil rubbings have a tendency to blur from friction with the envelope, so whenever you send a rubbing you should also write out all letters and digits that appear on the coin as an aid to identification. Two more important facts: the apparent metal of the unknown piece and the approximate grade. The latter two are the most frequently omitted items of information requiring a follow-up letter. For minting varieties other than doubling, pressings or rubbings often are quite helpful.

Q: Would you please tell me what this list of coins is worth?

Thank you for asking first, but it is impossible to evaluate coins or paper money without seeing the items. In fairness to our other correspondents, please limit your questions to six items at a time, and I'll try to give you an approximate range of values in different grades. The best suggestion I can give you is to take the coins in to a local dealer with the idea of getting them appraised, a service you may have to pay a small fee for, but which is not threatening to you or your coins. You don't have to sell them if you don't want to, if you make it clear you only want an appraisal. If you want to sell a coin, try several dealers for an offer so you'll get an idea of what the market for it is. I am always interested in new finds, especially if they are important enough to warrant photographing and reporting them in our publications, but I have to ask you, for security reasons, to write first before sending any coins or any item of possible value. A detailed description of a possible minting variety or "error" often will save the necessity of having to ship the coin back and forth. Return postage with questions is a must, please in the form of a loose first class stamp, unlicked and unstapled.

Q: If I send you a coin to be examined, what's to prevent you from keeping the piece or sending it to the Secret Service if it turns out to be a fake?

Ethics, in a word. While this may not be true of all hobby publications or authenticators, our policy has always been to return all coins sent to us, with full instructions as to how to properly dispose of the piece if it is a counterfeit or an altered coin. But, write first before sending anything of value to anyone. Unsolicited items are treated as gifts by postal regulations and do not have to be returned or paid for.

Q: "I read (heard) somewhere that such and such a coin was worth (a fabulous sum)." Would you comment?

This is a composite of frequent questions to this column. Please include a machine copy of the "source" of the statement whenever possible, as frequently there is either a modifier that affects the meaning of the statement, or there is evidence to indicate that the statement is from a dubious source or is incorrect. It's hard to refute or confirm a statement without the original at hand, and frequently such statements stem from sources that are totally lacking in knowledge of coins. All too often information is quoted out of context, or incompletely, making it next to impossible to determine the source, or its credibility. Give me as many facts as possible to work with and I'll try to give you as accurate an answer as possible. If the question is on something we published, then the page number, date of the publication, and the specific article or ad would be helpful. A machine copy of a newspaper or magazine article from other publishers is of tremendous help.

Q: Why don't you carry more reports of reader's coin finds. Lots of interesting coins are still being found in circulation, or with metal detectors.

These reports do make interesting reading and in the past we have featured quite a number of such finds. Unfortunately there is a tendency toward such a feature rapidly become a "can you top this?" competition, making it difficult to determine where reality turns into fantasy. If you are seriously interested in seeing your name in print, there are numerous ways of doing this, not the least of which is sitting down and writing an article that would be of interest to our readers. We are always looking for new writers who have a thorough knowledge of their topic and the ability to put it on paper. Submissions should be addressed to the editor, with return postage, or the manuscript will not be returned.

Q: Any chance of getting some better addresses for the coin shows you list? Some of them are pretty hard to find for a person from out of town.

That address thing is a pet peeve of mine since in so many cases clubs or show promoters merely list the name of the building or convention hall where the show is to be held. We had a rash of complaints about a major show with just that problem, compounded by a "map" which was less than helpful. The attitude seems to be, "You're supposed to KNOW where we are," which is not the best public relations for a coin show. It takes just a little extra effort to be helpful rather than snobbish about your show.

Q: Why don't you give an address when you mention someone who found a coin? There have been several cases where I would have liked to have written the person, both to congratulate him on his find and to learn more about the piece.

This sort of response is in the minority, as the overwhelming number of readers who contact us are adamant about our not using their address, and often even their name. Many collectors have learned through bitter experience that publication of their name and address becomes an open invitation to burglars or armed robbers. A significant number of my correspondents stress that they don't even want their name published for that reason, even though we never identify anyone other than by the state they live in at most, without specific permission. As an example, a person mentioned recently who has an uncommon name reported that despite that his address was not published, he received at least 20 phone calls from people who had tracked him down through the phone company. We are professionals, who respect your privacy, and want to ensure your personal security. For the same reason I urge readers never to discuss or mention their hobby on a postcard. The concept of personal security is the first thing a beginning collector should learn.

Q: What is your policy on anonymous letters?

I don't answer them. You are only hurting yourself if you just sign your initials, or a first name or leave your name off completely. I do not answer unsigned letters, since they give my computer fits. Quite a few questions never get into print, for one of a variety of reasons, including a topic that is not of general interest, so if you don't give me a name and address, there is no way I can answer your question. I do not publish names or addresses, nor do I sell or give them to anyone outside our firm. This is a professional publication, not an address mill.

Q: I have had a problem with a coin dealer, so I'd like to request that you publish his name so that other collectors won't have problems too.

Unfortunately, to comply with your suggestion we would leave ourselves wide open to some serious legal problems, as you can't just put into print everything you would like to say about people. We are strictly limited as to what we can publish in this area. If you have a complaint, document it fully and write directly to our Customer Service Department, which may be able to help. There have been several recent incidents on the online services and the Internet where collectors wanted to publicly blast dealers but libel laws can make it extremely expensive to vent your spleen in public, even if you're right. Laws vary from state to state, so what may be legal in your state might not be in ours.

Chapter 45

PROOF COINS, SETS, MINT SETS, SOUVENIR SETS

Although I've already used a number of questions on proof coins, sets, mint sets and souvenir sets, there are still plenty on hand for a section specially devoted to them. Deciding which chapter to put some of these questions in was difficult, as often a question could fit in several different places.

Q: Is there any information as to how the proof versions of the 1921 Morgan dollars came to be struck?

Farran Zerbe is quoted by one source as claiming that during a visit to the San Francisco Mint in 1921 to witness the striking of the first Peace dollars, the visit was marred by the arrival of Morgan dies instead. Zerbe claimed that to avoid disappointing him the officials polished the dies and struck "about two dozen" proof coins which he was allowed to buy and then pass on to collector friends around the country. There are a small number of known examples of proofs, but without mint marks, so the quote probably referred to the wrong mint. Walter Breen cited an unknown number and various reports of up to 200 struck, but at Philadelphia.

Q: Is there any special reason why the gold proof coins dated 1875 are so rare compared to other issues?

One possible point to speculate on is that in that year the Col. Mendes I. Cohen collection of gold coins was sold at auction. Several of the proofs brought less than they had cost when purchased directly from the U.S. Mint. It's interesting to speculate that this may have deterred the few collectors wealthy enough to buy the proofs from the Mint in that year, resulting in the present shortage.

Q: When did the 1936 proof sets begin to climb in value?

Almost right away. The issue price was $1.89. In a dealer ad in 1943 a set is offered for $40, with the 1937 set at $12.50. By 1973 the 1936 set had reached $900, with some ups and downs since the 1940s, peaking in 1980 at $10,350. Original cost was $1.81 plus eight cents postage. The quarter and half were face value plus 25 cents each handling, dimes face plus 10 cents, nickels and cents face plus 15 cents.

Q: Why didn't they leave the mint marks off the proof coins when they switched production from Philadelphia to San Francisco in 1968? The proof coins didn't have a mint mark before that.

The principal reason probably was the pressure that collectors had applied to get mint marks restored after they were outlawed in 1965. As to the argument on proofs with mint marks, I should point out that branch mint proofs with mint marks have been struck for well over a century, so there is plenty of precedent. There is nothing in the definition of a proof which precludes a mint mark. Some countries such as Israel even identify some of their proofs by using a mint mark which does not appear on the circulation strikes. There was one earlier regular U.S. proof with a mint mark: the 1942-P silver nickel proofs.

Q: How do I tell the difference between the 1960 large and small date proof cents? I can't tell from the pictures.

If you have an example of the two coins before you the differences are fairly obvious. Without the coins you have to depend on the photos. The key difference is that the 1960 small date proof cent shows the 1, 9, and 0 in the date all at the same level. In other words, if you put a ruler across the tops of the three digits they all would touch it. On the large date the top of the 9 sticks up well above the tops of the 1 and 0. If you look closely, the digits on the large 1960 (and 1960-D) date are actually larger than those of the small date, something which is not true of the 1970-S dates.

Q: At the 1990 ANA Convention in Seattle I saw a 1970 proof nickel in a set which was a strong golden color on the reverse. What would cause this?

San Francisco started striking proofs in 1968. The golden color was found to be a copper oxide which was caused by contact with the wooden storage boxes. When the cause was pinpointed the Mint switched to plastic storage boxes and cured the problem. The color has no effect on the value of the coin, nor does any other surface discoloration.

Q: I have discovered that both my 1975 and 1976 proof sets have the same Bicentennial quarters, halves, and dollars. Is this a mistake?

Both the 1975 and 1976 proof sets contained the Bicentennial quarters, halves, and dollars, so both are normal sets for the year. There were no quarters, halves, or dollars struck bearing a 1975 date.

Q: I got a proof coin from a local bank which had obviously been in circulation. How can that happen?

This surprises many beginning collectors. Proof coins frequently turn up in circulation, mainly as the result of thefts by children, or professionals, who spend the coins rather than try to sell them to a coin dealer. More than likely this is what happened to the coin you picked up, which would be classed as an impaired proof. Many dealers also break up proof sets and put damaged or marred coins into circulation. There were some past instances in the 1800s of surplus proofs being put in circulation by the Mint, but now they are all melted down.

The Mint produces only enough proof coins to fulfill the orders that it receives, plus a small number to replace defective sets or those lost in delivery.

Q: I found several rotated reverse coins in my proof set. What are they worth?

This has been a regular question from readers for a number of years. First, turn the set face up to make sure that all of the coins have the obverse positioned properly. In almost all cases the presumed rotated reverse turns out to be a case of the coin(s) being turned in the set. Minor rotations up to about 15 degrees (measured with a protractor) are common as the tolerances allow seven degrees for each die. Even if the rotation is somewhat larger this doesn't mean the coin is going to have some value, as the few collectors interested in rotations usually don't show any interest until it reaches at least 45 degrees.

Q: Why are single proof coins worth more than a complete set? My dealer says they aren't, but a glance at your price charts show they are.

You missed an important point in comparing the prices of proof or other cased sets and individual coins. Figured into the price of the separate coins is the labor cost for the time involved in opening the cases, and the cost of whatever packaging material is used to house the separate coins.

It's exactly the same thing as buying a car, or going to a parts house and buying the parts to build your own—you'll pay a lot more for the parts than for the whole vehicle.

Q: What was so special about the SMS that replaced the proof sets from 1965 to 1967?

SMS stands for special mint sets. They were supposed to replace the proof sets during those years. The Coinage Act of 1965 removed mint marks under the guise of preventing hoarding or speculating in low mintages from any given mint. San Francisco was picked to handle the special mint sets because they weren't as busy with striking circulating coins. Also, San Francisco was being used to strike proof Panamanian coins, as sort of a practice run for the resumption of proof production in 1968. The SMS coins were struck with more care than normal circulating coins and in some cases are prooflike in appearance, due to some polishing on the dies and apparently on the planchets. However, the majority of the coins were little if any better than the circulating strikes from the other mints.

Q: Were the 1965-1966-1967 special mint sets sold "over the counter" by the Mint, or just by mail order?

The unsold sets for all three years were sold over the counter at the mints in Denver and Philadelphia, the Assay Offices in San Francisco and New York, and at the Cash Division window at the main Treasury building in Washington. In early 1968 the Mint noted that it still had 62,000 of the 1965 sets, 114,000 1966 sets, and 27,000 1967 special mint sets which remained unsold.

Q: What's so unique about the 1970-D halves?

The 1970-D halves were struck only for the mint sets intended for collectors, marking the first time in U.S. coinage history that a circulation strike coin was issued for a purpose other than circulation. However, this did not affect the circulation status of the coin. The same thing is true of proof coins, which technically are legal tender, even though they are made only for collectors. 2,038,134 of the halves were struck, a mintage that was smaller than the 2,632,810 proofs for that year.

Q: What's a double mint set?

It's a set with two examples of each coin, so that both sides could be displayed. The first such sets were issued from 1947 through 1949. There was a gap for the Korean War, then the double sets were resumed in 1951 and issued through 1958.

Q: My 1968, 1969, 1970, 1972, and 1974 Philadelphia mint set envelopes all contain S Mint nickels or cents. How could this have happened?

It was all according to plan. Rather than include a third plastic envelope for the one or two San Francisco coins, they were added to the Philadelphia envelopes.

When San Francisco was striking circulating coins after the mint marks went back on in 1968, it was frequently necessary to combine coins from the different mints. In 1969 they had a total of 10 coins from the three mints, so they combined them to save packaging costs. There were PDS cents, DS nickels, PD dimes and quarters, and D halves. The mix, to avoid having more than two coins of the same denomination in the same envelope, resulted in three mints being represented in one envelope.

Q: In a recent column you mentioned the 1979 Mint packaged sets as being incomplete because they didn't contain the Anthony dollars. Wasn't that true of the 1971 and 1972 mint sets which didn't contain the Ike dollars?

You are right about the 1971 and 1972 sets. However, they are sort of a special case because the Mint had not had to contend with the dollar coins since they began producing the modern mint sets in 1947.

Q: I bought a 1983 mint set from a dealer, but you said that none were issued. Was I cheated?

The U.S. mint did not package any mint sets for 1982 or 1983. However, anyone can privately assemble a mint set and sell them, so long as they don't claim they are "mint packaged." Some dealers offered the souvenir sets from Denver and Philadelphia as mint sets, and these were "mint packaged," but they were not true mint sets. Crux of the matter is that when you buy a coin, you should pay for the coin and not the package it comes in. As a matter of fact, if you happened to be a *Coins Magazine* subscriber in those two years, you got a privately packaged set as a premium with your subscription. The official reason given for cancelling the mint sets for two years was economy. To meet its budget, the Mint dropped some 180 employees and cut the mint set program. The explanation at the time was that this was the one program that could be privately duplicated by obtaining new coins from the banks. The program was restored in 1984 after howls of protest from collectors who demanded mint packaged sets rather than those widely produced by coin dealers.

Q: Is it safe to leave my proof coins and mint sets in the packaging they were in when I received them from the Mint?

As a general rule the proof set hard plastic packaging is airtight, but the plastic envelopes used for the mint sets are not. Several world mints which use similar mint set packaging state specifically that it is not intended for long term storage. The coins would be better off in an airtight holder anyway. Collectors should be aware of the hazards of PVC, a softener used in plastics which breaks down into hydrochloric acid when it is heated. The hard plastic cases and such plastics as Mylar are safe for coins, but many of the world mints used the PVC-laced plastic envelopes for their coins for years.

Another important point is to check your coins that are in storage at least every six months. This does mean extra handling, but it helps you spot potential problems before they become severe.

Q: Why isn't there a uniform number of coins in the mint sets?

The same number of coins is not struck every year.

Q: What is the difference between a year set, a date set, and a date and mint set?

The name depends on the coins that are included in the set, and some other factors. For example, a year set or date set would consist of one of each denomination struck in a given year without regard to mint marks. A mint packaged mint set includes all of the coins struck at all of the mints with the same date, and packaged by the Mint. The same set from a source outside the mint is still a mint set, but not a mint packaged set, an important difference. A set of proof coins for a given year is known as a proof set. A type set is a group of coins of any year which are examples of the different types and series of coins struck, usually obsolete series.

Q: Which are scarcer, the polished device proofs or the frosted device proofs?

The frosted proofs are the scarcer, since they are from the first strikes with a new die. The rough surface wears away after a few strikes, giving the polished strikes. In recent years the Mint has used acid to roughen the die surface in the design, increasing the number of frosted proofs markedly.

Chapter 46

PROPOSED COINS

If all of the proposals for new coins over the years had become law, we'd be up to our elbows in coins of every kind, shape, and variety. Perhaps fortunately for the collector, the vast majority of the proposals never made it beyond the planning stage.

Q: What is a decad?

This was the name proposed for a copper coin by the Continental Congress in 1785-86. You and I came close to having a pocketful of these large copper coins, which were supposed to be equal in value to 1/100th of a Spanish milled dollar. It was detailed in a report of the Grand Committee of the Continental Congress in 1785, but before the report was adopted the paragraph defining the decad was deleted. However, Thomas Jefferson was involved in the solicitation of pattern decad dies from Thomas Wyon of Birmingham, England for the patterns now known as the Confederato "cents."

Q: Wasn't the bicentennial quarter an afterthought?

It was. The original proposal from the Administration was for a half dollar and a dollar. The quarter was suggested by Mint Director Mary Brooks after the original proposal was sent to Congress.

Q: I know that new mints have been proposed for a number of states, but has there ever been one proposed for North Dakota?

I didn't think so, since North Dakota is not exactly noted for any gold or silver production, but there actually was a bill submitted in 1964 in the Senate to establish a mint there. It and a companion bill introduced at about the same time to build a mint in Illinois, disappeared without trace in the halls of Foggy Bottom.

Q: Has Congress ever tried to legislate against coin collecting?

The closest call came in the mid-1960s, when Senator Bible of Nevada submitted a bill to outlaw coin collecting. It was based on the false premise that the collectors were to blame for the big coin shortage of the time.

Q: Was the $50 slug the largest planned coin in the California area?

Some reports suggest that $100 and even $1000 coins were discussed, and then abandoned. A $1000 coin would have contained 62.5 ounces of $16 gold, or roughly 5 troy pounds—a bit heavy for pocket change.

Q: Who was responsible for the proposal to issue $100, $50, and $25 gold coins that were to be called unions?

Secretary of the Treasury James Guthrie was the proponent of the three denominations, the $100 to be called a union, the $50 a half union, and the $25 a quarter union. The suggestion was made in response to a petition for production of a $50 gold coin by Californians in 1854. Oddly enough, the earlier $50 gold coins had been cordially hated because they were the only official coins being struck, leaving the business community without the small change they had enjoyed when the private minters were supplying $5 and $10 gold pieces.

Q: In answering another question you mentioned the gold union and half union coin proposals, but wasn't there a "silver" union as well?

I would bet that I could stump the vast majority of experts with this question, as I found only a single obscure reference to a silver union coin: it was the proposed name for the U.S. Trade dollar! Coincidentally, the suggestion came from California, the original source for the proposal for the gold $50 and $100 coins. In a letter to the Secretary of the Treasury, Louis Garnett of San Francisco suggested variously a "coin, disc.... or stamped ingot with the weight and fineness indicated." He went on to, "give it a title, as for instance 'Silver Union', differing from the coins representing our subsidiary and dollar of account. Also suggested was "silver arbiter."

Q: Wasn't there supposed to be a bicentennial gold coin?

A bill reached Congress in 1973, but it died in committee, along with the commemoratives. Authorization for such a coin was introduced with a bill to allow private ownership of gold, but the bicentennial gold coin fell by the wayside, dropped from the bill before it was made law.

Q: Were there any serious efforts to produce a smaller size dollar prior to the introduction of the Susan B. Anthony dollar in 1979?

Just how serious it was is a question, but there was actually a proposal dating back to 1928 to downsize the dollar. It came out of Colorado, where strenuous efforts were being made to revive the staggering mining industry. The proposal was to mix an ounce of silver, then worth only about 58 cents, with 47 cents worth of gold and three cents worth of alloy. However, the flaw in the proposal was that this was supposed to produce a coin only slightly larger, and 20 percent thinner than a half dollar, which would have been physically impossible as the full size silver dollar contained .77 ounce of silver. As early as 1925 the Treasury was experimenting with a plan for a smaller dollar, "possibly between the quarter and half dollar." Despite that there was ample earlier evidence from previous experiments that a gold-silver combination dollar was impractical, that was the course that was pursued, and failed again.

The Anthony dollar is still around—but most are in hiding.

Q: Was Susan B. Anthony the only woman candidate for a place on the SBA dollar of 1979?

She was far outnumbered, but not outgunned. Well before the final decision was made more than 60 other designs had been suggested to Congress, most of them American women.

Q: Were there any attempts to revive the Morgan dollar after 1921?

The abortive attempt to put the Peace dollar back in circulation with the striking of the 1964 coins is what sticks in the minds of most numismatists as the last circulating 90 percent silver coin, but there was a serious effort following the issue of the Ike and Anthony dollars to revive the Morgan design. Idaho's two Senators, James A. McClure and Steve Symms, along with Representative Larry Craig, introduced a bill to strike Morgan dollars for three years, dated 1983, 1984, and 1985. The bill also included provisions for a bullion coin, which was the only feature which ultimately received approval, the Morgan dollar idea getting dropped after a brief flurry of interest.

Q: Was the half dollar the only coin upon which Benjamin Franklin was supposed to appear?

If you are asking whether Franklin was proposed for any other denomination, he was proposed for the dime by a private group in 1939. The organization known as the Sons of the American Revolution passed a resolution to that effect. Congressman Hamilton Fish introduced the resolution in Congress, but it would be another decade before Franklin wound up on the half dollar.

Q: How come the United States never issued an FAO coin, like so many other countries did?

Many countries in the world issued coins using themes which matched the purpose of the Food and Agriculture Organization of the United Nations. The principal reason that the U.S. did not participate was that such a coin would require both Congressional approval and Mint support for the project. At the height of the FAO coin production, the U.S. Mint was adamant in its opposition to any commemorative coins, and Congress was more than willing to go along.

Q: Wasn't there an effort by the ANA some years ago to get a commemorative coin to honor the pine tree shilling?

At the 1949 convention, the ANA passed a resolution and appointed a committee to work to get a Pine Tree Shilling Tercentenary Commemorative quarter, to be struck in 1952 to mark the 300th anniversary of the 1652 coin. The measure was introduced in Congress in 1950, but—as usual—failed to pass.

Q: When was the U.S. two-cent piece first proposed?

The two-cent coin has a curious history. It was proposed in 1806 for the first time, but died because of the perennial copper shortage of that era, came up again in 1836, and was finally approved and struck from 1864 to 1873. During World War II proposals were advanced as a means of saving critical war materials for both a two- and three-cent coin. The idea was revived again in the mid-1970s when copper prices were threatening to make the cent cost more than its face value to make. At that time, the then Chief Engraver went so far as to produce a design for a new two-cent coin, a model which I spotted during a 1980 visit to his office in the Philadelphia Mint.

Q: It's my understanding that the 1943 zinc plated steel cents caused a lot of problems because they were mistaken for dimes in circulation. Was there any effort to correct the problem?

The coins were the topic of numerous complaints all over the country on this problem, and while the Treasury Department was sympathetic, its hands were pretty well tied by wartime conditions. There was serious consideration of darkening the coins or of punching a hole in the center, but that idea was quickly abandoned because of cost and other problems. The Treasury did agree to run the coins through a darkening process to change their appearance, "if a suitable process can be found," but that plan was cancelled when it became clear that the steel cents would be just a one-year experiment that had flopped badly, even if it did save critical war materials. The problem didn't make itself apparent until after the coin reached circulation, so while there was some popular sentiment for the coins to be modified, the idea of a hole in Lincoln's head was worse, so the idea never was taken too seriously.

Q: Wasn't there an immediate effort to reduce the size of the large cent right after it was first struck?

The first large cents were struck in 1793, and in 1795 when Henry De Saussure resigned as Mint Director, he recommended to President Washington that the size be reduced to discourage the already frequent practice by coppersmiths of using the cents as a source of the scarce metal. His recommendation was accepted, in 1856.

Q: Was Columbus ever proposed as a subject for a United States commemorative coin prior to 1892?

Columbus very nearly replaced Miss Liberty as the central design on our first coins, which in effect would have made all our coins commemoratives. The use of a Columbus design was advanced on January 1, 1793 by Elias Boudinot, a steadfast opponent of the Liberty design, then a Congressman, later to be the third Director of the Mint. His proposal lost when put to a vote, casting the die for the next two centuries of coinage. Boudinot was originally an advocate of using the visage of the President on the coinage. Mint Engraver James B. Longacre made another attempt with the Columbus suggestion some 35 years before the Columbian Exhibition. Longacre, in a letter to Mint Director James Ross Snowdon in 1857, made the proposal that Columbus be used on the new cents that were to be produced to replace the large cent. Longacre was careful to present both sides of the issue, pointing out the likelihood of criticism because Columbus was a native of another country and one which was a minority among the U.S. population at the time. The refusal by Washington of a place on the coinage was the major theme of his letter, as it would be until the inhibition against portraying actual human beings on U.S. coins was done away with in 1892.

Q: Didn't the Treasury want a half cent before World War I?

The Treasury recommended a half cent in 1912, and got the bill for the three-cent amended to include it. The proposed half cent was to weigh 30 grains. The three-cent started with a hole in the center, but it was dropped by the House. The whole idea was killed later by the Senate. Both coins were to be in the same alloy as the nickel.

Chapter 47

RARITIES, RARITY SCALE

The word "rare" is probably the most overused and overworked term in the hobby vocabulary. Interestingly enough, it is also a term upon which there is little agreement and even less standardization. This bickering has led to an astounding number of definitions, rarity scales, and verbal battles. But, that's not unique for a hobby term.

The unique 1870-S dime.

Q: How many 1870-S half dimes were actually minted?

The coin is listed as unique—one known. The mint records on the production of this coin are missing. It was first reported at the 1978 American Numismatic Association convention. Similarly, there are no records for the 1870-S dollar, although 10 are known to exist, as are one or two 1870-S $3 gold coins. One theory is that they were struck for the cornerstone of the San Francisco Mint.

Q: How "rare" is rare? In other words, is there a specific figure or range attached to commonly used terms such as "rare," "very rare," "extremely rare," etc?

We might say that rarity is in the eye of the person using the term. There is no single set scale for such verbal terms, which is too bad, as a single well-defined term would simplify collecting tremendously. However, there are so many degrees of rarity, depending on the specifications of a given coin, that a fixed definition is impossible. It is implicit that anyone using the term should at the same time give the appropriate definition for his readers.

1876-CC 20-cent coin.

Q: The story I heard is that the 1876-CC 20-Cent coins that have survived in Uncircu-lated grade were souvenirs saved by the members of the 1876 Assay Commission. True or false?

Possibly true, but there is no written evidence to support the belief, which I have seen quoted. You might say, "A likely story."

Q: Can you give me a list of some of the rarities in United States coins that are on the missing list?

This is only a partial list, but among coins that were reported to exist, but whose current whereabouts are unknown are the copper Nova Constellation 5 unit piece, last known in the possession of Samuel Curwin in London in 1784, and the second 1841-O half eagle, traced as far as King Farouk.

Q: In the literature of the hobby there are a number of references to examination, or even ownership of an 1895 circulation strike Morgan dollar. Does this jibe with present information?

It's generally agreed that there are no known 1895 circulation strikes, although there were 880 proofs. Experts, including Abe Kosoff, who "owned and sold one," Wayte Raymond, who mentioned in 1938 that they were "much rarer in uncirculated than in proof," and Stuart Mosher, one time curator of the Smithsonian numismatic collection, all have supported the presumption that a circulation strike exists. About the only logical explanation is that they were well-worn proofs, well-worn altered coins, or very clever alterations which escaped detection in the days of "eyeball" exams.

Q: Is there an "R" scale that is universal to designate rarity?

No. Dr. Sheldon initiated an R scale for the large cent. Variations have been applied to many other coins and series, some successfully, some creating more confusion than help. The writer who uses an R scale must define it for his readers, whether in a reference work or an ad.

Q: Do you have any information on a rarity scale using R, RR, RRR, etc. to designate the relative scarcity of a coin?

The R scale is a very literal one. A single R means rare. RR means rare rare, RRR is rare rare rare, and the pinnacle of rarity is reached with an RRRR, which probably means the piece is unique, or with only a couple of specimens known. Like most numerical rarity scales, it is both subject to interpretation and to individual usage by the dealer or author using the scale. The R scale is something you are more likely to run into in European numismatics, but it was used by some firms in the U.S. in the past.

Q: Is there any special reason why the 1877 Indian Head cent is so rare? It seems as if with that large a mintage it ought to be more common.

The 1877 had a mintage of 852,500. It was one of only two Indian Head cents with a mintage of less than a million, the other being the 1909-S which had a mintage of only 309,000, or less than half that of the 1877. Yet, if you compare the catalog values, the 1877 in most grades is worth double or more the price of a 1909-S. Contemporary reports indicate that those few collectors who wanted the coin bought one of the 900 proofs, but even in circulation the 1877 was difficult to find just a couple of years after it was issued. The suspicion exists that a significant portion of the 1877 issue was either melted down or lost in some accident, but there has never been any proof, other than the difficulties in finding one in circulation. The 1909-S was struck in the early days of the increasing interest in branch mint coins and was saved by collectors in large enough quantities to keep the market value down, even today.

The 1877 Indian Head cent had a mintage of 852,500.

Q: Is it possible to get a listing of the rarity scales used by some of the old-time researchers? I want to use them to determine the value of my coins.

There is no direct relationship between rarity scales and current market values, so there is no way to use them to determine the exact value of a coin. Some of the older references attempted to establish values based on the scale used, but they have been outmoded by discoveries of hoards of coins which in many cases have altered the rarity factor. Many new varieties have been discovered since the rarity scales were established, so you would be better off to use a price guide such as our *Coin Market* to determine general values and then consult with some of the specialty groups for information on the numerous die varieties which aren't listed in the regular price guides.

Chapter 48

RESTRIKES

Restrikes are controversial, to turn a phrase. Collectors pining for a rarity are pleased to obtain a restrike, or perhaps more accurately, a copy of the rare piece. Others damn them as fakes, made to fool honest collectors. In either case, the term is often misused, often misunderstood. That it has two meanings really confounds the novice.

Q: I have an 1803 dollar with a rotated reverse. Does that make it a restrike?

Because specific die rotations are one means of identifying some of the Mint restrikes of U.S. coins, the incorrect assumption is made that a rotation means it is a restrike, but the truth is that many of the early U.S. coins have rotated reverses. The specified rotations apply only to the specific denomination and date to identify restrikes.

Q: Just what is a restrike? Are coins struck with genuine dies always restrikes? Does restrike mean both a planchet struck (later) by original dies or a struck coin struck a second time with a different design?

The generally accepted U.S. definition is a coin struck from official dies but in a year subsequent to the date on the coin. If the dies were never used to strike a coin in the date year, then subsequent strikes are not restrikes. In all cases the status depends on the circumstances. Both definitions fit under restrike, even though the end product in each case is completely different. The struck coin classification perhaps would be better if it is considered as an overstrike, although then it can be confused with a double strike. As is obvious, we have some problems with terms. Then we need to note that this and similar terms have different meanings in other countries.

Q: Is the 1804 "restrike" cent a Mint product?

Most experts agree that it is not. It was made about 1860 using an altered and rusty 1803 obverse die and a reverse die for the 1818 cent. Despite that similar work was being done in the Mint in that era, the quality of the pieces suggests that the job was done elsewhere.

Q: Some 1980 proof coins were "restruck" in 1981. Are there any other modern instances of restriking?

The law specifies that coins must not be struck after the year of their date. One other instance was the clad coins, cents, and nickels with 1965 dates, struck until July 31, 1966. All of the 1966 dated clad coins were then struck in the last five months of the year. The silver 1964 dated coins were struck in 1965 and 1966, but were authorized under specific provisions of the 1965 Coinage Act. 1964 dated cents and nickels were also struck in 1965, and from December 1965 through July 1966, all with 1965 dates, then August 1, 1966 to the end of the year with 1966 dates. There were many examples during the 1800s, including the 1804 dollar.

Q: How do you distinguish between the original 1827 quarters and the restrikes?

The original marker is that it was struck with a reverse die which used a curled base 2 in 25 (denomination). The restrikes were made with an 1819 reverse with a square based 2.

Q: Has the U. S. Mint ever deliberately restruck a new variety? I know there have been deliberate reprints of misprint stamps, but have there been any coins?

So far, no. The Wall Street Journal claimed on the front page that the plan was to strike millions of aluminum 1974 cents to counteract the missing coins in Congressional hands. However, the 1.5 million already on hand were counted and melted. The one similar incident was the restriking of the 1856 Flying Eagle cents, which were sold to politicians.

Q: Were there any restrikes of the two-cent coins, especially the proofs?

R.W. Julian indicates there is a possibility of this, warranting further study of the series. The dubious area covers the 1873 proofs, as the Coinage Act of 1873 ended production of the coin.

Q: Are there any examples of U.S. coins "adjusted" after they were struck?

Perhaps not for weight, but some of the restrikes, such as the half cent proofs, are known with the knife edge filed off at the Mint, after they were struck.

Chapter 49

ROLLS

Back in the early days of our country, paper was too precious to waste on coins, so they were bagged and stacked, giving rise to the several stories of coin designs rejected because they wouldn't stack properly. When rolls came along, they were found to be an excellent method of keeping coins together and making counting almost automatic. For the collector, rolls are important too.

Q: Recently I found a large number of 1964 cents in circulation, which are brand new. Is the Federal Reserve just getting around to releasing them?

It's more likely that some collector dumped rolls of 1964 cents that he had saved, as there is only a slight premium for this very high mintage year.

Q: I was shocked to find that a local bank would not accept my rolled coins because I didn't have an account there—and wanted a premium for any rolls bought from them. How can they get away with charging for U.S. currency?

Such service charges can be a shock, but they are legitimate. The banks are charged shipping costs by the Federal Reserve, so they are passing the costs to the customer. Despite that coins are legal tender, the bank does not have to accept them if they don't want to.

Q: Are original rolls recorded anywhere?

Other than the occasional reports that appear in hobby publications, there is no official listing. We do have a record of a claim for the oldest, a roll of 50 French 1852-A gold 20 franc pieces discovered in 1979. An original roll is considered to be one that was wrapped, before reaching circulation, in its original wrapper. It may have been opened. However, rolls are a poor way of storing coins as the old wrappers contain enough sulfur to eventually blacken copper or copper-alloy coins.

Q: Are my original rolls of Anthony dollars in Federal Reserve Bank wrappers worth a premium?

They would get only a very slight, if any premium. Coins should not be stored in wrappers for more than a few months. Wrappers are intended for commerce, not for storing coins.

Q: What does the term "roll friction" mean?

Michael Fuljenz describes it as "a shiny discoloration," and goes on to identify it as occurring on Ben Franklin's cheek on the half dollar, starting just behind the nose and running up to the sideburns. The apparent cause is friction between coins as they move about inside a paper roll as it is handled. It is also found on Walking Liberty halves, the Standing Liberty quarters, and the Saint Gaudens' $20 gold.

Q: Are there any standards for the number of coins in a roll?

I think more tradition than standard. The usual rolls of coins number 50 cents or dimes, 40 nickels or quarters, and 20 halves or dollars. In my wrapper collection I have some off brand varieties for such amounts as 20 nickels or quarters.

Q: Was there a standard number of SBA dollars in a roll?

I know of at least three standards: 20 dollars to a roll, as was used for the Morgan, Peace, and Ike Dollars; 25 to a roll; or some banks even wrapped them 40 to a roll, just like quarters. The American Banker's Association announced when the SBA dollars reached circulation that the rolls would hold 25 coins. It wound up with the SBA dollars being handled in rolls of either 20 or 25.

There were several controversies, including whether to wrap them in rolls of 20 or 25. Also, the original government intent was to wrap them in pink wrappers, but that was shouted down and the Treasury went to grey.

Q: Tell me the trick to instantly figuring the per-coin price of a roll of coins?

For a roll of 20 coins, multiply the roll price by 5 and move the decimal point two places left in your answer. For example, a $10 roll would be $10 x 5 = $50, then moving the decimal over two gives you 50 cents a coin. For rolls of 25 multiply by 4. For 40 coins, by 2.5, or double the price and add half. For 50 coin rolls, double the price. Remember that in each case you must move the decimal point two places to the left in the answer.

Q: I see proof rolls offered by dealers for sale. Can I order rolls of proof coins from the Mint? Why doesn't the Mint sell proof coins by the roll?

The dealer rolls are made up by breaking open the regular sets and assembling enough coins to make a roll. The Mint sells proof coins only in sets. It's a popular practice to break up sets and make up rolls.

Q: Is there such a thing as a mint wrapped roll of coins?

Although you may be offered such a roll, it is a misnomer, as the U.S. Mint does not currently wrap any coins. They are distributed from the production mint to the Federal Reserve Bank either in bags or in bulk containers. The Federal Reserve Banks in turn may in some cases issue wrapped coins, but much of their deliveries either are in "original" mint bags, or rebagged coins, which may include circulated as well as new coins, or again in bulk. In recent years the armored car services have taken over much of the wrapping and distribution services previously performed by the Federal Reserve Banks. Fed wrapped coins are identified by the name on the wrapper. In some cases the distributors may use their own wrappers, or they may wrap coins for their bank customers with wrappers with the bank name. Best advice, look at the label, which may tell you something about the source. Coins of other countries are another matter, as several world mints with smaller production wrap all their coins before releasing them.

Chapter 50

SCAMS, HOAXES, RUMORS

Where there's money to be made you'll find the sharks circling, waiting to get their teeth into something valuable. Then there are the hoaxes, often practical jokes gone wrong. And rumors....How could we gossips live without rumors? As coin collectors we have more than our share of all three.

Q: My information is that any unusual coin found in circulation is either a pattern or a trial strike. Care to comment?

You would be surprised by the number of letters in my files, frequently from dealers, making that same assumption. The fact of the matter is that there are almost no documented cases of either a pattern or trial strike getting into circulation in this century, and not very many in the previous century. There are a variety of causes for an unusual looking coin, most of them problems with the minting process, or a counterfeit or fake, but don't make the mistake of immediately assuming that it is a pattern. Best to assume it's not, and has no value, then prove it.

Q: My buddy swears there are 1983 "copper" cents that are being hoarded by a couple of big dealers who cornered all that were made and plan the make a killing in a few years. Is it just a rumor, or what?

In 1983 there were all kinds of rumors about the existence of copper (brass) cents, and half the people in the hobby knew of "some dealer" or other who had some, a roll, or a bag. However, all efforts to track down a genuine example were fruitless, because they were all just rumors, and not fact. The editorial staff here spent a substantial amount of time and phone calls trying to track down the rampant rumors of such a discovery, but never documented even one coin. From a practical standpoint, it would be impossible for any individual or even a group of dealers to "corner" a given coin. If there are any bets on this, your buddy loses.

Q: Were there any plans to recall the nickel coins after the issue of the 1942 silver nickels and the 1943 steel cents?

There were all sorts of rumors, but nothing official. There were large stocks of nickel in the Emergency Stockpile of metals.

Q: My grandfather had a small trunk full of Indian Head cents when I was a boy. He always was ready to tell a story about hauling that heavy trunk to the Century of Progress World's Fair in Chicago in 1930 only to be told that the coins were worth only face value. What was the story behind this hoax?

I've found only a fleeting reference to it, indicating that someone unknown started a rumor that everyone should save their Indian Heads and bring them to the Fair to receive big money for them, but the story was in fact, a hoax. One suggestion was that it had been staged as a publicity stunt to advertise the Fair, but apparently the true instigator was never found.

Q: A generalized hobby publication that carries some information on numismatics said in an article that the Spanish dollars were called "pieces of eight" because the *exchange rate when the U.S. dollar was established was $1.08 cents. Somehow that doesn't sound right.*

This is an interesting account, but unfortunately it is a glaring inaccuracy. The Spanish dollar or 8 reales was called a piece of eight because of the 8 reales denomination, not because of its exchange value. The same article went on to claim that the dollar sign evolved "when the U.S. on bags of dollars got written with one letter over the other," which is just as false.

Q: Why is it that the initial issues of most U.S. coins have been surrounded with rumors and controversy?

A little research indicates that this is certainly true of almost every new series or denomination introduced. Each case would have to be taken on an individual basis, but the underlying reason seems to be that it is impossible to satisfy everyone. The dissatisfied commented, "I'll bet this coin won't last six months!" The first two words are quickly dropped and a rumor is born.

Q: Isn't there a story connected with the Jefferson nickel having to do with the flag being missing from atop the building?

For lack of anything better to do during the early days of World War II, the rumor got started that the designer of the Jefferson nickel (Felix Schlag) had forgotten to put the flag up on the building. The actual source of the rumor was traced to public ignorance, as many people assumed that the building on the reverse of the nickel was the White House, despite the clear MONTICELLO title below. People thought that since the flag always flew over the White House, and it was missing from the coin, then the coin was rare and valuable. As with many other new issues, people hoarded the Jeffersons in the firm belief that the government, once the mistake was pointed out, would recall the coins and make them valuable. But the building was in fact Monticello, and it never had, nor was it intended to have a flag on top of it. Another radio broadcaster was to blame for this one, no less a famous personage than Walter Winchell. His statement during a national broadcast caused so much confusion that the Treasury Department had to issue a denial. Winchell said the coins were being recalled because they forgot to put a flag on Monticello.

Q: What's the story on President Taft's head appearing on the first Buffalo nickels?

This is a canard advanced by a reporter for a Boston newspaper, who in reporting the distribution of the first Buffalo nickels in 1913, averred that it was possible to see the outline of a human face on the lower part of the buffalo's head, and claimed that it resembled President Taft. Not unexpectedly, it takes a rather vivid imagination to reach agreement with the report, which also claimed that the new nickels were both "much lighter" and yet "thicker" than the old V nickels they would replace. The reporter went on to claim that the pieces wouldn't work in vending machines, and as a result the initial issue was delayed by two weeks.

Q: Besides the false rumors about Joseph Stalin's initials on the Roosevelt dime and the hammer and sickle on the Kennedy half, wasn't there some kind of a similar rumor about the Standing Liberty Quarters?

There is a report citing a newspaper account of such an incident, although newspapers— then and now—rarely have the facts when they discuss numismatic topics. According to this source, a milkman received a dateless quarter in payment for milk he had delivered, and got the idea that it was counterfeit. He spread the word to fellow workers, and as the tale got around, the Russians were added to the mix, and blamed for the manufacture of the "fake." Word reached the Secret Service, who told everybody that the date had worn off the coin, and otherwise it was perfectly good, but, as the newspaper told it, the rumor keeps cropping up and the Secret Service keeps having to dispute it. People tend to believe what they want to believe, right or wrong.

Q: If a medal is described as .999 percent silver, does that mean it's pure silver?

Whoa! and NO! It means it is a fraction under 1 percent silver. The .999 by itself would mean that it was 999 fine, with only one part alloy, but that innocent little percentage mark changes the whole picture. This scam actually has been used to foist base metal bars and medals on unsuspecting or myopic customers.

Q: Enclosed is a clipping from a local shopper's guide. Is this story true?

The clipping stated that many years ago a number of gold coins were "printed" accidentally with the words "IN GOLD WE TRUST." All I can say is, "Nope! There isn't a word of truth in it." There isn't even anything that would come close. Not to mention that coins are minted, not "printed."

Q: Has the United States Mint every been involved in the use or testing of a process to transmute gold from some other metal?

Shades of alchemy! Yes, the U.S. Mint did get involved in just such a scheme, although not of their own choosing and it's probably an event that they would have preferred to have buried behind a veil of silence. The Patent Office rejected a patent from one E.C. Brice, of Chicago for a process of making gold. Under the law the applicant may demand the opportunity to demonstrate his process, a loophole that Brice used in an attempt to get his patent approved. The Patent Office, not having facilities, requested that the demonstration be done at the Mint laboratory. The Mint in turn appointed the Superintendent of the New York Assay Office, the Philadelphia Mint's melter and refiner, and the Bureau Assayer as a committee to oversee the test. After three weeks, the committee rather dryly reported, noting a "possible waste of labor," that "We have not seen the slightest evidence of any 'creation' or transmutation." The report went on to add, "The claimant failed in every instance to even recover all of the gold and silver known to be present in the materials." This all happened in 1897, long after the art of alchemy had been laid to rest in the middle ages.

Q: A friend of mine claims that ruby glass was produced by melting gold coins with the glass. Is this true?

I can't vouch for the source, but one writer back in the 1940s claimed that the Libbey Glass Co. tossed $20 gold pieces into the furnace to produce the distinctively colored glass known as ruby glass. Perhaps a technical expert in our audience can confirm or refute this particular piece of folklore.

Q: I have several 1864 cents which were handed down through my family with the information that they contain a good amount of gold. How can I find out what they are worth?

The story that a gold ingot got melted into the alloy for coins is one with a long beard, and in this case a foreign accent, as the story is based on a hoax involving (among others) the British 1864 penny, started by a pub keeper who was long on imagination and short on customers. You can check your own bronze coins in this case, for if they contained any gold they would weigh more than the normal 48 grains. The copper-nickel cents with the 1864 date weigh 72.0 grains. Another U.S. coin with the same false story was the 1811 cent, although it's very likely that the rumor has touched other dates as well. In the mid-1800s it was virtually impossible to find an 1811 because they were so carefully hoarded as a result of this rumor. What all these stories neglect is that the very minor amount of gold to be found in a single coin would be worth only a few cents at best, even at today's gold prices. At the time, with $20 gold, the value probably would have been less than the face value of the coin.

Q: Is there such a thing as artificial gold?

First, let me say that "There is no such thing as artificial gold." One 19th century hoax was the listing in *Lee's Priceless Recipes* by Laird and Lee in 1895. It told: "To make artificial gold, use Virginia platina 16 parts, copper seven parts, zinc one part. Put in crucible with powdered charcoal and melt and mix. Makes a gold of extraordinary beauty and value, not possible by any tests which chemists know of to distinguish it from pure virgin gold." This is obviously false. "Synthetic" gold is a pipedream. There is no practical way of turning any other metal into gold. The alloy described in the answer would in no way be mistaken for gold, probably the only qualification being a yellow color which might have been mistaken for gold on a dark night. Despite labeling this as a hoax, several readers wrote in for more information, apparently believing it was real.

Q: Supposedly there are some aluminum discs that date from the 1860s which have the name J.A. Bolen stamped into them. Are these pieces genuine?

No doubt your question is based on the unlikely existence of any aluminum discs in that era, when aluminum was still a great rarity and extremely expensive. Russ Rulau cites this, and a story of a Boston coin dealer who had access to the Bolen punches, who produced similar pieces as a practical joke on Maurice Gould, a counterstamp expert and competing coin dealer in Boston. He believes that the discs quite likely emanated from Boston, but still have collector interest because of the genuine punches used.

Q: What ever happened to the "$4 million" coin that was stolen several years ago?

Since we're still only at the $1 million level for a single coin, the silver dollar in question was stuck with the super inflated price tag by a South Dakota coin dealer, with the help of an Associated Press reporter, after the coin was allegedly stolen from a resident of the state. The story drew big laughs in the hobby. It was supposedly an 1821 silver dollar, but no dollars were struck between 1804 and 1836. There was of course no proof of the coin's existence. The most valuable coin at the time was listed at $230,000.

Q: Wasn't there some kind of a hoax associated with the Carson City dollars, something about them being "chop marked?"

It's an interesting, if dark sidelight on the coins of the Nevada Mint, but it revolved around one Abraham Curry, the man instrumental in founding Carson City and later getting the government to build a mint there. When Curry died, a popular scam in towns around the region was to tell anyone trying to spend a Carson coin that the CC mint mark was the "chop" of Curry's making the coins nearly worthless. The sharper would then reluctantly accept the piece at a fraction of face value to be added to his private hoard of CC coins which already had gained a reputation as being collector's items.

Q: You say there are "No genuine circulation full strike coins with two obverses or two reverses." Here's a newspaper item citing a silver dollar with a 1906 date on one side, 1909 on other.

This was a hoax in the 1912 newspapers. The article said that one side was struck at a time, but both sides of a coin are struck simultaneously. That and the dates are impossible, as no dollars were struck between 1904 and 1921.

Q: We've had lots of trouble over the years with misleading ads offering "silver" dollars, which turn out to be the cupro-nickel alloy instead. Any success in battling this scam?

Very little, and you might be surprised to hear that the Canadians have had the same problem, even taking a case to the Canadian Supreme Court, without success. In both countries, the argument used to sidle out of a potentially expensive ad writer's exuberance or ignorance is that "silver dollar" is a generic term, used so commonly as to no longer limit its meaning to true silver coins. Another way of saying that if you lie long enough it becomes truth.

Q: In reviewing my collection, I noticed that the $5 gold coin in my Statue of Liberty commemorative set doesn't match the catalog. Are there two varieties of this coin?

This collector fell victim to a misleading ad at the time the official coins were issued. The ad from a private "mint" offered a "set" containing the genuine half dollar and dollar but substituted a privately produced medal for the genuine $5 gold coin. The piece is not a coin and was not produced by the U.S. Mint so its only value would be any bullion that it might contain.

Q: I received a set of coins as a gift. I quickly discovered that the coins were not only worn, but they were cleaned and polished. Can't something be done about these scams?

There's little that can be done, as the firms that sell them do so outside the organized hobby. One thing that can be done is to deal only with dealers who regularly advertise in the hobby publications or on recognized computer online bulletin boards where their offers can be monitored.

Q: Wasn't there a contest to find mint mark letters on cents? Didn't Henry Ford offer a car for a 1922 cent?

One of the rumored contests was to find mint marks that would spell F, O, R, and D, then another S, O, L, and D. Since there are no U.S. mints that use F, R, or L for a mint mark, the story is an obvious hoax. This gets added to the "cute but truthless" stories. Someone else started the rumor that there were 200 1922 cents struck (without a mint mark) and that Henry had 192 of them, and was offering a new car for each of the other eight. This of course was just as false.

Q: I have another "Ford" story for you. Back in 1948 the Ford Motor Company stamped a quantity of cents with the script Ford logo, and put them in circulation, offering a new car for anyone who found one. Can you track this down?

I'm way ahead of you, thanks to a reader who furnished me documentary evidence that your story is false. In response to a query in 1978, the curator of the Ford Museum flatly denied that any such "deal" had been offered. From his letter, it is evident that numerous such unfounded rumors were started over the years.

Q: I still have a clipping from my local newspaper which says that a 1936 cent was sold for $25,000 because it was a mint "error." What ever happened to the coin, and are the 1936 cents I have found with a missing leg on the R in LIBERTY valuable?

The story of that 1936 cent was strictly a "bummer," as the coin in question was worthless. I happened to be the first expert who was allowed to examine the piece, and I determined that the coin appeared to have been altered, and was too worn to identify any possible minting variety. The alleged sale and promotion were used to help sell copies of a book written by the buyer. There was a recent attempt to revive the scheme by displaying the coin at an ANA convention in Baltimore, but the plans fell through. The 1936 cents you have are the result of a broken R on the hub used to make the die. There are several varieties, including ones with a second R with both legs over the one legged R. Yours do have a small value, depending on the grade, so are worth keeping.

Q: Are the needles that are offered to find buried coins worth buying?

This is an ancient scam that is continually revived, this time with coins as the bait.

Q: I've heard of a con game called the pigeon drop scheme, but how does it work?

This is one of the older confidence games around, but it still finds victims every year. A member of a group of con artists will approach a potential victim, or "pigeon," with a story that a large amount of money has been found. They usually show the victim the money, gold bars, coins, or whatever valuable they claim to have discovered. The victim is told he can share in the find simply by putting up earnest money, coins, bullion, etc. to establish his credibility. Once the sucker's money is in hand the con artists evaporate, along with whatever valuables were used for the scam.

Q: Were the zinc plated cents of 1943 a serious problem as far as confusion with the dime was concerned?

Contemporary accounts indicate that the coins were somewhat of a problem, although my personal recollection on the point is rather vague. One note of interest which does show that they were used by a few to make a profit was an item which was noted in the press at the time. The New York Post reported that the Third Avenue Railway company had been forced to install large magnets in the fare boxes to catch the "lead cents" that passengers tossed in, in an attempt to pay full fare with a single cent.

1943 steel cent.

Q: What is meant by "Ponzi schemes" in reference to purchases of coins or bullion?

A man named Ponzi in the 1920s bilked millions from investors by promising unusually high returns, then using new investment money coming in to pay the "interest" on earlier deposits. By publicizing the high returns he attracted even more money, until the bubble burst, leaving most of his victims broke. The term is applied loosely to any shady transaction where someone gets the use of your capital in exchange for promises of riches to be delivered "tomorrow." To avoid problems, always take delivery on coins or bullion that you buy, never letting anyone "keep" it for you.

Chapter 51

SETS

Q: How long since a complete set of Lincolns has been taken from circulation?

Probably prior to about 1960. Until then wheat cents were still plentiful in circulation, but they started disappearing with the issue of the 1959 memorial reverse cents.

Q: I have a complete set of Lincoln cents, lacking only the 1909-S VDB. Should I buy the coin to complete the set before selling the whole set?

If you are selling the set immediately, buying the key coin would be a losing proposition. If you are holding the set for future sale, then it might be worthwhile, but you will have to hold the set until the purchased coin has appreciated enough to offset the dealer's profit margin.

Q: What is the exact number of coins required for a set of Lincoln cents?

If someone tells you that a set is a set, they are wrong. Ask any group of coin dealers or collectors what constitutes a set of any denomination or series and you are likely to get as many answers as there are responses. In general, a set consists of one example of each date and mint. However, varieties are a matter of disagreement. While most, for example, would consider the 1909-S and 1909-S VDB cents as required for a set, despite being from the same year and mint, some would balk at including the 1955 doubled die, the 1972 doubled die, or the 1990 no-S proof cent. Some consider a set as just the circulating coins. Others include the proofs. Some demand that your set include an extra coin (two for the Lincoln cent) to show the reverse design.

Q: How many complete sets of early large cents are in existence?

Denis W. Loring, the National Secretary for Early American Coppers was kind enough to provide us with a complete and detailed answer, which I'll quote:

"With regard to complete sets of early date large cents. No one has ever completed a collection of all die varieties listed by Sheldon, as several of the "non-collectible" varieties are unique and owned by different people. Usually copper collectors refer to a collection of all 295 numbered varieties (plus six subvarieties, or differences in edge lettering) as "complete." Nine individuals have formed complete collections, two of which are still intact:

George H. Clapp: completed in the 1940s; donated to the ANS intact.
William H. Sheldon: completed in the 1940s; sold intact to R.E. Naftzger Jr. in 1972.
Dorothy I. Paschal: completed in the 1950s; dispersed privately by Raymond H. Chatham in the 1970s.
R.E. Naftzger Jr.: completed in 1972; in process of private dispersal by Eric J. Streiner.
Denis W. Loring: completed in 1974; dispersed privately by Dr. Robert J. Shalowitz in 1974.
Robinson S. Brown Jr.: completed in 1976; sold at public auction by Superior in 1986.
Jack H. Robinson: completed in 1989; sold at public auction by Superior in 1989.
G. Lee Kuntz: completed in 1989; sold at public auction by Superior in 1991.
John R. Frankenfeld: completed in 1991; intact."

Q: What is a "modern date obsolete U.S. coin set," that I found in a flea market?

A bit of double talk for describing a "20th Century Type Set." The set in question contains such coins as the Buffalo nickel, Franklin and 1964 Kennedy half, and silver Mercury and Roosevelt dimes. The coins may be "obsolete," but they are still legal tender.

Q: Why do dealers offer 13 coin "sets" of the SBA dollars? I count only 12 coins in a full set (circulation strikes).

The 13th coin is added so that the common reverse can be displayed with all the obverses. Besides the regulars, there are the extra 1979-P variety, the extra S and D mint marks for 1979 and extra S in 1981, making the total 16, including the proofs, and one to show the reverse.

Chapter 52

SLANG, NICKNAMES

Earlier I mentioned that coin collectors and dealers have their own secret language. A major part of this is the use of slang terms and nicknames, many of them dreamed up to cover a lack of knowledge of the minting process or to jazz up some common minting variety with a fancy sounding name and price to match. Needless to say, the collector needs to tread carefully when the terms being used are other than the proper technical language.

Q: I've seen "Akcidefects" mentioned several times. What does it mean?

This was cataloger M.L. Beistle's definition of "accidental die defects," referring to what we now class as die clash marks, or die clashes. The term was "coined" to combat the discredited "die suction" theory advanced as the cause for the markings. There are still references to die suction in some of our current or recent hobby literature, so the misinformation is still being spread.

Q: What is an "atheist cent?" I've seem some references to it in an old coin publication.

This is a nickname for a die break which occurred in the motto. Major die breaks covering parts of the In God We Trust motto are known for several years and mints, so this is not unusual. Values generally run from $5 to $15, depending on the size of the die break. The nickname arose from a coin which was missing the word "GOD." A major die break is one which extends from the edge of the coin across the rim into the field or onto the design. You will see major die breaks described as "cuds," which is yet another nickname.

Q: What is a "Black Beauty" nickel?

"Black Beauty" is a nickname that was applied to the nickels struck at Philadelphia in 1959, and may have been applied in other years as well. The coins attracted considerable attention at the time because they were assumed to be a minting variety. The color was either a surface discoloration, (which would have no value as that is not classed as a minting variety) or it's also possible that the alloy contained cobalt, which will cause nickel to darken in color. Cobalt is found in conjunction with some nickel ores, and is extremely difficult to separate from the nickel. If it was a surface discoloration, the probable cause was contact with sulfur fumes in the air or a sulfur compound that came in contact with the metal at some point. I'm inclined to favor the cobalt theory.

Q: What's a Black Dogg?

This was the nickname for the French Cayenne sous which circulated in the U.S. colonies in the 1700s. They were intended for New France, but spread into other areas, despite an aversion to copper coins, possibly the cause for the nickname. More than 500,000 were struck, but only 8,000 circulated in New France, the remainder being returned. At the time they passed for two pennies.

Q: What is a blanked die?

This term was used in the 1940s for what is known today as a die clash. This is mint language for a die which has been damaged by the opposing die (die clash) when they came together without a blank, or planchet, between them to absorb the blow.

Q: What were "blood thalers?"

These were German thalers of Frederick II of Hesse-Kassel who provided many of the Hessian mercenaries for the British for the Revolutionary War. The Hessian soldiers brought the coins to America, where the public decreed them stained with the blood of patriots.

Q: Any idea where the expression "to be buffaloed" came from? I believe it had something to do with an old trick preformed with a Buffalo nickel.

One source gives a trick which may have been the one that buffaloed a lot of bar flies. During World War I, a Buffalo nickel was dropped into a nearly empty beer stein when nobody was looking. The trickster asked for an empty stein, then announced that he could fill it with the contents of his glass. After bets were laid, he poured the dregs on the bar along with the nickel, and invited the bartender to "fill 'er up!" Worked every time.

Q: What's a "buzzard" cent?

The public has a habit of turning up its collective nose at new coin designs, and the Flying Eagle cent was no exception, quickly getting a sneer from the traditionalists.

1857 Flying Eagle cent.

Q: What is a "caved" die?

This is an old term for a die which has had part of the face sink, due to the pounding in striking coins. The Mint had periodic heat treating problems for their die steels, especially dies used in 1926, 1954-55, and the early 1970s. More recently the same effect is seen on the zinc cents. Today we commonly call it a "sunken die." It shows as a raised ridge, often beneath the letters in the motto around the rim.

Q: Do you happen to have a list of the common nicknames for our different coins?

This is probably not complete, but one writer lists the following:

Half cent:	half penny
Large cent:	penny, copper
Small cent:	nickel, eagle cent, Indian cent, Indian head cent, penny, copperhead, red, brass, Lincoln
3-cent:	nickel, threepenny bit, trime, fish scales
5-cent:	nickel, jitney, slug, buffalo, Jeffs
Half dime:	half bit, fip, picayune
Dime:	short bit, dim, dimo, dimmy, dis-mee (Incorrect pronunciation of disme), dimer, kopeck, thin
Quarter:	two bits, rough
Half dollar:	four bits
Silver dollar:	plunk, daddy dollar, cartwheel, iron man, simoleon, clam, smacker, shekel, bone, big boy, buck, spondulix, ferriswheel, deadman, hoop, sinker, washer, slug, wheel, bean, white bean, crown, silver baby, Beau or Bo. Recent—Carter quarters.
Gold coins:	bean, ridge, shine, sunbeam, gilt, ocher. Larger—yellow boys

$2.50 Gold:	yellow quarter
$5 gold:	half ned
$10 Gold:	ned, red
$50 ingots:	slugs

Q: Please explain what the "Copperheads" were.

Dissenters on the Union side during the Civil War formed a number of secret organizations which in one way or another aided the Confederate cause. Members used a cut down large cent, showing just the head, as a means of identification, and from this came the term, "Copperheads."

Q: What was, or is "country pay?"

Very often corn and other grains were used in lieu of money in colonial times. With coins short, it could even be used to pay taxes. The term continued in use, and may still be used in some parts of the Eastern Seaboard.

Q: What is a "crippled" coin?

A rare coin which has been damaged but is retained as a "filler" until a better specimen can be obtained is called a "cripple."

Q: I know that fanciful names were very popular for minting varieties in the 1960s, and that a number of different type coin designs have been nicknamed, but were there similar slang terms for die breaks on the older coins?

There are numerous examples in the old listings. One in particular that stands out is the 1817 cent, as there are at least four different dies which show a small die break above the Liberty head. These were variously called a dolphin, a snail, a mouse, or a rat head. Certainly not too different than the alligator, flying saucer, baseball bat, floating head, and other nicknames that confounded and confused variety collectors in the 1960s.

Q: Any luck on a definition of die burn? In regards to the recent question about the term "die burn," I have a couple of coins which exhibit burned areas from contact with hot dies.

In normal use the dies do not get to more than a couple of hundred degrees at most, so it would be virtually impossible for the dies to actually burn a coin. I'll be glad to examine the pieces you have found to try to figure out what did happen to them. A reader sent me an article which used this term several times, but without defining it. From my experience with die making and use, I'd guess that what he is referring to is the "orange peel" effect caused by worn dies, which gives nickel alloy coins a very rough field. It apparently is a Canadian term, so perhaps one of our readers up there can help out with a specific definition. David Lange suggested that it refers to the small mirror-like areas in the field of a coin resulting from repair work with a fine abrasive. Can anyone confirm this?

Q: What is meant by "die suction?"

This is a discredited term invented to explain the "ghosting" of design elements of a coin on the opposite side, or die clashes, as for example the Lincoln bust appearing as a hazy outline on the reverse of the wheat cents. The amateur experts of the day believed that coins were struck of molten metal and that the suction between the face of the die and the liquid pulled the metal into the die. We know now that this actually is design transfer from one die to the other due to the repeated pounding of striking coins. Only recently I learned that "die clash" is a British term, one of a few which has been adopted by U.S. numismatists with the same meaning.

Q: Silver dollars I know, but "Iron" dollars?

As a transplanted Yankee who grew up in New Hampshire, I can trace this back to New England, where a nickname for the silver coins was "iron" dollars. The reference was not complimentary, as they were disliked for their weight and bulk.

Q: How did the silver dollar get the nickname "cartwheel?"

This goes back to the old English coins, where large coins were called coach wheels or cart wheels. More recently the term has been included in "cartwheel effect," referring to the mint lustre similar in appearance to the shimmer of a turning wheel in a movie or on TV.

Q: I've heard the famous 1804 dollar referred to as the "bartender's dollar." Any special reason behind that nickname?

An ironic nickname, but not for the "original restrikes" which are the valuable ones. The epithet stems from the efforts of a person named Kennedy from Lowell, Massachusetts who very expertly converted 1800 dollars into 1804 dates, and then peddled the pieces in the 1880s using men dressed as tramps who told a sob story of wealth dissipated in drink, and offered their last "valuable" possession for a new stake. They quickly found that bartenders were the biggest suckers to fall for the line, and concentrated their efforts, leaving many an empty bar till in their travels.

Q: What is a Gypsy dollar?

This is one more name for the Maria Theresa thaler which one author claims was adopted by the gypsies of Europe as their universal coin. American gypsies in the early part of this century gold plated the big silver coins and sold them as European gold for close to $50 each.

Q: What is a "Bland" dollar?

Today's collectors would recognize them as Morgan dollars. Bland was a Missouri Representative who got together with Senator Allison to pass legislation which forced the Treasury to buy a minimum of $2 million a month of silver for coin dollars. The Bland-Allison Act of February 28, 1878 authorized the silver dollars and popularly they were named after one of the co-sponsors of the bill. Later they were called Liberty Head dollars, with Morgan's name attached to them as a fairly recent development.

A Bland dollar is a Liberty Head dollar is a Morgan dollar.

Q: Did you ever locate an answer to the question about the "Bo" dollars?

Bill Keffer did some digging for us, and reports that the term appears to have started in the French speaking areas of Louisiana. One story has it that a man named Franklin Beaux (?) was the first person to bring a quantity of silver dollars into the area of South Louisiana and introduced them into commerce there. Since "Beaux" in French would be pronounced "Bo," this seems a logical story to explain the term. Veteran coin dealer Jon B. Jolly writes, "...I'm now 65. My father owned a country grocery store in North Georgia and we used to get silver dollars from across the line in Alabama. At that place and at that time there was no confusion in our minds about this term. It was spelled 'BOW' (pronounced like 'GO') and meant, of course, a round dollar. I guess 'bow' isn't used much any more to mean round, but it certainly did 55 years ago in North Georgia." One source indicated that it was Cajun French slang for "good" dollar, or silver.

Q: What on earth is a "fandango dollar?"

It was the appellation applied to a short lived scheme to ship Colorado silver to Mexico to be minted into "dollars" to use up the mountains of unsalable silver resulting from the repeal of the Sherman Silver Act in 1893. The main backer of the idea was the Governor, Davis H. Waite.

Q: What's a "door hanger?"

I'm going to blame Burnett Anderson for bringing this bit of slang back from West Point. The mint workers use this nickname for a partially plated zinc cent planchet, supposedly because it got hung up in a bin door and didn't get the full plating treatment.

Q: Did early coin collectors make a distinction between "double cut" and "recut" dies?

There is some food for thought in the difference, as they listed dies as "double cut" if the doubling was part of the original die, and "recut" if the die had been in service for a time before the recutting occurred. Both terms actually referred to punching as well as cutting with an engraving tool.

Q: Was there a nickname for the 20-cent piece?

With some logic—"double dime." The term was widely used by early catalogers and dealers, especially Haseltine.

Q: What's a fish scale?

The silver three-cent piece struck between 1851-1873 was one. The principal reason for the nickname was its small size, plus its thinness. The Mint Director at the time, Col. Snowdon, tried to establish the coin as the "trime," but the label never caught on with the public. The other coin which got labeled as a fish scale was the Canadian silver five-cent piece, struck from 1858 to 1921. It's quite likely the nickname got started with the American coin as it was the first struck.

Q: What is a "force" die?

A force is actually more of a punch than a die, although they are similar in that the design on both the die and the force is incuse, or into the face of the tool. The term is probably pretty much obsolete, but it was once used to describe a tool which was classed as an embossing punch, as its use left a raised design on the metal being worked.

Q: What is "grandam gold?"

It's an obsolete term for hoarded money.

Q: What is a hamburger coin?

This was a lay press term applied to the first clad coins in 1965.

Q: Hammered coins I know, but "hammered dollars?"

As you indicate, hammered coins mostly went out with the introduction of the coin press in the 16th century. The hammered dollars were Spanish 8-reale coins defaced with a hammer by the Mexican authorities, and circulated in Texas when it was still under Mexican rule. Two reasons were given for the practice: the hatred for the Spaniards and anything representing them, and to keep the pieces from leaving the country. They passed for about 90 cents in United States money.

Q: Did you ever come up with a definitive definition for a "hay mark?"

This question has been kicking around for several years. At one time I thought perhaps it might refer to what we now call a filled die, missing design due to dirt and grease packing into the cavity in the die, which leaves a rough irregular surface on the coin from the embedded metal fragments. However, Walter Breen told me that it is an obsolete term for what we now call hairlines, the tiny scratches that result from cleaning, polishing, or buffing a coin. The term is still used in England to describe coins suffering this kind of damage.

Q: What is a humdinger coin?

There should be at least two answers to this, or perhaps one that refers to a similar name. Humdinger is a slang term for something that is very nice, or pleasing. It is also reported as the name applied to a coin, often a large cent, which had been holed twice and then threaded on a loop of string or heavy thread. By winding it up, and then working the hands back and forth in the loops, the coin would make a humming noise as it revolved rapidly.

Q: Please define "junk" silver.

The term originated as a description of damaged, badly worn, or mutilated coins, usually intended to be melted down for the bullion content. However, in recent years the meaning has been modified to include "common date" silver coins, or those with high mintages and minimal numismatic value. I always thought it meant U.S. silver coins, but one source indicates that back in the 1920s and 1930s, "junk" silver was a term reserved for low value world coins which might contain some silver, but usually less than 50 percent, or world silver coins that had no exchange value. The modern usage, referring to U.S. 90 percent silver common date pieces, came into regular usage in the 1979-1980 boom in the bullion market.

Q: What was the most popular nickname for the zinc plated steel cents of 1943?

Contrary to some published reports that they were widely called "silver," "steel," or even "zinc" cents, by far the most common slang term for them was "lead" cents. The public equated them with the still common lead counterfeits of the Depression years.

Q: Weren't all of the Liberty head coins called "Morgans" at one time?

This takes some explaining. The "Morgan" dollars, during the early years they were circulating, were not called that. They were either referred to as "Bland" dollars, or just "Liberty head" dollars. By the time of the general change in minor denomination designs (1892) the "Morgan" name had begun to be used, and most people called the new coins "Morgan" dimes or quarters or halves, simply because they had a Liberty head, even though they were the work of Barber. Several dealers and at least one editor of a numismatic publication contributed to the problem by referring to "Morgan" dimes, quarters, or halves in their ads, or in editorial copy. The coins were designed by Charles E. Barber, carry his initial at the base of the bust and correctly are referred to as "Barber" coins. Morgan got a lot of mileage out of designing the 1878 dollar, but had nothing to do with the 1892 coinage.

Q: What is an "Orphan Annie" dime? Didn't they disappear aboard a ship that sank off the East Coast?

This was the popular nickname attached to the 1844 dimes from Philadelphia, because they were a very low mintage (72,500) and Philadelphia was the only mint to strike dimes that year. Oddly, many of them must have been saved, because today they bring half of the price of an 1843-O dime, which had more than twice the mintage. That sinking story is just one of the unsubstantiated legends connected with this coin. The most likely cause for the disappearance of most of the dimes with the 1844 date is that a speculator bought the majority of them and shipped them out of the country to be melted for their bullion content.

Q: What is a Panamint Ball?

The original was a solid ball of silver bullion, weighing 750 pounds. It was conceived by Senators John P. Jones and William Stewart of Nevada as a theft-proof means of transporting silver from their mine in the Panamint mountains to Carson City. In 1964 a similar ball was shipped from Nevada to the Philadelphia Mint to be made into Centennial medals.

Q: Where did the expression "plug nickel" come from?

The original phrase was "not worth a plugged nickel." I believe the original source was the practice in the West of using nickels for target practice. A nickel that was hit by a bullet was considered as "plugged," and worthless. Earlier the term plugged traces back to an issue of tin coins with copper plugs in early England. The plug was supposed to be a deterrent to counterfeiting.

Q: When did they start the use of the "poor man's double die" nickname?

One of the earliest I can find is an ad in a 1962 coin publication. The nickname was—and still is—applied to mask a very common polishing variety of the 1955 cent which has absolutely no connection to, and far less value than the real 1955 doubled-die minting variety. It's a graphic example of why I advise not buying a nicknamed coin if the seller can't tell you what kind of a minting variety it is or how it was produced.

Q: What is a "posthole bank?" I've seen the term in connection with stories of coin finds with a metal detector.

The nickname was applied to the early day practice of homesteaders who were miles from any bank using the opportunity of a posthole dug near their house to bury coins or other valuables for safekeeping.

Q: Is "rap" a slang term, or a legitimate coin denomination?

My old Webster describes it as a slang term for an early 18th century counterfeit half penny in Ireland, and goes on to cite it as the source for the saying, "I don't give a rap."

Q: Here's an obscure coin nickname for you to dig up a meaning for us: a "Robertson."

Frey's Numismatic Dictionary missed this one, but the answer is that it was applied to clipped, mutilated, or fake gold coins of Spain, Portugal, and England. An infamous General Robertson was the English Governor of New York during the British occupation of that city, and he feathered his nest by demanding genuine coins in payment, and in turn paid out clipped coins for supplies. The nickname was applied first to the clipped pieces, and spread later to the other frauds.

Q: What is a "rolled fold" on a coin?

This may sound unbelievable, but the term was actually printed in at least one numismatic publication with a picture of what we know today as a die break, extending from the rim well into the field.

Q: I can't find a specific meaning for "shift." Can you help?

This is an obsolete term, which was used before machine doubling was recognized as damage to the coin rather than part of the minting process. It was frequently misused to apply to almost any of the some 20 forms of doubling that can be found on coins. The most frequent use was to hide a lack of knowledge of the real cause of the doubling. The closest to what you are asking here is die bounce, which occurs after the strike, producing worthless machine doubling damage. During the strike the dies and the planchet mesh like three gears, so there cannot be any movement of either the planchet or dies at the moment of impact, so obviously there can be no "shift" of either the dies or planchet. To demonstrate, put your hands together, fingers between fingers. Then try to move either hand sideways without moving the other hand. This is the way the die and planchet mesh during the strike, the relief of the coin sticking into the incuse design in the die.

Q: Which was the "ship on wheels" commemorative?

This was a slighting reference to the design of the 1892-93 Columbian Expo half. The reverse has a ship above two globes, which resemble wheels.

1892 Columbian Expo half dollar.

Q: Reading the ads, I am puzzled by many of the abbreviations and some of the words used. What does "slabbing" mean, for example?

Slabbing is a new slang term in the hobby, referring to the practice by some of the grading services of sealing a coin in a thick plastic case, or "slab," along with the grading information. The case is intended to protect the piece from handling damage, and in theory to keep the grading information with the coin which was actually examined. The coins are then traded and sold in the slab.

Q: Please define the term "sleeper."

A sleeper is a collectible which has been overlooked or ignored by collectors and dealers, but which is likely to show an increase in value. Many collectors make a habit of looking for coins which are really rarer than they are perceived to be, or that are underpriced for their rarity or condition.

Q: Where did the term "slider" originate?

Slider is a slang term that has embedded itself in hobby language, referring usually to a coin which, with a little wishful thinking, could "slide" up to a higher grade. Most consider it as a sort of between grade, but sliders are often abused by being relabeled as the higher grade to increase the profit margin. The term originated from the use of the old Wayte Raymond National Coin Albums. These had very thick pages with holes into which the coins were inserted and then strips of plastic slid into place on both sides to hold the coin in position. The movement of these strips across the coins quickly turned uncirculated coins into worn, scratched coins that no longer met the criteria for an uncirculated coin, so they were called sliders.

Q: What is a "splasher?"

The term is used to describe a test piece struck with a new die, usually on soft metal which tends to spread out markedly. It is a form of a die trial, usually uniface, in aluminum, or lead. The term probably arose from the false assumption that coins are cast, rather than struck, a misapprehension that still hasn't completely died out.

Q: Was one of our coins referred to as the "tombstone" coin?

While it was not a generally used nickname, some artistic circles charged the 2-cent coin with being "monumental art, engraved in the typical manner of a tombstone."

Q: What is a "trap" coin?

At first I thought this might be some sort of variation of the screw thalers which were hollowed out to serve as lockets, but "trap" is a slang term applied to coins which have hidden damage, something that doesn't show up except under strong magnification, or rim damage that is hidden by the holder or slab. It also seems to have been applied to coins that are overpriced.

Q: How about a trolley car coin? Which one do they mean?

It's slang or a nickname for the memorial reverse on the cent, which resembles one of the old streetcars. It was used disparagingly by the critics who wanted the wheat reverse retained.

Q: Today dealers talk about "raw" coins, the ones that haven't been encased in slabs, but what did the old-time dealers mean by a "virgin" coin?

A virgin coin in years past was a coin which had never been cleaned and thus was in its original condition, as modified by any wear. There is ample evidence that leaving coins alone and not trying to clean them will enhance their value, but this is a point that newcomers to the hobby learn usually only after they have made the mistake of ruining their coins by cleaning them.

Q: Is "William" a slang word having something to do with money?

I haven't heard it lately, so it probably comes under the heading of obsolete slang. "William" was used in several parts of the country for any piece of paper money, regardless of the denomination. The usage arose from the pun on "bill." Those Confederate notes which had blue backs, in contrast to the greenbacks of the North, were called "Blue Williams."

Q: What is "wood grain" toning?

It is a peculiar effect found on many of the early Lincoln cents, which after a time appear similar to the typical wood grain with light and dark streaks.

Q: Can you tell me, just what is a "Yankee dime?"

This is not exactly "coin of the realm." Back in the days when New England was still a group of colonies, it was the custom for girls to pay off a debt or favor with a kiss. These kisses, while not exactly cheap, got the nickname of a Yankee dime. While this sounds like a good story, it is somewhat curious that the term "dime" would be used, long before our first "disme" made its appearance. Perhaps the source got his time periods mixed up.

Chapter 53

STORAGE, SUPPLIES, EQUIPMENT, TOOLS, CLEANING

After you collect a coin, what do you do with it? Storing your collection properly, using the right storage media, having the right equipment such as magnifiers, and the nightmare of cleaning coins—all are grist for questions. To those of us who recognize the damage that cleaning can do, it's scary to see letters come in, or messages being posted on the online computer services, asking about how to clean up a collection before they sell it. What's even more scary is that these readers at least had sense enough to ask before doing it, but how many others are there out there right now scrubbing away......?

Q: How can I clean my coins?

Rule number one of coin collecting is—Don't clean your coins. Rule number two is—Always obey rule number one. Seriously, other than removing loose dirt or grease, any attempt to clean coins will permanently damage the surface, and reduce the value to collectors, sometimes to 50 percent or less. In words of one syllable, there is no safe way for the amateur to clean coins. Even professional cleaning is likely to permanently damage the coin surfaces, so with the exception of removing loose dirt or grease, our best advice is to leave your coins strictly alone. There is no product on the market that will safely remove encrustation or corrosion without permanently damaging the underlying metal. There are methods used by museums to clean coins that come out of the ground but they are expensive and still do at least some damage to the coin. If soaking the coin in a neutral solvent won't do the trick there isn't much else to try that won't leave you with a piece of worthless metal. There is no known process that will restore mint luster or improve the grade of a coin.

Q: Wasn't it at one time the accepted thing to clean and polish coins in a collection?

Read some of the old books from the 19th century, and you will find advice on how to clean, polish, rub, brush, and otherwise "prettify" your collectibles. The practice went out with moustache cups, but the general public assumes it is still current practice. I once had a collector bring me a large quantity of coins he wanted to sell that he had run through a rock polishing tumbler!

Q: I have a quantity of circulated silver dollars which are covered with dirt. How do I go about cleaning them up?

Plain soap and water is about the best for removing dirt. Don't rub the coins, rinse thoroughly afterward in plain water and then allow them to air dry, or pat them dry with a towel, but again, don't rub them. For encrusted dirt, try soaking in olive oil. Anything beyond this is going to do permanent damage to the coins and reduce their value.

Q: I've noticed some kind of grease on the coins I've taken from new rolls. Any idea of the source?

You will frequently find clear grease, and often very dirty grease adhering to new coins, which has been deposited on the coins during the minting process. Since this can contain damaging contaminants, it's a good idea to remove it with a neutral solvent before storing your coins.

Q: Will an ultrasonic cleaner be safe for my coins?

It's OK if you do one coin at a time, otherwise they may rub each other. Change the liquid frequently if the coins being cleaned are very dirty. This works only for loose dirt and grease.

Q: I have a quantity of silver art bars purchased in the 1970s which have tarnished badly. What can I clean them with?

The same rules that apply to coins apply here, except that most of your bars are, and probably will remain for the foreseeable future, worth more for their bullion content than their art. If you clean them, you will destroy the minted surface, and they will retarnish even more rapidly than they did originally. Special care is a matter of personal preference. There's no real need to protect the surface of regular bullion bars. But for the art bars, the dip will remove a part of the surface metal along with the tarnish, and will not prevent it from reforming, so you enter a vicious circle that will ultimately lead to a bar with a flat, ugly, altered surface, worth only its bullion value.

Q: I recently purchased a collection of Barber proofs, most of which have nearly identical parallel scratches on Liberty's cheek. Is there any special reason for this damage?

One source traces these slide marks to the albums which have thick "pages" with slides on one or both sides of the coin to hold it in place. If the coin isn't seated far enough in the hole, the slide will leave marks on the cheek, the high point of the design. The indication is that as many as three-fourths of the existing Barber proofs have been damaged in this way.

Q: My uncirculated nickels are stored in an album and recently I noticed they are starting to get spots on them. Is this the fault of the album?

Albums or boards are fine for circulated coins, but they do not provide the necessary protection needed to store high grade coins, especially for long periods. The key problem is that most are not airtight, hence they provide no protection from airborne contamination or handling, which is probably what caused the spots on your coins. The best long term protection are airtight, inert holders, such as the hard plastic holders. They cost more but they are designed specifically to protect coins for a long period of time. There are several brands on the market. There is also at least one album on the market fitted for airtight holders.

Q: I have a $50 bag of cents which I bought back in the late 1960s, which still has the mint seal on it, but no indication of the date or mint that struck them. Any ideas as to how to find out without opening the bag?

The value of the coins depends on the coin itself, not on how it is packaged, so you are needlessly protecting the packaging when you should have long since removed the coins and installed them in airtight inert tubes or holders. By this time it is likely that the coins have been permanently damaged by remaining in the bag, which provides no protection against contamination in the air. My advice would be to open the bag, sort out the salvageable coins—if any—and dispose of the rest. Keep the bag for a souvenir if you wish but that's about all it's good for.

(Updated) The coins turned out to be 1969 cents cataloging at 45 cents in uncirculated grade, or something more than $2000 worth in the $50 bag. However, from the samples that were sent to me, a large percentage had bag marks and scratches from movement within the bag while in storage, and quite a few more had spots and corrosion from their unprotected storage. Only a few were left which might be classed as uncirculated. While he didn't lose what he paid for the bag, he did lose out on the profit that proper storage could have earned him. My advice, repeated, is never to keep coins in a bag for long term storage, even if it is a "mint sealed" bag.

Q: In a recent article your publication warned against storing coins in places where there are extremes of heat or cold, or high humidity. If one must store coins in a home, where then is the best place?

If you stop and think about it, the least temperature extremes are in the living area of the house, where you keep the temperature somewhere near 70 degrees. This suggests a safe located in some part of the house that is kept at a reasonable temperature year-round. Cold or heat have no particular effect on coins, so severe changes in temperature in itself would not be damaging, but humidity and contaminants carried in the air will do damage, so those are the things you need to protect from. If your coins are stored in inert and airtight containers such as holders or tubes, they should be safe from most hazards—but how safe is your attic from burglars, fire, or severe weather?

Q: I have problems storing coins because of high humidity. Any suggestions?

Depends on the quantity and value of the coins. For a small number in an airtight compartment, bags of water-absorbing material such as silica gel will do the trick. For a room size collection, you'd need an electric dehumidifier.

Q: Many old-time collectors wrapped their coins in tissue paper and occasionally I see coins still preserved this way. Is this really a good way to protect your coins?

If there is a packing material that is on the market, it has probably been used to preserve coins at one time or another. However, tissue paper and most other papers contain sulfur, which is the leading cause of copper alloy coins discoloring, so despite its ready availability, it is not an ideal storage material. Neither is cotton batting, a favorite with non-collectors. This would be a good time to remind readers that the old practice of storing coins wrapped in aluminum foil is also bad for your coins. It all boils down to spending a little extra to get the proper packaging materials that have been specifically designed for the care and preservation of coins. The coin envelopes are made from a paper which does not contain sulfur, and some of the old tissue paper was specially made for the hobby without any sulfur in it, but there's no way to tell which is which.

Q: Is it all right to use plastic pill bottles for coins? Some of them are just the right size.

My standard recommendation is to use only those products which have been tested and found safe for coins. Plastic pill bottles may or may not contain harmful agents such as PVC—nobody knows, because they aren't intended for coins and thus haven't been properly tested. Additionally, the plastic may absorb potentially harmful chemicals from the pills stored in them. I've used the glass pill bottles (1960s) for coins, but they weren't satisfactory either as they broke easily because of the weight of the coins. For your own peace of mind, pay the extra cost for those products intended for coin storage.

Q: I have a lot of cellophane and wax paper envelopes left over from when I collected stamps. Can I use them for my coins?

Cellophane has a nasty habit of turning brittle in storage. Wax paper envelopes will not withstand the sharp edges of coins, which will cut their way out in short order, especially if you try to mail a coin in one. I once received a shipment of coins which had been put in cellophane and stapled to cards a decade or more earlier. When they got to me most of the coins were lying loose in the bottom of the box amid fragments of the envelopes. I guess I can't repeat often enough that the safe thing to do is to use only products which are designed and tested for safe coin storage. Household products, aluminum foil, plastic wrap, and other similar cheap substitutes can ultimately be the most expensive expedient you ever used.

Q: Years ago I bought a quantity of 2x2 cardboard holders which had to be assembled by placing the mylar window around the coin and then the holder was self-sealing. Recently I discovered that the coins stored in them had all slid down and now have glue on them. Is there any way to remove it?

If these are circulated coins, probably the best solvent you can try on your coins is nail polish remover, or you may be able to get acetone from your drugstore, but if you use the latter, do it in a well ventilated place. Try it on some of the lower value pieces first.

This points up a real problem, as many collectors don't realize that the 2x2 cardboard holders are not intended for long-term storage. The firm that made these particular holders I believe is no longer in business, but other forms of the cardboard holders are still plentiful. For long term storage your best bet for quantities of coins would be inert plastic tubes, which are airtight.

Q: I've noticed that some of the 2x2 cardboard holders I have purchased with coins in them have the staples very close to the coins. Is this a recommended practice?

This is a point where I seem to be in the minority in warning collectors not to follow this practice. Many coin dealers insert the staples within a fraction of an inch of the coin, apparently to deliberately make it difficult to remove them and thus void the "guarantee" surrounding their original holder. Both from the standpoint of threatening the coin with damage during staple removal, and equally important, during staple insertion, this is a practice which I strongly urge you not to follow. Most experts do recommend that you completely remove staples before taking the coin out, but they don't warn you of the hazards associated with placing them too close to the coin in the first place. Staples should always be flattened with a pair of needlenose pliers to avoid scratching the coin in the next holder. Don't economize with a single staple, as the first time you drop the holder the coin will come out the unstapled side, and don't plan to use a 2x2 for long term storage.

Q: In your column on stapling 2x2 cardboard coin holders you mentioned rust as a hazard. Doesn't only iron rust?

Rust is an oxide of iron, so you are correct, but a coin does not have to contain iron to be affected by the proximity of rust, such as that found on a rusting staple that is too close to the coin. The rust can stain the coin, doing essentially permanent damage to it. As we know from the recovery of the gold coins from the wreck of the S.S. Central America, rust stains can be removed from gold coins at least, but it requires very expert removal techniques that are not readily available to the collector or dealer.

Q: What are some of the plastics that are safe for long term storage?

The following plastics are considered to be inert and will not react with the air to damage coins: Polyethylene, polystyrene, acrylic, polyester (Mylar, Kodar) and cellulose triacetate. Use only products which have been designed and tested for coin storage. Raiding the kitchen for storage materials can be one of your bigger mistakes. Regardless of the storage medium used, check all your coins at least once a year, more often if you live in an area of extreme temperatures or high humidity.

Q: Isn't all the fuss about PVC a bit overblown? For instance, when I go to a coin show, the dealers have their coins in flips that contain PVC, as I come home with a bunch of them every time.

Dealers use the softer flips containing PVC for showing coins because they are not as likely to damage a coin that is removed and inserted in the flip several times by prospective customers. The hard flips can damage a coin's high points or even scratch them if the coins are not carefully removed or inserted. This still doesn't make them safe for long term storage. Even though I wince every time, I do recommend that the softer flips be used for mailing coins as the stiff plastic flips frequently split or crack, allowing the coin to come loose in the package or letter.

Q: What is meant by a "cloudy surface" coin?

Jeff Oxman's forthcoming "Silver Dollar Dictionary" defines it as the state or condition of the coin's mint luster, which has been dulled through contact with corrosive chemicals. Repeated or prolonged use of the chemicals as dips will etch the surface and give the coin a dull, cloudy appearance.

Q: Enclosed is an ad for an "industrial strength" metal cleaner. The company told me it won't harm a coin. Is it safe to use?

The product you are asking about has never to my knowledge been tested on coins. Given a lack of any recommendation I would strongly advise against using it. Any product capable of "polishing" metal does so by removing the surface either chemically or by the use of an abrasive. In either case this would reduce the value of the coin substantially, so why take the chance? Further, the instructions advise: "Use a damp cloth to clean the surface and a ... cloth to polish the metal." This is counter to the advice given for coins which is to never rub a coin with any material. To do so puts hairlines on the surface which reduce the value of the coin. Best advice, use a neutral solvent to remove loose dirt and grease, air dry, but never clean or polish your coins.

Q: I recently purchased an old-time collection. Examining the coins under natural light I discovered that many of the silver pieces have a distinct yellowish tinge. What would cause that?

Once more the messenger arrives with bad news. The most likely cause is that the coins were once cleaned with a commercial acid base metal cleaner and then were not properly rinsed afterward. The residue from the cleaner will eventually turn a yellowish color. Your coins should be examined in detail with magnification to determine just how much damage has been done by the cleaner, damage which is irreversible.

Q: How do I handle coins with cellophane tape on them?

Use acetone or nail polish remover. Don't use nail polish remover on high grade or proof coins. Next to cleaning, tape has probably wrecked more coins than almost any other misadventure at the hands of a collector. Any kind of adhesive attracts dirt and other contaminants, and when applied to a coin holds them firmly against the coin surface where they can do their damage. Never, ever put tape on a coin for any reason.

Q: Would you please explain the purpose and use of a touchstone?

The touchstone was a very valuable tool back in the days before accurate methods of assaying were developed. The touchstone was a piece of rock upon which pieces of bullion of a known fineness were rubbed, leaving a streak of the metal. Then the coin or other object to be tested was rubbed on the stone, and the two streaks were compared to match the fineness. In the hands of an expert the touchstone was claimed to be accurate to less than 1%, or .010 fine.

Q: What would you consider the most important tool for a collector?

There's no question as to the answer: a magnifier. Nobody should ever depend on the unassisted eye to examine a coin, especially if trying to grade it, or to determine if it is genuine or not. Best for such work is a 5X to 20X hand lens, which multiplies the image five to 20 times. For advanced work, your best buy would be a stereo-microscope with a zoom feature if possible, and a magnification in the 10 to 40X range. Expect to pay around $300 and up for a decent microscope.

Q: I have a microscope which can be set for either 600X or 1200X magnification. Which is best for examining coins?

Neither one! This is about like shooting ducks with a 16-inch cannon. Magnification is necessary when examining coins, but the proper range is between 5X and 20X, with 20X to 40X microscopic examination for preliminary authentication work. Any increase in magnification beyond that is useless to anyone except an expert trying to verify a soldered on mint mark or some similar task. My advice to any beginning collector is that the first purchase you need to make is a good hand lens, and then use it for EVERY coin you examine.

Chapter 54

TERMS AND DEFINITIONS

Besides the slang terms, there are technical terms and proper titles that are used. I've attempted to separate these two categories, but sometimes there's less than a fine line between them. As is so often said, more study is needed.

Q: What is an "aliquot" coin?

Aliquot is a mathematical term for a divisor which can be used to divide a greater number without a remainder, so an aliquot coin is one which is of a value which can be evenly divided into a larger coin or unit, as the quarter is 1/4 of a dollar, with no remainder. A 15 cent coin would not be an aliquot.

Q: What does a dealer ad mean when it says "coins sent on approval?"

The dealer will send you a selection of coins from which you can pick (or approve) those that you want, and return the rest. Once you are on the mailing list and establish your credit, you can expect regular shipments so it is necessary to exercise restraint, or you may get flooded with more coins than you can handle.

Q: Didn't the word barter once mean to cheat someone?

It may take an old dictionary to find that meaning, but it is correct. The English word barter comes from the old French "barater," which had two meanings, to trade goods, and to cheat, suggesting that not all early forms of barter were on the up and up.

Q: What is meant by "basining" a die?

Basining of a die occurs during the process of making it. The surface, or "face" of the die is shaped by abrasion, using a block of zinc known as a lap, which is either concave—to produce a raised and rounded field—or convex to produce a lowered or cup shaped field. The resulting die face is shaped to best promote the flow of planchet metal into all of the design. The amount of basining needed depends on the size, depth, and location of the design elements on both sides of the coin. This process is usually applied only to the Master Die, since this tool is used to shape the working hubs and from them the working dies, each of which will have the same convex or concave fields. There is some evidence that some of the Morgan dollar dies were individually basined and polished with the same, or similar laps in order to produce the mirror fields known as cameos. Most collectors assume the field of a coin (die) is flat, but there is a distinct curve, and a really flat field die is a rarity.

Q: How can a coin have "cabinet friction" if it was never housed in a cabinet?

The term arose from the old cabinets with multiple drawers once popular with U.S. collectors, and still very popular with European collectors. Research has shown that many of the markings described as cabinet friction are identical to those suffered by coins rubbing against each other in unopened bags.

Q: Is there any difference between a clogged letter and a filled letter on a coin? This came up at a recent club meeting and started a pretty hot argument.

There are two similar terms, "filled" and "clogged," which are frequently misused or substituted for each other by collectors, dealers, and even some price guides. A filled die is one which has dirt and grease filling the design cavities in the die face, preventing the coin metal from entering the design, resulting in weak or missing letters or numbers, such as the missing mint mark letters on some 1987 to 1994 quarters. A filled die always means that some of the design is weak or missing. A clogged die is one which has a small die break clogging the interior of one (or more) of the letters or numbers.

The die break appears as a raised area of the coin metal, so there is a very distinct difference between the appearance of the two effects on the coin—a filled letter is missing, but a clogged letter is there, with raised metal in it.

Q: I thought the definition of a coin included that it had to have a denomination. Some of the "coins" I've seen don't have any indication of value.

Walter Breen's definition is one of the best: "Originally, bullion formed into pellets or disks of standard weight, ... later similar items in any metal purportedly intended for circulation as money." As you can see, a denomination isn't necessary. Many of the early British coins were not marked, but passed by size or weight. A piece becomes a coin simply as a manifestation of the power of government to say it is a coin, or "whatever the issuing authority claims it to be."

Q: What's the difference between a restored coin and a restored die?

Restoration on a coin may mean anything from having the coin cleaned, to tooling it (using engraving tools to enhance worn design outlines), or even fresh engraving. A restored die may have much the same things done to it, polishing, re-engraving, etc., but from the collector's standpoint the two are entirely different. On a coin any such work is an alteration with zero collector value. However a coin struck officially with a restored die is perfectly acceptable to collect.

Q: Please explain what is meant by "Condition Census?"

This is a method of listing rare coins of a given date, mint, variety, etc. by listing the top six grades on the 1-70 scale, starting with the finest and listing the next best coins. As new discoveries are made, if their grade is high enough they may "bounce" one or more of the earlier listed coins. A typical listing for a given date might read 55-40-30-30-20-10, indicating that the finest known coin grades a 55, the second finest a 40, etc.

Q: What is a "dumb" planchet?

This is a Mint term for a planchet which has an internal crack or gas bubble, a defect which inhibits the normal "ring" of a planchet or struck coin.

Q: Are a galvano and an electrotype one and the same?

Strictly speaking, yes. However, in numismatic usage, a galvano is considered to be a pattern for a coin or medal which has been electroplated, while an electrotype is a copy of a coin made by plating two castings and then filling and fusing them together. European usage is to call an electrotype a galvano. To add to the confusion, both galvano and electrotype are also used as terms in printing.

Q: What is exonumia?

Some dictionaries would be prone to define exonumia as "Anything collected by an exonumist." Seriously, it is defined as almost anything that has to do with, or has some connection to numismatics, but which is outside the scope of the typical numismatic material, such as coins, medals, tokens, and paper money. For example a coin wrapper would be considered exonumia. The word was coined in 1960 by Russ Rulau, from Exo—out of, and nummus—a coin.

Q: How did fake coins come to be known as forgeries?

The word traces to the old French forgerie, meaning the working of metal. In turn that comes from the Latin "fabrica" or workshop, and "faber" or workman. Up until about the 19th century it had a perfectly innocent meaning, reflecting its roots as a common term in the metal working industry. At some point along the line the term was picked up and used to denote the making of something false to be passed off as the real thing, later more specifically to imitate or counterfeit a document or a signature on a document. Despite the more common current use in connection with documents, forgery is still commonly used for spurious coins because of the original meaning as a metal working term.

Q: Please explain the terms "inscription," "motto," and "legend."

There are an interesting group of intertwined definitions for these three numismatic terms. Webster defines legend as: "An inscription, motto or title, especially surrounding the field on a coin or medal. The ANA Dictionary defines legend as: "The inscription on a numismatic item," and is mute on both inscription and motto. The ANA Grading Guide says of inscription, "The legend or lettering," and for legend, "The principal inscription on a coin. "Motto" is "A word or phrase used on a coin." If you have that straight, consider the author who described inscription as "The lettering on the obverse," and legend as "The lettering on the reverse of a coin."

Q: Is "lamination" really a technical term, or is it another form of hobby slang?

It is a technical term of long standing. The definition as provided by the American Society of Metallurgists says: "Metal defects with separation or weakness generally aligned parallel to the worked surface of the metal." In coinage we apply it to thin layers of the coin metal which split off the faces of the struck coin, or off the rolled planchets.

Q: What is meant by a "legal receptacle" for a coin?

The term was used by the enabling acts for the various coins produced by the Mint, and refer to either a pay phone or a vending machine. The legal receptacles of the time were primarily responsible for the adoption of the billon alloy for the wartime nickels of 1942-45, although the original plan had been to make them with 50% silver, an idea that had to be scrapped when somebody figured out that the coins would then contain more than their face value in silver.

Q: What's a "Liberty Feathered Head?"

This was the name applied to what we now commonly call "Indian Head" cents. It apparently was in use at about the time the Indian Heads were replaced by the Lincoln cent in 1909. It may well trace to the story that the Mint's Chief Engraver, James Longacre, used his daughter wearing the headdress of a visiting Indian chief as a model, or to the fact that any female on a U.S. coin was considered to be Miss Liberty.

**"Liberty Feathered Head" was the name applied to what
we now commonly call "Indian Head" cents.**

Q: What is a "master" coin? Is this one struck with a Master Die?

A Master Die is almost never used to strike coins, except possibly die trials. A master coin is another, early name for a proof coin, used in the early 1800s.

Q: What are the names for multi-sided coins?

A: Trilaterial, rectangular, pentagonal, hexagonal, heptagonal, octagonal, nonagonal, decagonal, undecagonal, and 12 is a dodecagon. Then bet your friend he doesn't have a two-sided coin.

Q: Is there an "official" numismatic dictionary?

There are several numismatic dictionaries on the market, and the American Numismatic Association has an outdated version, last revised in the 1960s, but who is to say whether they are "official" or not? It's a hobby problem that needs to be solved. There is no official set of terms and definitions. Many have different, even conflicting definitions.

Q: Is there more than one definition for a proof coin?

From a technical standpoint, there are two different proof forms that are collected. One is the coin struck to "prove" the die, or die pair, frequently referred to as a test strike. The other is the much more common production proof, (with whatever finish) which is struck in quantity solely for collectors. An interesting argument develops, since proof coins with S mint marks are not "proving" any circulation coin dies. The original meaning was the same as that still used for paper money, a piece struck to test, or prove the dies. Over the years the term was broadened to include test pieces, presentation pieces, trial strikes, or almost anything else in the way of a numismatic item which meets the criteria stated in the question.

The definition of a proof has been changed and modified over the years, but one interesting opinion, not necessarily a universally accepted definition, quoted in the American Journal of Numismatics in 1870 states, "Proofs are coins or medals struck from the original die (Master Die) as it leave the hands of the die cutter (engraver) and are thus distinguished from specimens struck with dies which have been reproduced by pressure (hubbing process) from the original dies." The intent of the statement was to make a distinction between a coin struck with a handmade die, made by using punches and engraving tools, and a coin struck by a die which was the result of the making first of a working hub from the Master Die and then a working die. At the time, the use of hubs to make dies was still relatively new, as hubbing the dies didn't really become a major part of the process until the introduction of steam power in the 1830s, and wasn't completely adopted for all of the design until after the turn of the century. A proposal was made by Howland Wood in 1910 for standardized terms. Obviously unaware that U.S. Mint had for some time used hydraulic presses to strike proofs, Wood included the requirement that they be struck on a hand operated press. A significant omission was the failure to mention two strikes as criteria. Polished dies and flans (planchets) were included.

The modern definition is: "A coin struck on a specially prepared planchet, with specially prepared dies and struck two or more times."

Q: I'll bite, what is an "eternal" proof set?

This is an oddball item which cropped up during the transition period from the silver coinage to the clad coinage, while the Mint had shut down proof production (1965-68). Whether serious or a gag, someone proposed and actually prepared sample proof sets by buffing or grinding off the dates, suggesting that the set then would be good in any year. A similar suggestion which also didn't catch on was that the Mint strike only "decade" proof sets, with a single date (1970) or a dual date (1970-1979) which would be good for the whole ten years.

Q: What is a frosted proof?

Frosted proofs are the very first strikes from a new die, which show a roughened, or "frosted" effect on the design, surrounded by the mirror field. This is an effect which can be prolonged by periodically swabbing the incuse die design with acid to roughen the die surface. Frosted coins are worth a slight premium over the unfrosted ones, although in recent years the Mint has struck much larger numbers of frosted proofs.

Q: What is meant by a "minor" proof set?

In the middle of the 19th century, the Mint issued both full and partial sets of proof coins. The minor sets contained only the base metal coins: the cent, nickel three-cent, and five-cent coins.

Q: What's the difference between a "Roman" proof finish and a matte proof?

Walter Breen described the "Roman Gold" finish found on 1909 and 1910 U.S. proof gold coins as: "Surfaces light in color, midway between satiny and mirror-like, entirely without the granularity of matte or sandblast (proofs)." He also notes that "Waite Raymond used to call them 'brilliant matte proofs.'" The best description of it is that it lies along the scale from the rough surface matte proofs or sandblast proofs, then the satin finish proof, and then the brilliant, or mirror proofs. However some descriptions of the satin proofs would put them between the Roman Gold and the brilliant proofs, so there is room for variation. The exact method of producing both the Roman Gold and the satin finish proofs are unknown.

Q: What's the difference between patina and toning?

The American Numismatic Association defines patina as: "A green or brown surface film on ancient copper or bronze coins caused by oxidation over a long period of time." Toning is defined as: "Natural patination or discoloration of a coin's surface caused by the atmosphere over a long period of time." Artificial toning is considered to be any discoloration resulting from the application of chemicals or heat to speed up the natural process.

Q: As a newcomer to the hobby I am puzzled. Why is the edge of a coin commonly referred to as "reeded?" I don't find any dictionary definitions which come close, as either fluted, or serrated I think would be better choices.

Numismatics is a hobby where a lot of logic gets checked at the door, and this is one more good example. The closest definition of reeding is "An ornamentation by the use of half round molding, or a group of them, as on a column." One goes so far as to define reeding as "The opposite of fluting." Fluting in turn is "the concave channel as in a column." Since both refer to rounded surfaces, neither is correct when applied to the sharp edged, angular lands and grooves produced by the collar. Serrations are likened by one source to "the toothed edge of a saw," which isn't really a good fit either, but another says, "A formation or set of (single teeth or notches). That comes about the closest to the edge of a "reeded" coin.

Q: What's the difference between a "standard" and a "divisional" coin?

A standard coin is one which had unlimited legal tender value, while a divisional coin was good only for limited amounts as legal tender. Some definitions of a standard coin required that its metallic content be equal to its face value. All U.S. coins now are legal tender in any amount.

Chapter 55

TERRITORIAL COINS, PRIVATE ISSUES, STATE COINS

Q: What can you tell me about a Montana gold half dollar?

It's gold all right, but it's only 6 karat, and it was manufactured by the California Gold Manufacturing Company of Chicago in 1918. After a number were sold to dubious and devious merchants to use in various scams, the Government finally cracked down and confiscated the unsold "coins" and the dies used to make them.

Q: I have a California gold coin dated 1872. Didn't they outlaw them before that?

The government did, but couldn't make it stick in California. There are genuine 1872 coins, there are low grade alloy copies, and there are souvenirs that lack any gold content, all made with some of the same (obverse) dies, so you need expert help in determining what your particular piece is. If the reverse doesn't say "DOLLAR," or "CENTS" or some abbreviation of the words then you have a copy. There are several varieties without dates, at least some believed to be from the 1852-54 period.

Q: I have a $10 Baldwin and Company coin. Can you tell me what it's worth?

If your coin is genuine, showing a mounted rider with rope, it would be made of gold, and would be extremely heavy for its size, weighing about half an ounce. If it is one of the numerous worthless copies, it would be brass or some other metal and considerably lighter. I would suggest taking it to one of your local coin dealers to check, but don't allow the coin to be cleaned, scratched, cut, or otherwise damaged. Weight is the key non-destructive test. If it does turn out to be gold, let me know and I'll be able to help you further.

Q: Weren't the dies for the Oregon Beaver gold coins stolen at one time?

Two of the dies were stolen by burglars from the Oregon Historical Society in Portland in February 1959. One of the $5 dies and one of the $10 dies were in a display, with the other half of each pair in the vault. The thieves, who were captured with the missing dies a few days later, were ignorant of the fact that the dies they had could not be used to strike coins. Their plan had been to use them to make coins to sell to collectors. Recovered at the time of the burglary were a $5 and a $10 Beaver which were in a box which was dropped on a fire escape.

Chapter 56

RESOURCES

Numismatic News
Coins Magazine
World Coin News
Bank Note Reporter
Coin Prices Magazine
Numismatic Catalogs
Club Guide
Show Guide
Krause Publications
700 E. State St.
Iola, WI 54990

American Numismatic Association
818 N. Cascade Ave.
Colorado Springs, CO 80903-3279
(719) 632-2646

American Numismatic Society
Broadway at 156th St.
New York, NY 10032
(212) 234-3130

Bureau of Engraving and Printing
BEP Order Processing
PO Box 371594
Pittsburgh, PA 15250-7594
A sheet of 16 $2 notes is $43.50, or $45
with a cardboard frame. 16 $1 notes are
$26 and $27.50, including postage.
A 32-note sheet of $2 is $76.

U.S.Mint
Customer Service Center
10001 Aerospace Drive
Lanham, MD 20706
Tel. (202) 283-2646

If you have a question, please include a loose 1st class stamp and write to me at the address for Krause Publications above. Please do not send any coins until they are requested.

INDEX